P9-DZM-507

Admiral Halsey said it:

"THE COASTWATCHERS SAVED GUADALCANAL. AND GUADALCANAL SAVED THE PACIFIC."

Lonely Vigil is the untold story of the vigilant few who challenged a mighty military machine —and helped win World War II. It is a monumental and magnificent book, "suspenseful, bizarre, touching. A book that appeals to the romantic individualist in all of us."

—Publishers Weekly

"At last the Coastwatchers have an historian worthy of their feats. . . . Walter Lord's account is authoritative, enriched with human interest— and very good reading."

—John Toland

"Creates considerable excitement and raises a deep respect for those brave and wily men."

—Atlantic Monthly

SELECTED BY 4 BOOK CLUBS

more . . .

"A REMARKABLE STORY"
—San Francisco Chronicle

A masterful writer who has the ability to make the reader feel he is "there," Walter Lord is the highly-acclaimed author of such timeless best-sellers as *A Night to Remember,* about the Titanic, *Day of Infamy,* about Pearl Harbor, *Incredible Victory,* about the Battle of Midway, and other stories of great and momentous events. Now, with *Lonely Vigil,* he tells the never-before-told story of the forgotten heroes of World War II—the Coastwatchers of the Solomons.

"So much of this exciting tale is new to me. I knew some of these valiant men well. Walter Lord has brought them to life again."
—Samuel B. Griffith II
Brigadier General USMC (ret.)

"It's a remarkable story . . . compelling!"
—The Miami Herald

"A necessary and compelling tale."
—Time

Lonely Vigil

Walter Lord

A KANGAROO BOOK
PUBLISHED BY POCKET BOOKS NEW YORK

POCKET BOOKS, a Simon & Schuster division of
GULF & WESTERN CORPORATION
1230 Avenue of the Americas, New York, N.Y. 10020

Copyright © 1977 by Walter Lord

Reprinted by arrangement with the Viking Press
Library of Congress Catalog Card Number: 76-54257

All rights reserved, including the right to reproduce
this book or portions thereof in any form whatsoever.
For information address the Viking Press,
625 Madison Avenue, New York, N.Y. 10022

ISBN: 0-671-82176-8

First Pocket Books printing September, 1978

1 2 9 8

Trademarks registered in the United States and other countries.

Printed in the U.S.A.

FOR BETSY SCHOYER

Contents

Maps

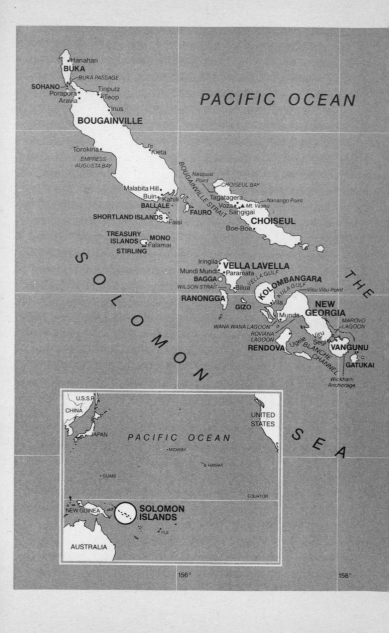

SOLOMON ISLANDS

REKATA BAY

SANTA ISABEL

Mata Mata

KILOKAKA HIDING PLACE

Mufu Point

Tataba

SAN JORGE

Mahaga

THOUSAND SHIPS BAY

S L O T

MALAITA

Auki

RUSSELL ISLANDS

FLORIDA ISLANDS

SAVOO

Tulagi

Cape Esperance

IRON BOTTOM

Lavoro

SOUND

Lunga Point

Berande Point

HENDERSON FIELD

Aola

Tangarare

Gold Ridge

GUADALCANAL

MARAMASIKE

Cape Hunter

CORAL SEA

Kirakira

SAN CRISTOBAL

SANTA ANA

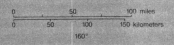

0   50   100 miles
0   50   100   150 kilometers

160°   162°

Introduction

Six thousand miles southwest of San Francisco, just below the equator, lie the Solomon Islands, scene of perhaps the bitterest fighting ever waged by Americans at war. Here, in 1942–43, the United States and its Allies battled the Empire of Japan for mastery of the Pacific.

Today, the visitor flying down from the former Japanese base of Rabaul finds it hard to believe that this great drama ever happened. The clear blue sky, where so many furious air battles were joined, is now at peace. No tracers, no shell-bursts—only the silent columns of cumulus clouds that pile up to infinity.

The sea is quiet too. It seems strange that an especially pretty channel should carry the grim name Iron Bottom Sound—until one remembers the many lost ships that lie there.

Far below, the islands doze in the sun. At 10,000 feet, the coconut palms of a coastal plantation look like rows of neat, green asterisks . . . in sharp contrast to the scarred and twisted stalks, leaning at crazy angles, that stood here not many years ago.

Landing on Guadalcanal at Henderson International Airport (once a muddy strip called Henderson Field), the traveler takes a bus to Honiara—a thriving town of 13,000—standing where there was nothing but an especially perilous stretch of jungle during the campaign. Now it is normal to stay at an air-conditioned hotel, shop at the supermarket, and hail a taxi that has a little light on the roof—just like London or New York.

It is only when going into the interior, or when visiting one of the other islands, that the visitor suddenly discovers that not so much has changed after all. The veneer of Honiara quickly disappears, and the timeless, changeless jungle takes over. There are no roads, only faint footpaths known to a few local natives.

Here, at last, one finds reminders of the great struggle. A hundred-yard walk in from the beach at Munda discloses rusting bulldozers, a shattered Japanese anti-aircraft gun, the wing of an American fighter plane. Wrenched from the fuselage, it somehow has the poignancy of the torn wing of a butterfly.

The oddest relic of all is one of the most difficult to reach. Fifteen miles in from Guadalcanal's north coast, up a mountain trail that teases the climber with an apparently endless succession of hillocks, there stands a ridge that offers a magnificent view of the coast and sea. At the edge of this ridge lie the remains of an old kerosene-run refrigerator.

It is no ordinary piece of junk. It is a legacy of the dark days of 1942, when the fate of the Solomons hung in balance . . . and when a small group of resourceful individuals, operating deep in enemy territory, gave immeasurable help to the Allied cause.

This book tells their story.

1

"STEAK AND EGGS"

The rusty little steamer *Morinda* sagged under the weight of the people scrambling to get aboard. A local doctor, hurling himself into the mob, dislocated his shoulder. Piles of luggage lay on the pier, abandoned by the planters, traders, missionaries, and minor officials who crowded the ship's rail. Tulagi, chief port and administrative center of the British Solomon Islands Protectorate, was in a panic—and so was the whole South Pacific.

Japan was on the march. On December 7, 1941, Tokyo's policy of expansion had finally collided head-on with Washington's policy of containment in the sunny skies above Pearl Harbor, and now the Emperor's forces were sweeping south. With chilling speed they struck not only the bastions of American strength but the whole jerry-built system of European possessions that for a hundred years had meant order and stability in the Pacific.

On December 23 Wake Island surrendered; Christmas Day, Hong Kong fell; January 3, 1942, Manila

went. On the 12th, enemy forces invaded the East Indies
. . . the 23rd, New Britain and New Ireland . . . the
30th, West Borneo. On February 1, in perhaps the most
unbelievable stroke of all, the Japanese laid siege to
the supposedly impregnable British base of Singapore
after surging down the Malay Peninsula with terrifying
ease.

Even more frightening than the collapse of the Allied
defense was the collapse of a great many preconcep-
tions that had stood inviolate for a century: the invin-
cibility of the Royal Navy; American technological
supremacy; the limitations of a purely imitative Japan;
the innate superiority of the Western fighting man; a
conviction that the oil, tin, rubber and other resources
of Asia somehow belonged by inheritance—if not by
divine right—to a few European powers; and an abiding
faith that the Far East would always accept this state
of affairs.

As these comforting beliefs crumbled in the face of
the enemy advance, Allied spokesmen desperately tried
to explain away the disaster. There was little mention of
the Japanese development of the aircraft carrier task
force, or the coordinated tactics that sank the mighty
British warships, *Prince of Wales* and *Repulse,* or the
fast-climbing Zero fighter plane. Instead, these easy
victories were ascribed largely to stealth, trickery, a
"simian" aptitude for jungle warfare. As *The New York
Times* described the conquerors of Malaya:

Many of them wear sneakers and swarm up the
boles of the coconut trees to the feathery fronds at
the top and act as snipers. They swing from the
jungle lianas like monkeys. They wade through the
swamps and become part of them. They infiltrate
the British strong points dressed in native clothes
or in few clothes at all.

The effect only added to the cold fear of those in the path of the advance. Frantic civilians, white and native, abandoned their towns, burned their plantations, and fled down the roads and trails on trucks, carts, bicycles, anything. Thoroughly demoralized, the Allied troops reeled back, sometimes laden with loot and liquor.

When Rabaul fell on January 23, it was clear that Japan would soon strike the Solomon Islands, a mere 200 miles to the southeast. Nor would this be a minor conquest: The Solomons were a majestic chain stretching like a necklace from Buka and Bougainville, just below the equator, to San Cristobal, 600 miles still farther to the southeast.

Administratively the islands were divided: Buka and Bougainville formed an Australian mandate; the rest were a British protectorate. But geographically the chain was really a single unit—a visually striking and even thrilling entity. Starting below Bougainville, the Solomons split into two parallel lines of islands—Choiseul, Santa Isabel, and Malaita to the north; Vella Lavella, the New Georgia group, and Guadalcanal to the south—both lines merging again at San Cristobal. In between ran a narrow corridor of water that cartographers called New Georgia Sound, but which seemed to any traveler more like a groove . . . or a gut . . . or, as it came to be called, "the Slot."

Near the southeastern end of the Slot, midway between Malaita and Guadalcanal, lay a small cluster called the Florida Islands. One of these—only two miles long—was Tulagi, seat of the colonial government.

The islands that lined the Slot were bulky masses of green, rising dramatically out of a sparkling blue sea. Rugged mountains towered above the strips of beach, and on Bougainville wisps of smoke rose from two live

Southeast end of the Slot, looking west. Cape Esperance, Guadalcanal, is at the extreme left; Savo Island in the center. (The Florida Islands lie just out of the picture, to the right.) Later known as Iron Bottom Sound, this was the scene of the opening battles in the struggle for the Solomons. (National Archives)

volcanoes, blending with the huge cumulus clouds in the sky. The vastness of nature loomed everywhere, and even a large vessel steaming along the Slot looked like a toy against the spectacular backdrop of mountains and clouds.

They were islands of beauty—and remoteness. Discovered by the Spanish in 1567, they were so far removed from the world's trade routes that they were lost and not found again for 200 years. During the nineteenth century occasional European explorers added a legacy of English, French, and German place names, but no formal government existed until the British established their protectorate over the Southern Solomons in 1893.

Nearly fifty years later the islands remained largely empty and unknown. Only 650 white settlers, mostly planters and missionaries, lived in an area of some 60,000 square miles. Tulagi had perhaps 40 or 50 Europeans, although it did include those perquisites of English colonial life, a Residency, a cricket pitch, and a small golf course.

Even the jungles were largely empty, except for mosquitoes, lizards, agile crocodiles along the river banks, and an occasional bush rat as big as a rabbit. Over 100,000 natives lived wild, secluded lives. Mostly very black Melanesians, they had little contact with the settlers or even with each other—some 40 different dialects were in use. Head-hunting was not unknown, and few white men had done very much exploring. Choiseul was probably the least charted island in the world.

But that was the way the settlers wanted it. Men came out here with the deliberate purpose of getting away from the ordinary world. Some had a restless, independent streak; some had a past they longed to forget; some hoped to spread the Word of God. For a few the Solomons weren't the answer, and they just drifted—often lost in drink—little more than beachcombers. But for most this self-contained world was the end of the rainbow. In the words of one new arrival:

I realized that here was the place where one might truly live and learn, a place altogether different, and above all, a wild free place where men succeeded only by their own strength, courage, enterprise and intelligence.

And now it was crashing down around their heads. Defense was hopeless. The antique firearms collected by the British colonial government were no match for the invaders. In the whole chain there were only two small units of regular troops: a 24-man unit of Australian Imperial Force commandos stationed at an unfinished airstrip on Buka to the north; and a similar A.I.F. unit guarding a minor Royal Australian Air Force patrol plane base in Tulagi harbor.

In this desperate situation, word was spread that the steamer *Morinda* would sail one last time for Australia on February 8. Abandoning their holdings, terrified settlers from all over the Solomons poured into Tulagi, where the ship would make its final stop.

The refugees had a glimpse of the dark days to come even as they waited on the dock. Shortly after the *Morinda* hove into view at 11:00 A.M., a Japanese Kawanisi flying boat appeared overhead. As the steamer dodged into an estuary, the Kawanisi casually made two bombing runs on her. There were no hits, but this was due to luck rather than any show of defense. There was no ground fire at all.

The panic was on by the time the plane flew off and the *Morinda* finally docked. All afternoon the refugees fought to get aboard, while the captain fretted about lifeboat regulations and tickets. It was after 8:00 when the ship gave a farewell blast on her whistle, cast off, and headed southwest for Australia.

Quiet once more settled over Tulagi. The only trace of the afternoon's tumult was the pile of abandoned luggage still lying on the dock . . . heaps of government records left behind in the rush . . . a few forlorn planters who missed the boat . . . and, of all things, an incoming passenger.

It should have pleased Martin Clemens to be coming in when everybody else was leaving. He had a great instinct for the dramatic and radiated a charm and urbanity that irritated some but appealed to many. A Cambridge oarsman with aristocratic tastes, he had come to the Solomons in 1938 as a young Colonial Office cadet. On leave in Sydney when the Japanese attacked Hawaii, he instantly sensed that this was the end of a way of life. He symbolically tore a pound note in half and tossed it into the harbor from a Sydney ferry.

Now he was back in Tulagi, ready for his next assignment. The Resident Commissioner, a bewildered elderly Englishman named William Sydney Marchant, ordered him to take over the district office on the island of Gizo to the northwest. But Gizo was already no-man's-land, and Clemens pointed out that it would be suicide even to land there. In the end he persuaded Marchant to let him go to Guadalcanal, largest of the British Solomons and just twenty miles to the south. Here he might be able to do some good.

On February 11 he crossed over, joining District Officer D. C. Horton at Aola, a tiny settlement on the north coast that served as administrative center for Guadalcanal. His arrival was a godsend to both Dick Horton and his assistant, Henry Josselyn. They had long wanted to leave the Islands and join the armed services. They quickly broke in Clemens, and by early March they were gone.

Martin Clemens was now the sole British official on Guadalcanal—a position that was anything but enviable. He was not only supposed to keep the flag flying as the colonial world crumbled around him, but in taking over the Aola station, he also assumed another responsibility that would hold him on Guadalcanal indefinitely. He automatically became a link in the Islands Coastwatching Service.

Developed by the Royal Australian Navy after World War I, the Service aimed to establish a network of observers who might keep an eye on the country's vast unguarded coast in case of war. Gradually the area was expanded to include New Guinea, the Bismarcks, the Solomons, and the rest of the strategic islands that girdled Australia's northeast coast. Since there was little defense money in the economy-minded '20s, the observers were volunteers drawn from local government workers, planters, traders and missionaries.

With the 1930s came the threat of Japanese expansion and the appointment of the Australian Navy's first full-time Director of Naval Intelligence. Commander R. B. M. Long was an affable career officer whose cherubic appearance concealed a brilliant mind and a skill at political wire-pulling. He saw gaps in the Coastwatching system, and the outbreak of the European war in 1939 gave him the budget to do something about it. He put the problem in the hands of an old Naval College classmate, Lieutenant Commander Eric Feldt.

It was a happy choice. Feldt tended to be distant and overly correct with his naval colleagues, but he was utterly in tune with the temperamental and individualistic "Islanders," as the longtime white residents of the Southwest Pacific were called. Squeezed out of the Navy by peacetime cuts in 1922, he had gone to New Guinea himself and was warden of the Wau Goldfield when called back for wartime duty. He knew the islands and the people thoroughly, and they knew and trusted him.

Feldt regarded the islands as a "fence" around Australia, with gaps and holes to be filled. Arriving in New Guinea on September 21, 1939, he began fixing the fence, and by mid-1941 the job was done. Over 100 Coastwatching stations stretched in a 2500-mile crescent from the western border of Papua New Guinea to Vila in the New Hebrides. Control stations at Port Moresby, Rabaul, Tulagi and Vila coordinated operations in their respective areas, and these in turn reported to Feldt's headquarters at Townsville in northern Australia.

All the stations were equipped with "teleradios"— remarkably durable sets that would transmit either by voice or by telegraph key. They worked on storage batteries and had a range of up to 400 miles by voice, 600 by key. They were efficient but clumsy, for even when broken down into their component parts of speaker, receiver, and transmitter, each part weighed some 75–100 pounds. Then there were the batteries, the charging engine, and the benzine to run it. In all, it took twelve to sixteen men to carry a set any time it had to be moved.

At the outset, however, this didn't seem especially important. No one expected the Coastwatchers to be on the move. They would not be operating behind enemy lines; they were really lookouts or spotters, in friendly territory, watching for any sign of hostile ships or

Lieutenant Commander Eric Feldt, organizer of the Coastwatchers. An old Islander himself, he seemed to know everybody in the South Pacific. (Courtesy Mrs. Eric Feldt)

planes. For sending messages, Feldt taught his Coastwatchers a simple cipher system called the "Playfair
code," which required no equipment other than a list of
key words. It was not especially secure, but nobody
thought that mattered. The information would be of
only transitory value and, again, the men would be in
no danger of capture.

Those neat assumptions collapsed in the shattering
aftermath of Pearl Harbor. Quickly punching through
Commander Feldt's fence, the Japanese controlled New
Britain, New Ireland, and the whole Bismarck Sea by
the end of February 1942.

These were harrowing days for the Coastwatchers in
the path of this avalanche. Some, like the ebullient
Keith McCarthy on New Britain, made hairbreadth
escapes. Others, like C. C. Jarvis on Nissan, had time
for one last message—UNKNOWN SHIP STOPPING AT
LAGOON ENTRANCE—then vanished forever. All found
themselves suddenly facing the probability of operating
behind enemy lines. But whatever their fate, Feldt insisted on one point: They were meant to watch—not
fight. To drive the point home, he called the network
"Ferdinand," after the famous fictional bull who pre-
ferred flowers to the arena.

March, and the Japanese began moving into the Solomons. The enemy had taken a few weeks to tidy up
earlier conquests; so the move came a little later than
expected, but it couldn't have been more threatening.
The chain flanked the northern coast of Australia and
pointed like a spear directly at the supply route from
America. Control of the Solomons meant control of
the New Hebrides and New Caledonia, and that in turn
meant control of the approaches to Brisbane and
Sydney.

Eric Feldt deployed his men accordingly. He planted
eight teleradio stations in the Solomons area, six directly

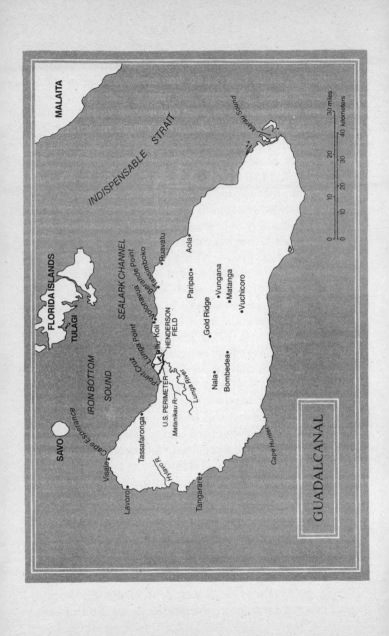

in the path of the Japanese. Two were on Bougainville; another in the central Solomons; and three on Guadalcanal, next-to-largest of the islands and the most likely place for an enemy airstrip.

Of the three Coastwatchers on Guadalcanal, Martin Clemens at Aola was in the best position to cover the eastern end of the island. Eighteen miles to his west— about midway along the northern coast—Pay Lieutenant D. S. Macfarlan of the Royal Australian Navy manned another teleradio at Berande, a rubber plantation owned by the South Pacific trading firm Burns Philp. All the way west was the third Coastwatcher, F. Ashton Rhoades, manager of the Burns Philp copra plantation at Lavoro.

Stocky, cheerful Don Macfarlan had been a buyer with an Australian dry goods chain before the war. Called up as a naval reservist in 1941, he landed more or less by chance in naval intelligence. Here he was picked up by Eric Feldt and sent to Tulagi to coordinate Coastwatching activities in the area, and to serve as naval liaison with Resident Commissioner Marchant.

As the Japanese advanced into the Solomons in March 1942, Marchant shifted his headquarters to Auki, Malaita, a hundred miles farther east; and Macfarlan—acting on previous instructions from Feldt —moved to Guadalcanal. Unlike most of the Coastwatchers, he had no experience in the area, but he had a unique advantage. He quickly came under the wing of Kenneth Dalrymple Hay, an oldtimer who managed the Berande plantation.

Stubborn, independent, and immensely wise in the ways of the Islands, Hay characteristically refused to join the exodus south. He watched the panic with contempt, then retired to Berande and began collecting an immense amount of abandoned Burns Philp stores.

Macfarlan joined him, and the two spent most of April shifting supplies to three secret caches in the interior. When the Japanese came, their plan was to retire to an eminence called Gold Ridge, fifteen miles inland and 2800 feet up. From here, there was a magnificent view of the coastal plain and the waters offshore. While Martin Clemens watched the east, they would handle the middle part of the island.

"Snowy" Rhoades, concentrating on the western end of Guadalcanal, came from a prosperous Sydney family. He had been wounded in World War I, fallen on hard times in the '20s, and finally caught on with a Lever plantation in the Solomons in 1933. Gradually he learned to recruit natives, shoot crocodiles, and get the most out of a grove of coconut palms. By now he was a thorough Islander—tough, caustic, and highly individualistic.

Rhoades had been earmarked for Coastwatching work by Eric Feldt over a year ago, but there weren't enough teleradios to go around. That was no longer a problem, and on March 24 Don Macfarlan headed for Lavoro with Clemens and Hay. They assembled a teleradio, strung the aerial, worked out codes and schedules, and the new recruit was ready for business.

April was a month of tense waiting on Guadalcanal. The Japanese had now moved into Buka, Bougainville and the Shortland Islands. They stepped up their air strikes on Tulagi. Squadrons of land-based bombers joined the Kawanisi flying boats that staged the earlier raids. The RAAF patrol plane base in Tulagi harbor reeled under the blows.

Watching from a lookout atop a giant banyan tree at Aola, Martin Clemens wondered how long it would be before the Japanese landings began. Of the three Coastwatchers on Guadalcanal, he was farthest removed from the enemy line of advance, yet Aola was the seat of government—wouldn't the Japanese head there first? He began preparing a fall-back position in the hills behind the station.

Meanwhile, as district officer, he struggled to maintain some semblance of British "presence" on the island. It was a life of ludicrous contrasts: One minute he was trying to fight the war; the next he was settling some native marital dispute, for his authority touched everything. On April 21 he met the problem of sagging morale in characteristically British fashion: He staged a cricket match.

At Berande 18 miles to the west, Macfarlan and Hay continued moving supplies to the secret caches they had established in the interior. Hidden at Koilo, for instance, were 110 cases of food, 93 bags of rice, 200 cases of kerosene, 40 drums of benzine, and at one point 50 cases of whiskey.

Even at this late date Macfarlan was also attempting to expand his Coastwatching network. He gave a spare teleradio—patched together by the RAAF at Tulagi— to Leif Schroeder, an old Norwegian trader who operated a store on Savo, a smallish island between Guadalcanal and Tulagi. Another set went to Joe Martin, a half-caste on Choiseul, but he could never make it work, and the Japanese were now too close for Macfarlan to go up and teach him.

At Lavoro, Snowy Rhoades tried to run his plantation as usual, with occasional interruptions when Japanese planes raided Tulagi. Being all the way west, he was generally the first to see them. Then he'd break off and flash a quick warning to the A.I.F. commando unit guarding the patrol plane base. It did little good; they had nothing to shoot back with, and could only crouch in their shelters as the bombs rained down.

April 29, the days of waiting ended. That morning the RAAF radioed Macfarlan that a large concentration of Japanese ships had been sighted heading for the Solomons. On May 1 especially heavy raids hit Tulagi. One damaged patrol plane was towed across to Aola, and Martin Clemens wondered how, on top of his other problems, he could hide a two-engine Catalina. Some 300 natives finally dragged it up on the beach and covered it with palm leaves.

On the 2nd, Coastwatchers to the west of Guadalcanal reported a Japanese seaplane carrier and escorting corvette in Thousand Ships Bay, Santa Isabel. That was only 60 miles from Tulagi. The RAAF advised Macfarlan that they were evacuating the patrol plane base, and the A.I.F. commandos began destroying supplies, equipment, anything that might be of use to the enemy.

At Berande Don Macfarlan assessed the latest ship sightings and decided the time had come to move to Gold Ridge. He piled his gear into the plantation truck, and during the afternoon Ken Hay drove him cross-country several miles into the interior. At Bamboo Creek a dozen native carriers were waiting. They took over the gear and disappeared with Macfarlan up the winding trail that led into the hills. Hay returned to Berande, planning to join him later.

Back at the plantation a visitor was waiting. Snowy Rhoades had piloted the company launch down from Lavoro in search of supplies and news. On Hay's return from Bamboo Creek he got plenty of both, and the two men sat for a while on the plantation house verandah watching the smoke boil up over Tulagi.

Now it was dark, and the glow of many fires spread across the evening sky as the commandos continued their demolitions. There was no time to lose: If the latest sightings were correct, enemy warships would be arriving any hour. Despite the danger, Rhoades decided

to get back to Lavoro. He loaded the launch and at
9 o'clock chugged off into a beautiful moonlit night.

Martin Clemens was winding up an especially hectic
day at Aola. There were records to pack, supplies to disperse, defenses to organize, the crew of the damaged
Catalina to feed, three boatloads of fleeing Chinese to
deal with—and everything seemed to happen at once.
Now, as the glare of the flames seared the sky over
Tulagi, he tried to remember the code signal that meant
the station there, VNTG, was closing down for good.
Was it "eggs and sausage"? "Liver and bacon"? Something like that, but his weary mind drew a blank.

Suddenly word came that he was wanted at the radio
shack. He rushed in and learned Tulagi was coming on
the air. The background noise was appalling, but as he
bent low over the set, he could hear a faint, desperate
voice calling, STEAK AND EGGS, DAMN IT, STEAK AND
EGGS, DAMN IT, VNTG CALLING VQJ4, STEAK AND
EGGS.

Now he knew, but that was all he knew, for the voice
faded and there was only static. Had VNTG sighted
Japanese ships? Were the Japanese already ashore,
bursting into the station? Had the RAAF and the commandos gotten away safely? Shaken and worried, nobody slept in Aola that night.

In the first gray light of May 3, an ancient coaster
wallowed in, clearing up the mystery. It carried the
RAAF personnel, who reported the commandos had
also escaped on another ship. Even as they slipped out
of Tulagi harbor, they saw four Japanese warships
sail in.

Clemens gave everybody breakfast, and the Tulagi
men then sprawled on the lawn in exhausted sleep. He
tried to persuade their commander to keep them on
Guadalcanal and form a guerrilla band, but the man
was an aviator who wanted only to get back in the air.

The Coastwatcher's standard 3-B-Z teleradio. Considered a marvel of compact efficiency in this pre-transistor era, it was a mass of knobs and dials and weighed nearly 300 pounds—not counting batteries, charging engine, and fuel. (Admiral Nimitz Center)

By evening the group was gone, heading south on their little ship.

No time to mope about that. During the day the damaged Catalina was scuttled; three schooners loaded with Chinese refugees were sent to safety; most of the native families living on the post were evacuated. Whatever else he was doing, from time to time Clemens would dash to the teleradio, twiddle the dials, trying to keep in touch with Don Macfarlan, en route to Gold Ridge . . . or Snowy Rhoades, isolated at Lavoro . . . or the control station at Auki on Malaita, which relayed his intelligence to Townsville. The best vantage point was the lookout post, high in the banyan tree, where a native blasted away on a conch shell every time Japanese planes appeared. Occasionally Clemens himself climbed the ladder for a look. The weather was thick, but he made out two big ships—apparently transports—steaming into Tulagi harbor.

Actually only one of the ships was a transport, but Martin Clemens was right in his hunch that a major Japanese landing was under way. Its early conquests digested, the Empire was now on the march again. The plan was to seize both Tulagi and Port Moresby on the southern coast of New Guinea.

This would give Japan control of the Coral Sea. Her bombers could then range from Port Moresby, hammering bases in Australia itself; while from Tulagi and its adjacent islands, the Fleet Air Arm could devastate New Caledonia, the Fijis, and Samoa, imperiling the supply lines between Australia and the United States. Combined with the "decisive fleet engagement" at Midway that Admiral Isoroku Yamamoto was already planning, the result should win the war for Japan. The Allies would see the futility of fighting and negotiate a peace on Tokyo's terms.

The twelve ships assigned to the Tulagi phase of the operation left Rabaul on April 29, and it was the vanguard of this force that arrived in the early hours of May 3, just as the last defenders were clearing out. By 8 A.M. troops were swarming ashore from the transport *Azumasan Maru*. With them, acting as guide and interpreter, came a Japanese named T. Ishimoto. He had lived on Tulagi for years, working as a carpenter . . . and as a quiet observer for His Imperial Majesty's government.

The Japanese landings on Tulagi meant a whole new set of worries for the Coastwatchers on Guadalcanal. Would the enemy come right over? Nobody knew, and there was certainly nothing to stop them. Prodded by two strafing enemy float planes, Ken Hay decided to close down Berande and join Don Macfarlan on Gold Ridge right away. He spent the day packing up and that night loaded his truck to capacity. Hay liked his comforts and even included a kerosene-run Electrolux refrigerator. He then went to bed but was soon awakened by the beam of a ship's searchlight probing his house. It suggested he was leaving none too soon.

At Aola to the east, Martin Clemens had no sleep at all. He spent the night answering false alarms and checking his jittery native sentries. He was still at it around 6:30 A.M. on May 4, when a blast from the conch shell announced the approach of the day's first planes.

But this time was different. Sweeping in from the south, 40 dive bombers and torpedo planes, all bearing the American white star, poured down upon the Japanese shipping in Tulagi harbor. Great balloons of fire and clouds of black smoke boiled up into the sky, as the watchers at Aola looked on first in disbelief, then in ecstasy. Some one began beating the station drum, and to Martin Clemens it seemed to say, "Come and see, come and see!"

Unknown to Clemens or any of the Coastwatchers, U.S. Navy code-breakers had learned about the Japanese operation, and now Admiral Chester W. Nimitz, Commander-in-Chief of the Pacific Fleet, was deploying his forces to meet the threat. Under Rear Admiral Frank Jack Fletcher the carriers *Lexington* and *Yorktown* raced to the scene, and the planes hammering Tulagi were from the *Yorktown,* hovering about a hundred miles to the south.

That was just the start. Wheeling west, Fletcher now went after the other prong of the Japanese advance, the Port Moresby Invasion Force. In the Battle of the Coral Sea that followed, U.S. carrier planes sank one enemy carrier and seriously damaged another. American losses were even greater—*Lexington* and two other ships sunk, *Yorktown* badly hit—but Fletcher's

purpose had been achieved. At 9:00 A.M., May 7, the
Port Moresby Invasion Force turned back to Rabaul.

But the Japanese on Tulagi remained, far less crip-
pled than they looked to the excited watchers on Guadalcanal—or to old Leif Schroeder, the Coastwatcher
on Savo. He had the best ringside seat of all. In fact,
he was too close, for several Japanese survivors from
sunken patrol boats soon came swimming ashore.
Schroeder took to the bush, but not his assistant George
Bogese, an educated native medical practitioner. Bogese
tended two badly burned sailors, and when a Japanese
patrol arrived to pick them up, he asked to be paid for
his services. He was immediately arrested and taken to
Tulagi as prisoner. Here, under threats of execution,
he was soon telling who the Coastwatchers were, and
where they were stationed.

It was just as well Martin Clemens didn't know. He
was discouraged enough already. During the evacuation
of Tulagi, there hadn't been time to think about himself. There were the Australians and all those Chinese
to ship south. Then, during the Japanese landings he
was so busy he barely realized that Don Macfarlan had
left the coast for the hideout on Gold Ridge. Finally
came the American strike, and who could think about
anything else that day? But now they were gone too—
everyone was gone but the Japanese—and Clemens suddenly came face to face with his own situation.

He had never felt more alone. The empty district
officer's house, with its simple furniture of "government oak," seemed bare and cheerless. The last beer
had vanished from the Electrolux in April. On the radio,
through some atmospheric quirk, he could only get a
BBC program aimed at West Africa. Restlessly, he
turned to the wind-up phonograph, which boasted a
miscellaneous collection of records left behind by various officials through the years. Normally he played the

Tony Martins, but on one of these first, lonely nights he absentmindedly put on a lugubrious number called "When You're a Long, Long Way from Home." It was too much. He broke down and cried.

He was frightened too—and not just of the Japanese. A month earlier a prospector named Wilmott had been axed to death in his bed by a native. Was it an isolated incident, or did it presage an uprising in the wake of the ignominious flight of the European settlers? Every night Clemens went to sleep half-convinced he wouldn't wake up in the morning.

But he struggled on, certain that his own staff was loyal, whatever the feelings of the population. To start with, he had eighteen native constables under Corporal Andrew Langebaea, an earnest man who liked to stamp to attention with a crash that shook the office pilings. Langebaea became a sort of chief of staff, in charge of organizing a scouting force drawn from his constables and fresh recruits from nearby villages. They quickly proved both brave and resourceful. A native named Bingiti was soon making regular canoe trips to Tulagi, bringing back the latest on what the Japanese were doing.

Clearly the scouts were willing enough. More difficult was the problem of teaching them to report what they saw. Most of them spoke only pidgin English— hardly suited to modern warfare. Beyond that, how could a man recognize a truck when he had never seen one? How could he tell the difference between a cruiser and a destroyer when he normally called all naval vessels "men o' war"—apparently a carry-over from the distant days of Captain Cook and the early explorers. Trial and error gradually produced a series of curious but workable frames of reference. A gun barrel "all same fella beer bottle" proved to be a 3-incher.

As yet, Andrew Langebaea's scouts had brought no

The District station at Aola, Guadalcanal, where Martin Clemens struggled to maintain the authority of the British Empire. As the Japanese approached, he took to the hills and assumed his new role as Coastwatcher. (Courtesy D. C. Horton)

intelligence suggesting the Japanese might be coming over to Guadalcanal, but Clemens was taking no chances. Up in the hills behind Aola he was already preparing a fall-back position at a tiny village called Paripao. His native clerk, Daniel Pule, bustled about the Aola office, packing and listing the files and records. Pule—a born bureaucrat—wanted to bring every last form and voucher along, and Clemens never really managed to convince him that the time had come to consider burning rather than saving carbon copies.

May 13, and all preparations were suspended by the unexpected arrival of Brother James Thrift, one of several Catholic missionaries who had remained on Guadalcanal, convinced that they could carry on their work in spite of the war. Sailing in from his mission station down the coast, Thrift was accompanied by two American flyers from the carrier *Yorktown*. Lieutenant Leonard Ewoldt and his radioman, Ray Machalinski, had run out of gas and crash-landed at sea after the raid on Tulagi. Washed ashore on the southern coast of Guadalcanal, they had been taken by friendly natives to Thrift. Now, as Clemens came forward to greet them, Ewoldt's very first words were, "Could you please get us back to Pearl Harbor?"

"I'll see what can be done," Clemens replied in the best unflappable British colonial tradition.

He was as good as his word. In three days Ewoldt and Machalinski were on their way south in a launch manned by Chinese volunteers. At San Cristobal a schooner was waiting, which took them to the New Hebrides, where they ultimately caught a ride back to their squadron.

Mid-May, and the tireless scout Bingiti paddled the 20 miles from Tulagi with the disturbing news that George Bogese had been captured and was talking. Obviously it was time to clear out, and at 1:30 P.M. on the 19th Clemens closed the office and headed for the bush.

There was nothing furtive about the departure. Led by the station dog Suinae, it was almost a gala procession. Some 190 carriers had been recruited to bring along the last of Daniel Pule's beloved files. Sixteen men staggered under the big office safe, crammed with £800 in silver. Another dozen struggled with the teleradio, now broken down into its various parts. Michael the cook and his boys labored under their loads of clanking pots and pans; while Anea, perhaps the world's meekest jailer, escorted his civil prisoners. Since Clemens was not only a Coastwatcher but also the district officer on Guadalcanal, jail, courts, treasury, the whole official apparatus had to be within reach.

Andrew Langebaea and Daniel Pule remained at Aola to keep in touch with the native scouts. In addition, Andrew took on a very special assignment. Ever so carefully he planted a potato garden over the first hundred yards of the path leading toward Paripao. By sunset it was impossible to find a trace of the track, or to know that any one had ever gone off that way.

Reaching Paripao at 5:30, Clemens found everything ready for him—a leaf hut combining house and office, other huts laid out nearby, a wireless mast with palm fronds lashed to the top for camouflage. He quickly set up the teleradio and renewed contact with Macfarlan on Gold Ridge, Rhoades at Lavoro, and the overall control station on Malaita.

One problem remained. Tulagi couldn't be seen from the house, so a good lookout post was needed. Next day Clemens found a suitable spot: a 50-foot tree at the edge of the village. Cane loops were nailed to the trunk for footing, and at the top he built a camouflaged platform, six feet by six feet, complete with railing. Here a sentry always stood watch, occasionally lowering a bucket for food or betel nut, searching the horizon with an old pair of field glasses, and blasting on his conch shell when he saw anything unusual.

But at first there was little to see. A week slipped by, and still no sign of the enemy. Clemens whiled away the time clearing a chicken yard, target-shooting with his .22, and reading three treasured volumes of Shakespeare's comedies, tragedies and histories that he always carried with him. Henry V met the French on Saint Crispin's Day and Birnam Wood came to Dunsinane, but still no Japanese crossed to Guadalcanal.

Then on May 27, a rumor that enemy patrols were ashore at Tenaru, fifteen miles to the west, and on the 28th Clemens's scout Koimate panted up the hill with the first details: The Japanese came in two launches . . .

they were ashore only a few hours . . . then one launch headed back to Tulagi, the other west toward Lunga.

Near the western tip of Guadalcanal Snowy Rhoades learned of the landing too. By now he had been joined by Leif Schroeder, ferried over from Savo by native canoe, and the two men were operating together. They moved back from Lavoro to a leaf house about two miles into the interior, but they were on the coast every day, and Rhoades was on excellent terms with a cluster of Catholic missionaries who had clung to their station at Visale. Bishop Jean Marie Aubin, like most of the Catholic missionaries in the Solomons, vaguely hoped to maintain a sort of Christian neutrality in this temporal struggle, but it was hard to be neutral when your friends were in danger.

Rhoades learned that more and more Japanese patrols were coming ashore . . . that they were looting houses, joy-riding on horses, and shooting cattle, which they then dressed and took back to Tulagi. So far, pretty innocuous. Then, early in June, Bishop Aubin slipped him a message that put a more disturbing light on things. A Japanese observation post, complete with radio and machine gun, had been established at Sapuru, only a few hills away.

Don Macfarlan, now established with Ken Hay on Gold Ridge, was also aware of the mounting Japanese activity. June 8, a body of troops arrived from Tulagi, and neat rows of tents sprouted on Lunga plain. On the 19th a destroyer anchored off the beach and began ferrying more men and supplies ashore.

On June 20 Martin Clemens's scout Chimi confirmed the destroyer and brought first word that the Japanese had built a wharf. That afternoon clouds of smoke hung over Lunga, as troops began burning off the tall Kunai grass that covered the plain.

"It looks as if the Nips are going to stay," Clemens noted in his diary that night, and all the Coastwatchers knew that a whole new phase was about to begin. From now on they would be operating deep behind enemy lines. How they would fare, operating alone on an island against an enemy army, only time could tell.

2

ALONE

What were the Japanese up to? Martin Clemens, Don Macfarlan and Snowy Rhoades tossed the question back and forth as they prepared for the dangerous days ahead. The three men were in frequent if erratic contact, sometimes by the teleradio, sometimes by native runners who darted back and forth over the trails that laced the hills and jungles.

In view of reports that the Japanese troops were vandalizing and befouling the neat plantation buildings on Lunga plain, Clemens wondered whether they really intended to stay after all. But then why the wharf? Perhaps only to ship things off the island.

Snowy Rhoades was wondering too. When the Japanese began burning the grass, he thought they might be clearing land for an airfield, but as the days passed, there was still no sign of construction. And the wharf? On July 1 he radioed that it was only for loading meat.

On Gold Ridge, Don Macfarlan was equally puzzled. As late as July 3 he speculated that the Japanese were clearing land just to get timber for rebuilding Tulagi.

"After all," he wrote Clemens, "it is feasible to suppose they are short of billets."

July 6, all doubts were dispelled. That morning a twelve-ship Japanese convoy came steaming down the Slot and anchored off the mysterious wharf. While destroyers screened the work, the freighters and transports disgorged 4 heavy-duty tractors, 6 road rollers, 2 generators, an ice plant, 100 trucks, a completely equipped infirmary, and dozens of cases of a soft drink labeled Mitsubichampagne Cider. The miracle of the bulldozer had not yet been revealed to the Japanese, but for earth-moving they brought along the beginnings of a miniature railroad: two tiny locomotives and a dozen hopper cars.

Two construction battalions also streamed ashore, along with 400 fighting troops to guard them. The Coastwatchers knew none of these exact figures, but their native scouts made them well aware of what was going on. Judging from the equipment, Snowy Rhoades's first hunch was right: The Japanese were building an airstrip. From Townsville Eric Feldt urged his three men to find out everything they could about it.

The new Japanese move meant a drastic change in the life style at Gold Ridge, 2800 feet up and directly behind Lunga plain. Don Macfarlan and Ken Hay were ensconced in a comfortable five-bedroom house built as headquarters for the European manager of a gold-mining company. The firm hoped to capitalize on the strain of gold that had been found both on the ridge and in the Sorviohio River valley below, and at this point nobody yet realized how little gold was really there. The European manager was now gone, but a capable Fijian named Kelemende Nabunobuno remained as caretaker, and he served as a sort of host for the visitors.

The tone of the place was set by Ken Hay. A legen-

Don Macfarlan, who watched the Japanese from Gold Ridge, 2800 feet above the enemy airstrip being built on Guadalcanal. Photographed later, after his return to friendly territory. (Courtesy Don Macfarlan)

dary island character, he was a man of gargantuan girth, impassioned kindness, implacable grudges, and a thousand money-making schemes. He traded in any kind of merchandise. He organized currency-exchange deals with the fleeing Chinese traders. Quite naturally he was also involved in the current gold-mining operations. He believed in living well, as attested by the Electrolux refrigerator, hauled up the mountain by a dozen natives and now the showpiece of the establishment. Hay wasn't about to let living in the bush destroy the good things in life—he even insisted that his butter be served in ice.

Macfarlan was the working stiff in this combination, trying to serve as coordinator of all Coastwatching work on the island, carefully keeping his teleradio operating under the worst conditions. Both Rhoades and Clemens often found their sets out of order, but never

Macfarlan. His transmitter was always dry, his batteries always charged. No wonder that at the control station on Malaita, and at Feldt's headquarters in Townsville too, he became a sort of epitome of reliability.

But even the most efficient intelligence agent is only as good as his information, and it was here that Macfarlan was especially lucky. The Fijian caretaker Kelemende had excellent contacts. The native "police boys," mostly provided by Clemens, proved daring and resourceful. One got a job as a cook in the Japanese officers' mess at Lunga, stayed for four days, and brought out highly useful information on the camp layout.

The Japanese themselves made these infiltrations easy. In their rush to get the airstrip built, they turned to native labor:

NOTICE NO. 1—All inhabitants on this island must be ordered by Japanese Government to cooperate for Japan. Any inhabitant against it should be severely punished by Japanese Martial Law.

ORDER NO. 1—Men only over 14 years old or less than 50 years have to work for Japanese troops at some places on this island. After a month's labor they will be given the identity as a civilian on this island. During work for Japanese troops, they will be supplied with meals, etc.

Ishimoto, the interpreter and guide on Tulagi, now crossed over to Guadalcanal. Promoted to a sort of political affairs officer, he took on the job of putting the order into effect. It was not an easy task. Few of the natives could read, but they were shrewd, and when the order was read to them, they quickly grasped that they were not going to be paid. Their only return for a month's labor was to be given "identity as a civilian on this island"—whatever that meant.

Nevertheless, a trickle of cowed natives began reporting for work, and mingling with them came some of the Coastwatchers' most resourceful scouts. Clemens's man Dovu got work as a carrier, helped bring stores from the beach to the airstrip site . . . and made careful note of everything he carried.

There were some close calls. In a rash moment the bureaucratic Daniel Pule took a job helping unload a small schooner at Taivu. As he sweated away, Ishimoto himself suddenly appeared. With head bowed in the best Japanese tradition, he politely inquired, "My friend, I've known you before at Tulagi?"

Pule's heart was in his mouth. Indeed Ishimoto had often seen him at Tulagi and might well connect him with the government. He tried to indicate that he couldn't speak English and gestured for a cigarette.

"You're a liar," Ishimoto said coldly, all politeness gone.

Pule desperately clung to his pose. He gestured that he was hungry and wanted some food. Ishimoto seemed a little more convinced and had some rice brought over. Pule now tried one more bit of pantomime: He wanted some betel nut. Hesitantly Ishimoto indicated he might go to a hut some yards away. Once there, Pule fled and was safely out of sight by the time Ishimoto realized he was gone.

In another encounter, one of Macfarlan's scouts found himself closely questioned by a Japanese officer—not Ishimoto, but one who also spoke good English. The scout managed to convince the officer that he was just another English-speaking native, but as he turned to go, the Japanese casually asked if there were any Europeans in the hills. When the scout replied, "None left—

all gone away," the officer, who had perhaps learned his English in America, simply snorted, "Bullshit."

It was all too clear that the Japanese knew a great deal about the Coastwatchers on Guadalcanal. From the coerced medical assistant George Bogese—and perhaps from radio intercepts—Ishimoto knew at least some of the names and would ask affectionately for the whereabouts of "Mr. Snowy" or "Mr. Mac."

Early in July Rhoades passed along a rumor that the Japanese were planning to use paratroopers to trap Clemens and Macfarlan. Knowing the tangled, jagged terrain, neither man worried much about that, but it was different when Rhoades also reported that the enemy planned to use bloodhounds. There was something especially chilling about the thought of being tracked down by dogs, and the Coastwatchers gave the matter considerable attention. Rhoades urged Clemens to put citronella on his heels and walk in streams; he himself scattered arsenic along the trails leading to his hideout.

But it was Macfarlan who had the real secret weapon. Ken Hay kept a mongrel bitch named Suzy, and it was said that if her droppings were spread across the path to Gold Ridge, this would draw any bloodhound away from the scent he was following. The theory was never tested, for actually the Japanese at no time used dogs to track the Coastwatchers. They did use watchdogs to guard their facilities, and these were apparently what inspired the rumor.

These were especially grim days for Martin Clemens at Paripao in the hills behind Aola. On July 4 word had reached him that Japanese patrols were coming ashore at Taivu, nearest point on the coast and only seven miles away. He immediately doubled his sentries and began pulling farther back the following morning.

He traveled light now. The big safe and office records had been hidden in a tunnel dug into the hillside, and the party consisted only of two scouts in the lead, a dozen carriers, Michael the cook with his helper, and Clemens himself bringing up the rear. All that day and the next he climbed deeper into the interior, soaked by the rain, slipping and sliding in the mud, sweating from the heat, his throat as parched as his clothes were drenched.

Finally, on the evening of the 6th, the little group reached an isolated toothlike rock, hundreds of feet high, connected to the surrounding hills by a thin ridge only four feet wide. Atop the "tooth" perched a tiny native village called Vungana. It looked as safe as Edinburgh Castle and the view of the coast was magnificent. Here, Clemens decided, he would make his next stand.

Yet the outlook was anything but cheerful. Native loyalty in some villages was beginning to waver. The Japanese were reported coming down the south coast behind him. His radio batteries were low. He was running out of water. On July 8 he radioed the Malaita control station a gloomy assessment of his situation. CANNOT DO VERY MUCH GOOD FOR VERY MUCH LONGER. HAVE YOU INSTRUCTIONS?

He began to think about getting off the island. There were a couple of boats hidden on the south coast; maybe he could reach them. That same day he radioed Gold Ridge, asking whether Macfarlan intended to evacuate and suggesting that the government ketch be left for Clemens himself, "if need be."

Back came a laconic "Yes."

The strain grew, and on the 14th Clemens asked in his diary a rhetorical question that caught all his weariness and discouragement in just four words: "O Lord, how long? ? ?"

Martin Clemens with six of his scouts. Andrew Langebaea, "chief of staff," stands on Clemens's left; Daniel Pule, chief clerk, on his right. (National Archives)

Snowy Rhoades felt the pressure too. Ishimoto had visited Visale "looking for Europeans," and while Bishop Aubin managed to fend him off, there was no telling how long the old man could play dumb. Nor could the Japanese fail to notice the track that Rhoades had by now beaten between the coast and his hideout in the hills.

July 9, he decided it was time to move. Traveling mostly at night, a party of 24 carriers brought his rice, kerosene, benzine, and the teleradio down to the west coast of the island. Here everything was loaded into his launch—hidden for just this emergency—and again traveling by night, he headed down the coast.

Twelve miles, and Rhoades was at the mouth of the Hylavo River. Here he unloaded his gear onto the beach, sent the launch away, and began waiting for a fresh group of carriers who would meet him at dawn. It was still dark, so he hid his supplies under some coconut fronds and lay down in the sand for a nap.

The sound of a diesel engine woke him up. There was no chance to run for cover without being seen, so he rolled under some leaves and waited. In a few seconds he could make out a Japanese barge edging along the shore toward him. Aboard were about forty soldiers and the ubiquitous Ishimoto. Rhoades hardly dared to breathe—if he was seen he was lost—as the barge crept within a hundred yards. Then, finding nothing, it chugged on down the coast.

An hour later the carriers arrived with two canoes, and Rhoades was on his way up the Hylavo. A two-mile paddle, another mile of walking, and he finally reached his new hideout—a leaf house built in the foliage near the river bank. Here at last he felt safe for the moment.

At Gold Ridge the situation looked so dangerous that on July 8 Eric Feldt ordered Don Macfarlan to fall back to "the most inaccessible part of Guadalcanal" and keep radio silence until needed again. Macfarlan lingered on, but he began preparations to withdraw and even talked evacuation with Martin Clemens.

The place seemed dreadfully exposed. Nor was security helped by three more refugees. The newcomers were F. M. Campbell and his two teenage sons Jack and Pat. Campbell had been an early district officer who married a native girl, retired to grow copra, and was now mining gold on land leased from the government just below the ridge. Along with another doughty individualist named Andy Andresen, Campbell had continued prospecting, regardless of the war swirling around him. As the Japanese swarmed onto Lunga plain, he complained in a note to Martin Clemens, "It's all very upsetting and not conducive to the health or good gold-digging."

At last, as Japanese patrols began fanning inland, the Campbells decided they should, as young Jack later put it, "forget prosperity and head for Gold Ridge." Andresen remained at his house by his claim, but he led scouting parties for Macfarlan, occasionally coming up to the ridge to discuss the latest developments.

There were now nearly a hundred people clustered on Gold Ridge, counting Macfarlan's scouts, Hay's servants, and about thirty natives brought along by the Campbells. Only Macfarlan and the scouts had much to do. The rest settled back, relaxing uneasily, surrounded by danger for literally hundreds of miles. They argued, drank, hunted, practiced target-shooting, and played endless games of rummy with a worn deck of cards supplied by Martin Clemens.

So many people doing so little couldn't help being conspicuous, and it was probably a group of them loafing together that finally attracted the attention of two Japanese Zero float planes on the morning of July 12. Down they roared in a strafing run as the Gold Ridge group dived for the bush. The hideout had been discovered.

Macfarlan decided to move back at once. Two hours of frantic packing, and they were on their way. They headed south, made about four miles, and camped for the night. Shortly after dawn they were on their way again, down into a dark valley . . . then up the next range to the top of Mount Jonapau . . . then down again into the valley behind that. It was back-breaking work, especially for the lumbering Ken Hay. Finally they tied a rope around his waist, raising and lowering him over the roughest places like so much bulk cargo.

July 14, they straggled into Bombedea, a primitive native village on the banks of a swift stream called the

Sutakiki. Here Macfarlan decided to make his new camp. He had by now put two whole mountain ranges between himself and the Japanese. That should be enough, and if not, there were good escape paths leading to the south coast. The Campbells joined him, while Hay and Andresen moved into nearby settlements.

The natives gave them anything but a warm welcome. Most of the villagers vanished into the hills, refusing to work at the camp or supply any food. They had paid taxes for years, explained a committee of elders, and here was the government running away. Macfarlan said he was willing to pay for what he needed, but they told him his money was no good. Japanese money was what they wanted now.

The situation looked desperate. Gold Ridge was gone. Food stocks were low. The natives were hostile. Macfarlan was now stuck in a gloomy valley where he couldn't even see the sun, let alone the Japanese. On the 15th he radioed the grim details to Eric Feldt at Townsville. Back came an encouraging but cryptic answer:

GOOD WORK BAD LUCK. POSITION NOT AS BAD AS APPEARS. STAY IN BUSH BUT DO NOT REPEAT NOT TRANSMIT FROM ANY POSITION WITHIN TEN MILES OF YOUR CAMP. STICK IT OUT FOR FOUR MORE WEEKS AND I WILL RESCUE YOU BUT DO NOT MOVE TO BEACH UNTIL INSTRUCTED.

For good measure, a separate message was relayed from the Deputy Chief of the Naval Staff at Melbourne, promising, "It won't be long now"; and the control station at Auki assured Martin Clemens, "Things are happening for the best."

"There is a big stunt brewing," Macfarlan wrote Clemens on the 19th—his first cheerful letter in days—

and on the 21st he elaborated: "It is only a matter of a few weeks, and we will be in the money again. . . . My advice is, sit pat—either come here or keep in close touch with us and wait for the big event."

For Martin Clemens the outlook wasn't nearly so rosy. His carriers had vanished; his teleradio wasn't working; and worst of all, he learned from the natives that Ishimoto had visited Aola for the first time with a lugger full of troops. They had torn apart the office, dug up Andrew Langebaea's garden, and carried off his potatoes. Andrew himself underwent a stiff grilling, but he was wearing only a pair of shorts and managed to pass himself off as a bush boy.

Suddenly Vungana no longer seemed like Edinburgh Castle. With Ishimoto now concentrating on the eastern end of Guadalcanal, Clemens felt terribly exposed in this lofty perch. He decided to pull back once again, hoping for someplace less conspicuous.

At 9:00 A.M. on July 19 he started off, heading ever higher and deeper into the interior. On the 20th the path faded out, and the party continued up a river, usually waist-deep against a swirling current. His last pair of shoes gave out, and for a while he hobbled along on bruised and bleeding feet. One of the scouts finally made him a pair of sandals out of a mail bag, and Clemens ruefully recalled the regulation against damaging government property.

Late that afternoon they climbed a nearly perpendicular rock-face to reach a village of just four huts called Vuchicoro. At last he felt safe again and ordered the party to make camp. It was pouring rain and the radio still didn't work; so he whiled away the time rereading his Shakespeare. As a substitute for supper he made up the menu for the first dinner he'd have if he ever got out of this alive: Toheroa soup from New Zealand, Lobster

Newburg, and duck with green peas. Then he munched
a soggy piece of hardtack and curled up to sleep.

Snowy Rhoades was in trouble too. One day as he
sat in his leaf hut up the Hylavo River—the place that
seemed so safe—he was visited by a native who had
been working on the Lunga airstrip. The native brought
word from the Japanese commander saying they knew
where Snowy was; they were coming to get him, and
when they did, they wouldn't execute him; they were
going to cut off his hands and feet.

"That's when I decided to sleep with a pistol under
the pillow," Rhoades later recalled. He did more than
that. A friendly native told him about a secret cave
two miles deeper into the jungle, and he lost no time
moving there. Arriving, he found it was not so much a
cave as a long ledge of overhanging rock, but it was
perfect for his purposes. Adding a leaf "verandah," he
had room for himself, twenty carriers, and all his stores.
As was his invariable custom, he hid the teleradio in a
separate place—this time in a leaf hut a mile away.
Making sure that its location was known only to the
four natives who built it, he once more felt relatively
safe.

At Bombedea, Don Macfarlan was again beset by
doubt. Food was low, and the carriers were deserting.
There were reports of a 500-man Japanese force coming
down the south coast—this could cut off all escape.
When Eric Feldt said to stick it out for four weeks,
that didn't seem long, but the last ten days had been
hell, and now it seemed a lifetime.

"We are all living on hope," he wrote Clemens on
July 28. "If nothing happens before the weekend, I
intend to flit. I would suggest you do likewise. Patrols
are approaching the Ridge, and I don't intend to wait

here until I can't get out. . . . I may be wrong, but I am going to get out before it is too late."

But of course he stayed. Every once in a while a man discovers he can go beyond the limits he sets for himself—can endure more than he ever dreamed he could —and so it was with Don Macfarlan. His deadline, Friday, July 31, came and went—and still no sign of the Allies—but he did not "flit," as he liked to put it. Instead he found himself writing Martin Clemens, "We will hang on for a few more days as you suggest. . . . I suppose we must have faith."

So it was back to the teleradio and the latest information he could get for Townsville. Kelemende slipped up to Gold Ridge again for another look at the Japanese airstrip. They were working on it 24 hours a day now. The construction crews used great flarelike lights at night. The runway, a scout reported, was red clay and gravel over grass. It looked almost finished.

Clemens and Rhoades had their scouts out too. In three months these primitive natives had learned a lot about the ways and toys of civilization. They now reported trucks and tractors and destroyers with breezy familiarity. Yet there were mix-ups. On July 29 Bingiti reported planes "with wheels" on Halavo Beach at Tulagi. If true, this meant there was a second Japanese airstrip. Clemens's teleradio was working again, and he immediately relayed the report to Townsville.

To Macfarlan this was simply incredible—Halavo Beach was only 20 yards long—and he was right. It turned out that some Zero float planes were resting on bogie wheels, and Bingiti's informant mistook the bogies for landing gear.

On August 1 Daniel Pule sent Clemens a particularly detailed report with a map of Lunga plain showing tents, workshops, bomb sheds, and a wireless station. Trenches and dugouts were neatly marked in red pencil.

There was no way to forward the map, but Clemens radioed the information to Townsville. Back came an urgent query for the exact location of the wireless station. Clemens managed to oblige in ten minutes.

Still, how much longer could they last? Macfarlan was now living mainly on potatoes and a melonlike fruit called pau pau, Clemens on taro root and an occasional pumpkin. Native support was falling apart, and this could be fatal. With it, the Coastwatchers might somehow luck through; without it, they were lost. So far they had managed, but the native chiefs were practical men who couldn't afford to stick with a loser, if the Japanese were really going to take over the island.

The Tassimboko villagers were now openly pro-Japanese, and some of the settlements around Visale were leaning that way. At his cave near the Hylavo, Snowy Rhoades learned that the local chiefs had held a meeting and decided he was too much a liability to have around. They were sure he would ultimately be caught and the neighboring villages wiped out for harboring him. The solution was to liquidate him themselves first and take his head to the Japanese.

At this point a chief named Pelisse objected. Rhoades had a rifle with a thousand rounds and was a good shot besides. Even if they attacked at night, many of them would be killed. As for himself, he had promised to help Rhoades, and he would keep his promise. On this note the chiefs deferred their decision . . . but for how long? And how many Pelisses were there on Guadalcanal?

On August 3 Don Macfarlan decided to join Martin Clemens for what might turn out to be a last stand. He had no carriers and wrote Clemens, begging him to send any he could round up. "I know it is tough, but if you can't do it, then I'm afraid I have no chance."

Daniel Pule, Martin Clemens's chief clerk, today lives in retirement on New Georgia. He stands here (left) with Alesasa Bisili, a mission schoolboy in 1942. They are holding the torn wing of an American plane—part of the debris of war that still litters the Solomons. (Author's collection)

But even in these dark hours the Coastwatchers somehow managed to keep up a steady flow of information for the insatiable brass at Townsville and the control station at Auki on Malaita. Headquarters was no longer offering soothing advice to lie low. On August 4 Auki fired off a particularly urgent request: "Any reliable additional information as to number, type, location troops; positions, types and calibre of guns to be sent now."

During the next 31 hours Clemens sent eight different messages giving his scouts' latest information on Japanese troop billets, mess facilities, bomb and fuel storage, trenches, and the planting of a naval gun for coastal defense.

Macfarlan was having less luck. At 3:30 P.M. on the 5th he gloomily reported, CANNOT OBTAIN ANYTHING RELIABLE. NATIVE REPORTS VERY CONFLICTING. . . .

Then, five hours later, pure gold. The competent Fijian Kelemende was now back on Gold Ridge and had his own contacts out. Two of them had been drafted by the Japanese to work on the airstrip. They had escaped during an Allied bombing raid, and Kelemende rushed them down to Macfarlan on the Sutakiki. From the information they supplied he radioed the most complete picture yet of the situation on Lunga plain:

ONE APPROX 6-INCH GUN ON HILL BEHIND LUNGA STOP AA GUNS ON SAND BEACH LIGHT CALIBRE APPROX 2 INCH OF THESE SCOUT SAW THREE LUNGA SIX KUKUM BUT ARE OTHERS STOP NO ARMED FIGHTING VEHICLES OBSERVED STOP RUNWAY IN POSITION PREVIOUSLY MENTIONED BUT IS GRAVEL AND CLAY FROM NEARBY HILLS NOT CEMENT STOP UPON 31ST JULY WHEN NEAR COMPLETION RUNWAY HIT ALSO ROAD ROLLER BUT ONE STILL REMAINS STOP HANGAR IN COURSE CONSTRUCTION NEAR RUNWAY STOP AS NEAR AS CAN BE GAUGED FROM

TENT AND HUT ACCOMMODATION FOUR THOUSAND
TROOPS OF WHICH HALF LABOR CORPS. . . .

It was just the kind of information needed by the
Allied invasion armada, now ploughing north through
the Coral Sea toward Guadalcanal. This great force was
the immediate result of the danger posed by the Japanese airstrip, but its genesis could be traced much
further back.

The Solomons had caught the eye of Admiral Ernest
J. King, Commander in Chief United States Fleet, as
long ago as February. He saw both the threat they
posed in Japanese hands and the opportunity they
offered as an Allied strong point in a step-by-step re-
conquest of the Pacific. Trouble was, the Allies had
agreed that the defeat of Germany came first, and both
President Roosevelt and Army Chief of Staff General
George C. Marshall were cool to any operations that
diverted men and resources from Europe. If necessary,
Marshall's planning chief, Brigadier General Dwight
D. Eisenhower, was even willing to let Australia go
down the drain.

Nonsense, King argued, the Americans couldn't just
stand by while the Japanese gobbled up island after
island. It was all very well to beat Hitler first, but certain minimum steps had to be taken to stabilize the
situation in the Pacific. Ernie King was a man of ruth-
less determination. "They always call on the sons-of-
bitches when they're in trouble," was the way he is
supposed to have explained his own appointment as
COMINCH. But he was enormously respected. All
spring he kept hammering away for a limited offensive
in the South Pacific, and in the optimistic atmosphere
that followed the great American victory at Midway
his persistence finally won out.

By July King's War Plans Officer, Rear Admiral

Kelly Turner, had developed a plan calling for, among
other goals, the capture of Tulagi and the simultaneous
occupation of an airfield (or airfield site) on the north
coast of Guadalcanal. King and Nimitz quickly approved, and Turner was put in charge of the Amphibious Force. Christened WATCHTOWER, the Tulagi
landings were set for August 1—only a month off.

July 4, and the whole scheme picked up tremendous
momentum. That day Nimitz's industrious code breakers deduced that the Japanese were planning major
landings on Guadalcanal. Coastwatcher messages and
aerial reconnaissance soon made it clear that the enemy
was already doing just what the Americans planned to
do—build an airstrip on Lunga plain. This airstrip, eyed
so avidly by both sides, suddenly became the focal
point for the whole operation. It was what made
Guadalcanal—code name, CACTUS—so important.

Yet no one seemed to know anything about the place.
When Vice Admiral Robert L. Ghormley, Commander
of the South Pacific, informed Brigadier General A.
Archer Vandegrift that his First Marine Division would
be landing on Tulagi and Guadalcanal in five weeks,
the General was utterly astonished. He didn't even
know where they were.

On July 22 the Marines sailed from Wellington, New
Zealand, and few military enterprises have ever begun
under greater handicaps. Some components of the division had yet to join up. There wasn't time to load all
their equipment. Space was so tight they had only ten
days' supply of ammunition. No one yet knew much
about Guadalcanal. There were no good maps, and an
aerial photographic mosaic of the island had been lost.
Admiral Ghormley pleaded for more time, and King
grudgingly moved the landing date back to August 7—
but not a day beyond that.

From the 28th to the 31st the operation was rehearsed on the tiny Fijian island of Koro. Everything seemed to go wrong, and Vandegrift consoled himself with the old theatrical maxim that a bad dress rehearsal means a good opening night.

On the evening of July 31 the whole force weighed anchor and headed northwest for the Solomons under Admiral Fletcher, the officer in tactical command. At last the breaks began coming their way. The weather turned hazy, and no Japanese patrol plane caught even a glimpse of the huge armada—over 80 ships spread out over the sea in a giant circle. Nor did any enemy submarines run across this choice target. The sea remained calm, the voyage completely uneventful.

Late afternoon, August 6, and Fletcher's carriers—*Saratoga, Enterprise* and *Wasp*—peeled off with their escorts to take their covering position south of Guadalcanal. The rest of the ships ploughed on. Dusk, and on the thirteen transports nearly 17,000 Marines settled down for a last night at sea. On the mess deck of the transport *American Legion* the juke box blared away, while a young Marine, his body glistening with sweat in the stifling heat, did some exaggerated jitterbugging. On the flagship *McCawley* Kelly Turner moodily thought of a passage written in 1939 by the British military analyst Liddell Hart: "A landing on a foreign coast in the face of hostile troops has always been one of the most difficult operations of war. It has now become almost impossible."

On Guadalcanal Captain Tei Monzen of the Imperial Japanese Navy had good reason to be pleased. The 2571 construction troops under his command had done wonders in the month they had been building the airstrip on Lunga plain. The field was nearly finished. Repair shops, bomb sheds, a fine medical clinic, and a pagodalike administration building were ready; only a small middle section of the runway remained to be graded. Around the field a criss-cross of serviceable roads connected the positions of the 400-man force assigned to defend the base.

It was time for a small celebration. On the evening of August 6, Monzen ordered an extra ration of *sake* for all hands, and it was announced that thanks to their industry and patriotism, planes would start landing in a few days.

In the mountains to the east Martin Clemens spent a fruitless day. His scout Bingiti had just returned from Lunga, but the man was exasperatingly vague. Yes, he thought the strip could now be used. No, he wouldn't say any planes had actually landed there—but he wouldn't say they hadn't.

It was all very frustrating. Clemens had left his perch on Vuchicoro, hoping he could operate more effectively at Matanga, a village closer to the coast. Today it didn't seem to make much difference where he was. He felt disgusted and depressed. He was hungry and his feet hurt. Starting his diary entry for August 6, he asked rhetorically, "Is nothing going to happen after all?"

This same evening Pat and Jack Campbell, the teen-age sons of the old gold miner F. M. Campbell, stood on Gold Ridge, looking down at the field. They had come up from Bombedea to see if anything new was going on, but to their surprise all was dark. For the first time in days the Japanese weren't working by flare-light. Contemplating a wasted trip, the boys joined the Fijian caretaker Kelemende in the manager's house and went to bed.

Jack woke up before daybreak on Friday, August 7, and just couldn't get back to sleep. For a while he tossed and turned, but it was useless. Finally he slipped quietly out of the house so as not to disturb Pat or

Kelemende, sat down on the grass near the crest of Gold Ridge, and stared into the empty night.

Soon the first hint of dawn streaked the eastern sky, and gradually he could make out the dark bulk of the Lunga plain stretching below him toward the coast. It was going to be a cloudy day, so it was still fairly dark when suddenly, a little after 6 o'clock, a series of flashes erupted from the sea. Next, the distant boom of guns, and then more flashes and explosions as shells ripped into the shore.

Pat and Kelemende came bounding out of the house, and the three of them watched in excitement. Still more flashes, and as the day grew brighter, they could see that the channel between Tulagi and Lunga was literally covered with ships. Cruisers and destroyers lay close in, pounding the shore, and behind them waited an array of freighters and transports. Beyond these, other warships were pounding Tulagi across the channel.

Now there were planes too . . . sweeping in from the south . . . dive-bombing the beaches . . . raking the shore with machine guns. A gasoline dump exploded, sending an orange balloon of flame into the sky.

Down in the valley of the Sutakiki Don Macfarlan could see none of this, but he heard the gunfire, saw the waves of carrier planes, and knew what it all meant. The days of worry and waiting were over—Feldt had been true to his word—deliverance was at hand. Snowy Rhoades at his "cave" and Martin Clemens at Matanga could also hear the guns and see the planes, and they too felt a surge of immeasurable relief. Twisting the dials of his teleradio, Clemens caught snatches of carrier jargon and bursts of American slang. "Calloo, callay, oh, what a day ! ! !" he scribbled in his diary at noon. "On combat radio I hear Tulagi is taken, and at 1205 Marines land on Gavutu. Wizzard ! ! !"

For the American commanders leading the assault,

The Allied anchorage at Guadalcanal, sketched August 8 by Martin Clemens from his lookout at Vungana. Date, filled in later, is off a day. (Courtesy Martin Clemens)

it was hard to believe it could go so easily. They had taken the Japanese completely by surprise. It was late morning before any fighting developed, and then—as so often happens in war—the pattern was quite different from what had been expected. All the advance planning assumed that Guadalcanal would be hard, Tulagi easy. Actually the reverse was the case. Most of the Japanese combat troops in the area were on Tulagi and its neighboring islands. Holed up in caves and dugouts, they fought to the last man.

No such problem on Guadalcanal. The Japanese were mainly construction troops with little stomach for fighting, and the 400-man defending garrison couldn't make much of a dent. Together they all fled west into the bush. The Marines pushed in and along the coast, incredulous at first, then exhilarated. Would it all be this easy?

Not if Vice Admiral Gunichi Mikawa could help it. Like everyone else at Rabaul, the commander of the Japanese Eighth Fleet had been caught off guard by the blow. Now he quickly hammered out a counterstroke. Planes scheduled to raid New Guinea would attack the Allied shipping off Guadalcanal instead. All submarines would concentrate on the Solomons. A transport-load of troops would head there right away. Mikawa himself would pull together all available warships—five heavy cruisers at Kavieng, two light cruisers and a destroyer at Rabaul—and attack the Allied force.

At 9:30 the planes were on the way. Twenty-seven high-level bombers, followed by 17 Zero fighters, took off from two different airstrips, wheeled into formation, and headed southeast. It was the shortest course possible—a straight line to Guadalcanal, passing over the southern coast of Bougainville.

3

"FORTY BOMBERS HEADING YOURS"

High on a steep slope called Malabita Hill near the southern coast of Bougainville a middle-aged man in white shirt and shorts peered through a pair of round spectacles at the planes passing overhead. At first glance Paul Mason looked like a bank clerk who had somehow strayed into the jungle. He was small; his mild blue eyes seemed to abhor violence; and he had a self-effacing diffidence that would seem far more appropriate in an office than in the bush.

This was, however, deceptive. Mason was born in Sydney but had been in the Solomons since 1915. And although he was indeed small, he had the strength of an ox and an endurance that was the wonder of even the old Islanders. He had other assets too that specially fitted him for his present work. He was an expert at repairing and operating radios. As manager of the Inus plantation on the east coast of Bougainville, he knew both the area and the natives intimately. When he volunteered for Coastwatching work at the start of the war, Eric Feldt eagerly snapped him up.

With Mason in the south and the Assistant District Officer Jack Read in the north, Bougainville would be well covered. For incidental support the two Coast-watchers could look to the A.I.F. commando unit that had been guarding the unfinished airstrip on Buka. Driven off by the Japanese, these men were now operating on Bougainville as small reconnaissance teams under their commander, Lieutenant John H. Mackie.

So far nothing much had happened. Mason first stationed himself behind the town of Kieta, working informally with four of Lieutenant Mackie's commandos. After the Japanese raided Kieta on March 31, the commandos withdrew to Mackie's camp to the north, and for several days Mason was alone with two natives. Then, about April 10, he was joined by four more of Mackie's men, who had been routed by a Japanese patrol from their station at Buin on the south coast.

This proved an unhappy combination. The usually mild Mason was in a snappish mood—perhaps because he felt the commandos had been careless in almost letting themselves get caught at Buin. To make matters worse, one of them, Sapper Douglas Otton, had a badly infected leg and naturally was of little use. After a week of it the commandos left, hoping to work their way north and join the rest of Mackie's detachment.

"Slim" Otton soon realized he just couldn't go on. His leg was acting up, and like it or not, he would have to go back to Mason. One of the others, a happy-go-lucky wireless operator named Harry Wigley, then said he'd stay too; so the group split up, with Otton and Wigley returning to Mason's camp.

To their surprise, Mason was all smiles. It turned out he had a special dislike for the two men who had gone on north, but nothing against Otton and Wigley. From now on the three men formed a happy, cheerful team. "Wig" did the radio work; "Slim" processed the intelligence; while Mason, as he modestly put it, "sat back mostly giving free advice."

His first decision was to re-establish the observation post at Buin. From here they could keep an eye on the Japanese naval anchorage in the Shortland Islands and cover almost any traffic starting down the Slot. Malabita Hill, a few miles behind Buin, offered the perfect vantage point, and Mason opened shop there around May 1.

He was just in time to see a segment of the Japanese fleet setting out for the big fight developing in the Coral Sea. After that, there was little to report for a while, but still plenty to do. The camp was short of everything, and much time was spent on the teleradio trying to arrange a supply drop by one of the big RAAF patrol planes based at Cairns in northern Australia.

The flyers were willing enough but inexperienced at this sort of work. The first drop was 70 miles off target. Undaunted, Mason borrowed a bicycle from a native,

Paul Mason, photographed with Wang You, one of the many natives he worked closely with on Bougainville. (Courtesy Mrs. Paul Mason)

pedaled and walked to the drop site. He found nothing;
so it was 70 miles back again—all for the exercise.
Eventually the RAAF's aim improved, and Buin received not only food but other supplies, including a
petty officer's cap and insignia to give Mason naval
status.

In July, Eric Feldt suddenly ordered them to move
inland, lie low, and keep radio silence until ordered
back on the air. This suggested they were being saved
for something big.

At the same time, to confuse any Japanese eaves-
droppers, Feldt gave Mason new call letters. Once back
on the air, he was to use the first three letters of his
sister's married name. This could only refer to Mrs.
John Stokie, wife of a New Britain planter; so from
now on the station was STO.

August 5, orders came to move back to the coast
and start reporting all enemy movements to the southeast. Speed was essential. Plain language must be used,
even though this made it easier for any Japanese listening in.

By the morning of the 7th Mason was operating
once more from Malabita Hill. Around 11:30 he caught
the drone of approaching planes. In another minute 27
twin-engined bombers flashed by—Admiral Mikawa's
initial response to the American landings on Tulagi
and Guadalcanal. Mason carefully counted the planes,
rushed to the teleradio, and flicked on the emergency
X-frequency. At 11:37 he called, FROM STO, 27 BOMB-
ERS HEADED SOUTHEAST.

Some of the Allied ships caught the message direct
from Paul Mason—they knew about X-frequency and
were tuned in. Most got it by a complicated but highly
effective relay. Port Moresby, the control station for
the Bougainville Coastwatchers, flashed it to Towns-

ville, which sent it to Canberra, which shot it back to Pearl Harbor, where CINCPAC's big transmitter broadcast it over the whole Pacific. One way or another, every ship in the invasion fleet got the word within 25 minutes.

On the carriers south of Guadalcanal quick calculations were made. Buin was 300 miles away . . . cruising speed of the Japanese medium bomber was 160 knots . . . that allowed nearly two hours to vector out the Grumman Wildcat fighters, stack them west of the landing area, and put them in position to pounce. They needed every advantage: They packed a lot of fire power, but the Zero could still outmaneuver them.

Down below the unloading stopped. On every ship the gunners stood waiting.

At 1:15 some fighter pilot gave the "tally-ho," as the Japanese bombers appeared west of Savo. They were flying in a wide and stately V-formation; the Zeros, which had started later, had now caught up and were flying cover. At 1:20 the Grummans poured down on them, and two minutes later the ships opened up. Here and there Japanese planes spiraled down trailing smoke. The rest came on, but they were shaken and their bombing was wild. "Rather a poor shot," dryly commented Captain Ferncomb of the cruiser *Australia*.

About an hour later nine dive bombers damaged the destroyer *Mugford* in a brief attack, but the combat air patrol soon drove them off. Thanks to Paul Mason's timely warning, the Japanese lost at least sixteen planes —a sobering statistic for the generally overconfident command at Rabaul.

Off Guadalcanal the transports resumed unloading. By nightfall 11,000 Marines had landed. Ashore, the troops were fanning out west and southwest, still against virtually no opposition. The advance party bedded down in a grove of palms and amused themselves cracking coconuts.

At enemy-held Rabaul, too, it was a quiet night after the day's excitement. Only the ordnancemen were busy, arming the bombers with torpedoes for a new attack on the Allied invasion fleet in the morning.

At 8:00 A.M. on the 8th the planes began taking off —some 44 torpedo bombers and fighters altogether. With the torpedo planes going first, they took off in stages, wheeled into position, and once again headed southeast on a direct course that would take them over Bougainville.

Five miles behind Aravia, a small mountain village in northern Bougainville, Coastwatcher Jack Read bent over the dials of his teleradio. This morning, August 8, was his first opportunity in two days to tune in. He had been so busy the day before that he just took a chance that nothing much was happening.

He was, in fact, always busy. A dark, wiry, brisk man of 36, Read had been in the New Guinea public service for twelve years, but had never been on Bougainville until November of 1941. He had arrived then as assistant district officer at Sohano and never really had a chance to know the area before the war was upon him. In a way, he had been trying to catch up ever since.

As the Japanese swept south, he was faced with the job of evacuating the families of the European planters. They were all difficult, and three of the women flatly refused to go. It was the same with the Catholic missionaries, who included 24 nuns. Bishop Tom Wade of Providence, Rhode Island, was one of those idealists who believed that the Church could remain aloof from the war and enjoy the respect of both sides. A few of the missionaries, like Father Albert Lebel at Tinputz,

Jack Read, on northern Bougainville, was in ideal position to spot Japanese air strikes coming down from Rabaul. (Courtesy Jack Read)

were under no such illusions, but most took their cue from the Bishop and tried to carry on. Read made it clear that they did so at their own risk, but in his heart he knew he couldn't shrug them off so easily.

When the first Japanese bombs fell on January 23, 1942, Read moved from his exposed station at Sohano to the hills behind Aravia. Next, a quick trip to Kieta on the east coast, where the remaining Europeans had panicked and fled, and the natives were looting the town. Read restored order, then headed back to Aravia, checking the various plantations and missions along the way. By now Lieutenant Mackie's commandos were camped nearby, and when their communications collapsed, Read took on their radio traffic as well as his own.

March 31, and the Japanese began landing at Buka Passage. The move trapped Mackie, who was visiting an outpost on the island of Buka with several of his commandos. Read rushed a warning to them, then arranged their rescue with the help of a resourceful Fijian missionary named Usaia Sotutu. In the dead of night Sotutu put Mackie and his men into a canoe and slipped them back to Bougainville.

The Japanese soon got wind of all this from natives living on the Passage, but Read had his natives too. Sotutu organized a scouting network of "mission boys," and a giant bearded constable named Sergeant Yauwika had marvelous contacts. The teleradio churned out a steady flow of information to Eric Feldt, particularly on the unfinished Buka airstrip, which the Japanese had taken in March and were now busily completing.

July 14, and Read was told, like Mason down south, to lie low and keep radio silence until further instructtions. And, like Mason, he was given new call letters to use. They would be his daughter's initials. This could only refer to Judy Eleanor Read, so from now on the station was JER.

Then nearly three weeks of watchful waiting. But unlike Mason, Read didn't have to move back into the interior. He was already there. He had picked out his observation post at Porapora in April, but it was so good—2500 feet up and rarely any clouds—that he decided to save it. The natives could never keep a secret very long; so why risk blowing it too soon?

But now the time had come, and by the morning of August 8 Read had packed his supplies, lined up his carriers, and was almost ready to go. It was at this point that he decided to tune in one more time before dismantling the teleradio for the journey. He aimlessly turned the dial to the 7-megacycles frequency, where he could sometimes pick up interesting aircraft traffic.

The air was alive with the chatter of American carrier pilots and their ships. They were tossing about place names on Tulagi and Guadalcanal, and it was thrillingly clear that the "big show" was on; in fact, that Tulagi was already won. Read sat glued to the set, relaying the news to the natives who crowded around, and it was Sergeant Yauwika who first heard a new sound . . . a dull, throbbing roar that grew louder every second.

Planes, many planes, were approaching from the northwest. The view was blocked in that direction, and in their excitement several natives shinned up the trees. Then, seconds later, the planes were there for all to see. A great formation of Japanese bombers raced across a break in the jungle, only a few hundred feet overhead . . . then a second group right afterwards. Read caught a brief but lasting impression of red discs—of propeller blades flashing in the sun—as he tried to count them.

He twisted the teleradio dial to X-frequency and called Port Moresby. For agonizing minutes he could get no one. Finally some other Coastwatcher in New Guinea picked up and passed on his message for the Allied invasion fleet:

45 BOMBERS NOW GOING SOUTHEAST

Admiral Kelly Turner caught the relay of Read's warning about 10:40 A.M. He immediately ordered the transports to stop loading and get under way . . . the cruisers and destroyers to take up defensive disposition . . . all hands to prepare for an air attack.

South of Guadalcanal the hovering carriers caught the relay too. Once again all available fighters took off for the Slot, while the task force's combat air patrol climbed and orbited for an interception west of Savo.

This time they were fooled. The Japanese did not

come straight down the Slot. Instead, they curled north around the Florida Islands so as to come in from the east. They fooled not only the waiting Grummans but the fleet's radar operators too.

The cruiser *Australia* saw them first, 23 torpedo planes sweeping in from the east at noon. They were skimming the water—some only 20 or 30 feet high—aiming straight for the transports. But Jack Read had given Kelly Turner 80 minutes' warning, and the Admiral used them well. The ships were all moving, circling at high speed, and the screen threw up a devastating curtain of fire. Two, six, no one knew how many Japanese planes exploded into the sea—they were falling everywhere. Only three managed to run the gantlet, and only one torpedo struck home. It hit the destroyer *Jarvis,* stopping her dead.

Coordinating their attack with the torpedo planes, eight Japanese dive bombers now came plunging down. But a circling ship is hard to hit, and all their bombs were misses. Desperately, one of the bombers slammed into the transport *George F. Elliot,* leaving her a blazing wreck.

In ten minutes it was all over. Here and there a Japanese plane straggled homeward up the Slot, but they still weren't safe. The Grumman fighters—originally caught out of position—tore into the survivors. It was after 2 o'clock when they again passed over Jack Read on Bougainville. He had trouble counting them coming down, but now it was easy. There were only eight.

Deep in the mountains of eastern Guadalcanal, Martin Clemens moved forward to Vungana, where he could get a better look at the show. Rising early on the 8th, he climbed to the lookout and was rewarded by an amazing panorama. Ships stretched everywhere;

Japanese torpedo plane skims the water off Lunga Point during the great air strike of August 8, 1942. Thanks to Jack Read's timely warning, 36 of 44 enemy planes were shot down. (National Archives)

landing craft bustled to and from the shore, trailing wakes that looked like white brushstrokes painted on a canvas of blue. For practice, he counted up to 25 of them through his binoculars.

He watched the air strike at noon too, and was awed by the immensity of it all—the puffs of smoke that filled the sky . . . the flashes of every conceivable color . . . the bedlam of every imaginable sound. He was so excited he forgot to eat, and considering how hungry he was, he must have been excited indeed.

As the calm of evening finally settled on the scene, he jotted his impressions in his diary, closing with the words. "And so ends another splendid day."

Splendid indeed. The Marines overran the main Japanese camp, captured all sorts of supplies and equipment, and at 4:00 P.M. took the greatest prize of all—the almost-completed airstrip. With understandable optimism General Vandegrift wrote his wife that evening, "The fighting is over now, and we have the place we set out to take."

Then an urgent message arrived from Admiral Turner, summoning him to the flagship *McCawley*. It turned out that Admiral Fletcher, worried about fighter plane losses, planned to withdraw his carriers immediately. This was appalling news. It meant the Amphibious Force would have to go too, with the freighters and transports still largely unloaded.

There followed a brief discussion about a Japanese force sighted that morning by a patrol plane off the east coast of Bougainville. Since the pilot thought he saw two "seaplane tenders," the force was probably going to Rekata Bay on Santa Isabel island, where the enemy was developing a seaplane base. It might mean trouble in a day or so.

The conference broke up at 11:55 P.M., with Vandegrift heading for Tulagi on the minelayer *Southmore* to check the supply situation there. He had just settled down in the wardroom for a cup of coffee with the skipper, when a sailor shouted down the speaking tube, "Commodore, you better come up here. All hell's broke loose."

Admiral Mikawa had arrived. In a remarkable combination of audacity and plain good luck his seven cruisers and single destroyer had burst through every Allied barrier protecting the Guadalcanal landing area.

Now the fox was in the hen house. At 1:38 A.M. on the 9th the torpedoes hissed from their tubes, and at 1:43 the cruisers' main batteries opened fire. At the same moment, spotter planes dropped flares silhouetting the Allied ships, and the Japanese flagship *Chokai*'s searchlights snapped on. They revealed a scene of surprise and confusion—guns still trained in, sailors scrambling frantically about the decks of the screening warships.

In six devastating minutes Mikawa ravaged the South Force, guarding the shipping off Guadalcanal. The cruiser *Chicago* had her bow blown off; the *Canberra* turned into a blazing, sinking wreck. Then he wheeled left and headed for the North Force, protecting the transports off Tulagi. About 1:50 the hail of torpedoes and shells began again, shattering the cruisers *Astoria, Quincy* and *Vincennes*.

Another twenty-five minutes, and it was all over. Continuing to bear left, Mikawa rounded the north side of Savo and headed back up the Slot. At trifling cost, he sank four cruisers, badly damaged a fifth, and turned the screening force into a shambles.

Kelly Turner had originally planned to unload all night and leave at 7:30 A.M., but Mikawa's visit upset that timetable. Now they unloaded all morning and began pulling out in the afternoon.

By 7:00 P.M. the whole force was gone—eighteen transports escorted by what was left of the screening force. Still in their holds were half the Marines' food, all their barbed wire and sandbags, all their heavy earth-moving equipment, except for one bulldozer that somehow reached shore. As they watched the last of the ships disappear to the southeast, the Marines needed no one to remind them that they were now alone.

The Coastwatchers on Guadalcanal were blissfully unaware of this sudden change in the fortunes of war. In the early hours of August 9 Don Macfarlan saw flares, gun flashes, and occasional searchlights from an observation post he had established on Mount Jonapau. It was clearly a sea fight, but he had no clue as to the outcome. At Vungana Martin Clemens saw and heard gunfire too, but he was equally mystified. "May be a naval battle off Savo," he noted laconically in his diary.

Snowy Rhoades knew even less. At his cave on the other side of the island, he could only hear the rumble of distant guns. He guessed correctly that he was cut off from the landing area by the Japanese garrison retiring westward, and there was really nothing he could do at the moment.

Macfarlan and Clemens, on the other hand, now had to decide whether to stay put or come down and join their liberators. For Macfarlan the choice was easy. His naval orders said to remain in the bush, and that's what he would do. For Clemens it was not so simple. Like Macfarlan, he was a Coastwatcher working for the Navy, but he was also district officer, the only government official on the island, and he wanted to be near the center of authority. Beyond that, there was his yearning to be where the action was. What seemed dangerous but strangely satisfying work yesterday now struck him as drearily tame. "It's too anticlimactical sitting here like birds in the wilderness," he complained in a note to Ken Hay on the 13th.

Late that afternoon he found the solution. A U.S. Marine Corps Field Message arrived from his friend Charles Widdy, manager of the Lever Brothers plantations in the Solomons, who was serving the expedition as a guide:

American Marines have landed successfully in force. Come in via Volonavua and along the beach to Ilu during daylight—repeat—daylight. Ask outpost to direct you to me at 1st Reg. C.P. at Lunga. Congratulations and regards.

Hardly official instructions, but good enough. Clemens packed up the teleradio, organized his carriers, and at 7:35 on the morning of August 14 started downhill for the beachhead.

The guard at the Marine outpost just east of Volonavua raised his rifle but held his fire. The little group marching down the beach toward him on the morning of August 15 was like no military formation he had ever seen. Two rows of nearly naked natives, closed up and rifles at the slope, were stepping along with smart precision. Leading them, accompanied by a small dog, was a white man in tattered shirt and shorts, but wearing an immaculate pair of black dress oxfords.

Martin Clemens was entering the American lines. It had taken two days to come down from Vungana, because there were isolated Japanese units roaming about, and he didn't want to run into them. Then, when he finally reached the coast, he realized he still wasn't safe. He was about to face the biggest danger of all—trigger-happy Marine sentries.

He had no identification, knew no password. The best course, he decided, was to put on as snappy a show as possible. He hoped the Marines would be convinced that whoever he might be, no Japanese would approach in this way. So he closed the column, dressed his ranks; and as his own contribution he squeezed into the oxfords, which Macfarlan had sent him some time ago. They were much too small—hurt his feet dreadfully—but if it contributed to the overall effect, no sacrifice was too great.

The strategy worked. The Marine guard, after what seemed a lifetime, lowered his rifle and beckoned the group in. As he came forward, Clemens suddenly felt a queer lump in his throat and wondered what it would be like to speak to some one in his own tongue again.

He had tried to rehearse what he would say before he got there, but now the words wouldn't come. He could only whisper his name.

The guard relaxed, gave him a cigarette and a piece of chocolate. In seconds a mob of Marines milled around, every one asking questions at once. Later he visited D-2, the division intelligence post, and finally had a meeting with General Vandegrift himself. The General was quite taken by this urbane newcomer who had appeared so casually from nowhere, and assigned him to his intelligence staff. From now on Clemens would supply the Marines with scouts and guides, while continuing to collect information through his innumerable native contacts.

That evening he had a sentimental reunion with Charles Widdy, helped along by a bottle of *sake* and two miniatures of brandy. Clemens was still so excited that he didn't feel the liquor at all as he and Widdy talked the night away. But they did grow louder and louder, until finally at 3:00 A.M. a weary Marine yelled at them to knock it off.

Then the letdown. As he turned in at last, Clemens suddenly felt a surge of emptiness and disappointment. He had looked forward to this day for months, and in his misery had even conjured up visions of a beer, a hot bath, a soft bed. Now here he was without any of these pleasures; only a foxhole in a coconut grove that he had to share with Widdy. It was ludicrous to have expected more, yet it was still an anticlimax.

Clemens soon learned there were other things too that fell short of the high hopes he held on his mountaintop. The Allied force, which looked so triumphant from Vungana, turned out to be a beleaguered garrison. With the loss of sea and air support, and so much equipment, General Vandegrift had pulled his troops into a compact beachhead designed mainly to protect the airstrip.

From the center of the strip it was never more than two and a half miles to the perimeter in any direction, and to the south it was only a few hundred yards. Overhead, the shallow V-formation of the Japanese bombers was an all too familiar sight. The promptest warnings from Mason and Read did little good as long as there were no fighters to intercept them.

The first step was to get the airfield in flying shape. Marine engineers worked day and night filling the gap in the center of the strip, lengthening the runway, chopping down trees that blocked the approach. Captured Japanese trucks and grading equipment proved a godsend, as did stores of rice and "liberated" *sake*.

The engineers were still hard at it on the evening of the 15th, when four U.S. destroyer-transports slipped in from the New Hebrides—the first ships to arrive since Kelly Turner's departure. Banking on assurances that the strip was ready, they brought 400 drums of aviation gas, 300 bombs, 120 maintenance personnel, and an air operations staff.

Looking slightly out of place among the rest came Lieutenant Commander Hugh Mackenzie, Eric Feldt's deputy for the area. Mackenzie had graduated from naval college with Feldt, then retired in the '20s for a life in the South Pacific. Back in the Navy in 1940, he became Feldt's assistant and later served with credit during the disastrous retreat from New Britain. Brave and cheerful, he hated routine. As a friend later put it, "He knew no fear, and no organization either." Yet he had a good overall grasp of things, and most important of all, he knew how to get along with Americans.

Now he had come to set up a Coastwatcher headquarters right on Guadalcanal. The network could then receive and disseminate emergency messages direct, rather than rely on the somewhat cumbersome relay system currently used. To help him, Mackenzie brought along a naval assistant, a civilian radio expert, and a native refugee from New Ireland named Henry Rayman Martin, who had attached himself to Mackenzie at Vila as the only person he could find who spoke his brand of pidgin English. It proved a fortunate association, for Rayman was a skilled and intuitive mechanic.

They got their first taste of the tense atmosphere on Guadalcanal a few minutes after landing. A Marine sentry almost bayonetted the dark-skinned Rayman when he couldn't pronounce the password "Lilliputian."

Next morning Mackenzie started looking for the right location for the teleradio. All the good places were already taken, and he was finally stuck with a spot nobody else wanted—a dugout built by the Japanese just north of the airstrip. It would obviously be on the receiving end of every enemy raid.

The dugout itself also left much to be desired. It was really a narrow covered trench about 50 feet long, but only five feet deep. No one could stand up straight in it. Along each side ran a ledge cut into the soft black earth. This was used both for sitting and for storing equipment, including the precious teleradio. The roof was of coconut logs covered with Japanese sandbags, and Mackenzie soon discovered it leaked.

Alongside the dugout he erected a Japanese tent, ripped and torn by shrapnel. It too was available because nobody else wanted it. The tent served as both an office and a refuge when the air in the dugout got too thick. Three radio operators, lent by the Marines, slept here; while Mackenzie himself bunked in a Japanese shack about a half mile away.

It took only a day to install the teleradio, string the aerial between two palms, and plug a field telephone into the central exchange, called "Texas Switch." On the morning of August 17 Mackenzie proudly opened for business, using the call letters HUG for local traffic and KEN when contacting the outside. This proved confusing, and eventually the station became simply and universally known as KEN.

It came on the air none too soon. On the 18th the Japanese staged their first air raid aimed directly at the strip, now christened "Henderson Field" in honor of a Marine squadron leader lost at Midway. Jack Read, as usual, gave nearly two hours' advance warning. KEN phoned the alert to Air and Division headquarters; warning flags fluttered; a bicycle siren wailed; and everything ran like clockwork—except that there were still no fighters to intercept.

As the Japanese bombers unloaded, the staff of KEN had their first experience with Hugh Mackenzie in an air raid. He wouldn't take cover. Fascinated, he stood on the steps of the dugout watching the show. Even though a Marine was cut in two about 50 yards away, he seemed oblivious to the danger. The staff concluded that here was a fine leader, if only some miracle kept him alive in the days ahead.

That night the embattled Marines learned they faced a brand-new peril. Sometime after 11:00 P.M. outposts along the beach noticed a break in the soft, steady rhythm of the sea lapping the sand. Heavy waves came rolling in—obviously the wash of ships passing eastward at high speed. The sharpest eyes could see nothing, but three hours later the outposts heard the wash again—this time the ships were passing westward.

A Japanese night landing to the east seemed a good bet, and early on the morning of August 19 Martin Clemens was asked to supply native guides and scouts to help find out. Daniel Pule was assigned to a Marine patrol, and a little later Sergeant Major Jacob Vouza led out a native patrol on his own.

Vouza was a colorful character. Physically big by Solomons standards, he had served for years as a police

Sergeant Major Jacob Vouza, Martin Clemens's legendary scout. Guiding a Marine patrol, he is seen here wearing U.S. battle fatigues. (Courtesy Norris H. Allen)

constable on various islands in the chain. Autocratic and headstrong, he had been reprimanded more than once for taking the law into his own hands. Most recently he had been stationed on Malaita, but with the outbreak of war he had been sent back to his home island, Guadalcanal, without explanation. At first Clemens feared the effect such a stormy personality might have on his own team of natives, but his worries were groundless. Vouza rose to the occasion and quickly became a valuable addition to the scouting network. After the Allied landings, he entered the Marine lines proudly wrapped in a Union Jack, still working for Clemens as a scout and a guide.

Leaving on the 19th, Vouza led his patrol south, then circled east and back north to the coast. He was carrying a small American flag that some Marine had given him as a souvenir, and he decided that it might be a dangerous thing to have on him if he should run into any Japanese. He turned off alone for Volonavua, planning to hide it in a house there and then rejoin his group.

Too late. He walked right into a Japanese patrol. They found the flag and took him to the village of Tanevatu for interrogation. Here Ishimoto appeared and began asking questions about American troop strength and disposition. When Vouza just shook his head, the guards tied him to a tree and beat him with rifle butts. Still no answer, so they stabbed him in the chest with their bayonets, and an officer slashed his throat with a sword. Again, no answer. Finally they left him for dead, still tied to the tree, and hurried on west. It was getting dark now, and they had serious business to attend to.

Their goal was no less than the recapture of Henderson Field. They had been landed as the advance echelon of a much larger force, and their commander, Colonel Kyono Ichiki, thought they could do it all alone. Now he was approaching from the east with 800 men, hoping to take the Americans by surprise. It was one of his patrols that caught Vouza.

Another had considerably less luck when it was ambushed by a party of Marines, and soon General Vandegrift had enough information to guess what was up. He quickly adjusted his defenses, then got an unexpected boost around sunset on August 20. Flown in from a carrier, twelve Marine dive bombers and nineteen Marine fighters bounced down on Henderson Field.

About 1:30 A.M. on the 21st a bright green flare announced the start of the enemy attack. From the operations dugout at Lunga, Martin Clemens listened to the bedlam and watched the tracers ricochet across the sky. The guns were still blazing when, just before 7:00, he got an urgent telephone call from Lieutenant Colonel Edwin A. Pollock's command post at the front. A badly wounded native had staggered through the enemy lines and was asking for him. Clemens grabbed a jeep, and taking along Daniel Pule, raced to the scene.

It was Vouza. Somehow he had wriggled loose from the tree, then stumbled and crawled three miles back to a Marine outpost. Now he lay on the ground, nearly fainting from loss of blood, too weak even to sit up. Still, he refused any treatment until he could report everything he had seen.

Clemens and Pule dragged him behind the jeep, and Vouza poured out the best information yet received on the Japanese strength and weapons. Clemens relayed it on by field telephone, while the fighting continued around him. Even as he talked, a bullet smacked into the jeep.

Vouza had more to say, but now it was personal. He firmly believed he was dying and dictated a long last message to his wife and children. Clemens took it all down, writing with one hand and holding Vouza's hand with the other. As he finished, Vouza collapsed and was rushed to the field hospital.

Banking on his information, a Marine force now crossed the Ilu River to the south, falling on Ichiki's left flank and rear. Surprise was complete. The Japanese found themselves hopelessly trapped in a coconut grove, pinned against the sea and the main Marine line.

By 5:00 P.M. it was over. The Marines always called it the "Battle of the Tenaru," mistaking the river. But whatever the name, the first Japanese attempt to retake Henderson Field ended in disaster. At a cost of only 43 killed, the Marines virtually wiped out Ichiki's whole force. The Colonel himself survived long enough to contemplate briefly the price he had paid for overconfidence. Then he burned the regimental colors and committed hara-kiri.

Amazingly, Jacob Vouza lived. At the Marine field hospital the doctors sewed him up, pumped him full of new blood, and in twelve days he was back on his feet. But for the first few hours it had been touch and go, and he was unconscious most of the time. Just before being placed under the anesthetic, he came to long enough to mutter, "I didn't tell them anything."

After Colonel Ichiki's disaster the Japanese began a steady build-up of their scattered forces on Guadalcanal for a new try at dislodging the Marines. Major General Kiyotaki Kawaguchi, a magnificently mustachioed infantry officer, was put in charge of the attack. He drew up a complicated plan calling for separate landings east and west of the perimeter, to be followed by a coordinated assault from both directions.

Starting August 28, Rear Admiral Raizo Tanaka began ferrying the men south from the Shortlands. He relied on quick, darting destroyer thrusts which he appropriately called "Rat operations"—and which the Americans, with equal flair, called the "Tokyo Express."

At his lookout on Malabita Hill near the southern tip of Bougainville, Paul Mason had a magnificent view of the Japanese anchorage in the Shortlands, and on August 29 he radioed unusual activity: 5 WARSHIPS, EITHER CRUISERS OR LARGE DESTROYERS, SUDDENLY STARTED FOR THE SOUTHEAST AT HIGH SPEED AT 1245.

From time to time Mason reported more of these forays, and the overworked flyers at Henderson Field did their best to intercept. Tanaka, a smart tactician, quickly learned to gear his departures so he'd remain beyond the range of the Marine bombers until dark. Then he'd barrel in at flank speed, land the troops, and be on his way back home, again out of range, by sunrise. But if it wasn't always possible to capitalize on Mason's messages, they were no less important. They clearly indicated another attack was coming soon.

These were busy days for Jack Read too. He managed to borrow one of Lieutenant Mackie's radiomen, Corporal H. L. Sly, to help on the routine traffic, but plane sightings he always handled himself. The Japanese air command at Rabaul was doing its best to neutralize Henderson Field, and every morning when the weather was right, flights of bombers and fighters passed over northern Bougainville. Perched in his observation post at Porapora, Read would meticulously count them . . . then open up on the teleradio, now linked directly to KEN:

August 29, 8:25 A.M.: 18 TWIN-ENGINE BOMBERS, 22 FIGHTERS NOW HEADING SOUTHEAST.
August 30, 9:25 A.M.: 15 PLANES, MAY BE FIGHTERS, JUST PASSED GOING SOUTHEAST VIA EAST COAST.
August 31, 8:45 A.M.: 18 TWIN-ENGINE BOMBERS, 23 FIGHTERS NOW EN ROUTE YOURS.
September 1, 8:55 A.M.: 18 BOMBERS, 22 FIGHTERS GOING YOURS.

Listeners in the stifling dugout marveled at the calm, unruffled voice of this man so deep in enemy territory. They were fascinated by the pithy brevity of his words. The warning "40 bombers heading yours," used on one of these occasions, became a sort of catch-phrase on Guadalcanal as a dry summation of impending peril.

Read was off the air almost as soon as he came on—Japanese radio direction-finding was a constant worry—but his few brief words were always enough. As his voice crackled over the receiver, one of the Marine operators would scribble the message down and hand it to Hugh Mackenzie. The commander would then relay it over the direct phone to Air Control, now located in the picturesque "Pagoda" just north of the

Henderson Field, Guadalcanal, the great prize captured from the Japanese. Early warnings, flashed by the Coast-watchers on Bougainville, were invaluable in helping U.S. forces hold the strip. (National Archives)

airstrip. Then a call to D-2, and another to Texas Switch, to be passed on to all antiaircraft units.

Read's signals usually gave about two hours' notice, but communications were erratic on Guadalcanal, and it took time to alert pilots, bring them to the strip, and generally get the defenses organized. When the Japanese were about 50 minutes off, the warning flag went up on the Pagoda, the bicycle siren sounded, and the fighters began taking off. Later the dive bombers and some Army P-400s (next to useless in fighting Zeros) also took off, but their job was simply to stay out of harm's way.

The Grumman Wildcats carried the burden of the defense, and they were tough little fighters indeed. But they were slow climbers, and it took 45 minutes to reach 30,000–35,000 feet—the altitude they needed to get the jump on the faster and more maneuverable Zeros.

Their wait was never long. Straight down the Slot the Japanese formation would come, the bombers almost invariably in their wide, shallow V, the Zeros roaming above and below them. Picking the moment for attack was the skipper's art, but when he gave the signal, the fighters plunged down on the enemy formation, hurtling by the top layer of Zeros, and boring in on the bombers.

Every fight was different, yet somehow always the same: the Japanese formation, shaken and broken . . . bombers fluttering down out of control . . . Zeros turning grimly on their tormentors . . . dogfights in and out of the towering columns of cumulus clouds, watched with fascination by both sides below.

And then, two hours later, Jack Read would be on the air again, counting the aircraft as they limped back to Rabaul. They were rarely in formation now—just straggling along—and sometimes he saw only three or four planes.

In the midst of these great aerial battles the Marines got a welcome assist. On August 31 the first air search radar arrived and was immediately installed at Henderson Field. The manual said the range was 125 miles, but 80 miles was more like it—much too close to give the hard-pressed fighter pilots the time they needed. Jack Read remained their priceless secret weapon.

Yet the Tokyo Express continued to run, gradually building up General Kawaguchi's force to 6000 men.

By September 12 he was ready, and that night a red rocket burst in the sky just south of Henderson Field. It was the signal for a coordinated attack from the east, west, and south; but the General neglected to take the jungle into account. It made such exquisite timing impossible, and the result was a piecemeal assault that ended in disaster. Colonel Merritt Edson's First Marine Raiders had a close call on "Bloody Ridge," but the Marine lines held, and Kawaguchi was repulsed on all fronts. In two days he lost over 1200 men, as against Marine casualties of 143 killed and wounded.

So the perimeter was safe. The Marines had defeated the second Japanese attempt to retake Henderson Field and throw them off the island. But they were so battered, so exhausted, and still so lacking in the tools of war that they were unable to follow up their advantage. Paradoxically, the victors remained penned up, while the vanquished controlled the island.

An ugly stalemate now developed. The Americans controlled the air, leaving the Japanese unable to mount an offensive powerful enough to dent the Marines' perimeter. But the Japanese controlled the sea, leaving the Americans unable to land enough men to break out of the perimeter. Until the Japanese could knock out Henderson Field, or until Nimitz could regain control of the sea, there seemed no way to get off dead center.

While the battalions and regiments remained at loggerheads, a far more mobile—more personal—kind of warfare was breaking out on the other side of the island, which would introduce a most remarkable individual to the Coastwatching fraternity.

4

THE GOOD SHEPHERD

It all began on August 15 when Snowy Rhoades, operating on the western end of Guadalcanal, heard from a native that an American flyer had landed in a rubber raft at nearby Tiaro Bay. Taking no chances, Rhoades sent Leif Schroeder, armed with a .45, to investigate. Schroeder found the flyer about fifty yards from the beach, but his uniform was in tatters, and the man himself was so sunburned that it was hard to tell whether he was American or Japanese.

The castaway seemed equally suspicious of Schroeder, and for long seconds the two men stood examining each other uncertainly. Finally the flyer made up his mind, walked boldly up to Schroeder, and announced he was American.

It was Machinist William H. Warden, fighter pilot from the *Enterprise,* who had been shot down during the landings on the 7th. For a week he had paddled about the Slot, going first to the Russell Islands—where he found no one—and then on to Guadalcanal. He made contact with some natives almost at once, but they knew no English; so it was impossible to tell them who he was. They finally decided he was American, not because of the way he talked or looked but because some of the stitching on his yellow raft happened to be in the shape of a star. To the natives of Guadalcanal, anything with a star was American.

Identification settled, Schroeder now led Warden back to the cave, where he was greeted by a somewhat grumpy Snowy Rhoades. Most of the Coastwatchers liked to operate alone—the fewer "boarders" the better—and Rhoades was no exception. Nor did it help that Warden had badly sprained an arm when he tripped over a rock on his way to the cave. That made him even more of a liability.

Fortunately there was medical help nearby. Father Emery de Klerk, in charge of the Catholic mission station at Tangarare—only ten miles down the coast—was a skillful medical man, and on August 15 Rhoades wrote him, asking whether he would come up to the cave and take a look at Warden's arm.

De Klerk was on a trip to Visale at the time, but the message was relayed to him, and he promised to drop by on his way back. Sure enough, he appeared out of the jungle on the 21st. By this time Warden not only had a bad arm but was feverish and immensely depressed, and his first glimpse of his benefactor could not have been very encouraging.

Father de Klerk was only 5 feet, 4 inches tall—a meek and somewhat ineffectual-looking Dutch missionary of 36. It was easy to believe that here was a man of great piety, but hardly very practical. A devoted follower of Christ, perhaps, but not much of a leader himself.

He was, in fact, quite different. After seven years at Tangarare, his position made him an important figure in this isolated area. As priest, he tended the spiritual

needs of some 1500 natives. It was not unusual for him
to hear 150 confessions a day while making his rounds.
As head of the Church's ten schools in his district, he
presided over the only education there was. As doctor,
he had a "practice" of some 1500–2000 patients. His
specialty was giving injections against yaws, and he
applied his needle with the skill of an expert who had
given over 21,000 innoculations through the years. He
easily met the natives' only two tests: He didn't hurt
and his medicine worked.

But his greatest strength lay in the fact that he identified with the natives completely. He understood and
respected the matriarchal system that governed the island's tribes. He recognized their property claims and
cheerfully conceded that Tangarare really belonged to
them. He demonstrated his sincerity by ploughing almost all revenues back into the station. Nor did he
favor his Catholics. Protestants and pagans found they
received the same education and medical treatment.
Finally, he paid the natives the supreme compliment of
mastering their complicated Gari dialect.

More and more the natives turned to him for advice
and leadership, especially on matters involving the war.
The whole business was quite beyond them. Most had
no conception of nationality, and terms like "Japan"
and "America" meant nothing. Both sides were "white,"
with the Japanese merely the "new whites."

For his part, Father de Klerk didn't put much stock
in nationality either. He was not pro-Allied; he was
pro-native. As a practical matter he simply wanted
what was best for his flock. The old colonial regime had
its faults, but it seemed infinitely better than anything
the Japanese might offer, judging from their performance in Malaya and the Philippines.

So he went his own way, applying only the test of
what was best for his flock, not caring too much

whether that was in line with official policy or not. When Bishop Aubin, the elderly Belgian who presided over Catholic affairs in the Solomons, advised his missionaries to be "neutral" and give their parole to the Japanese, Father de Klerk wanted none of it. The Japanese were bad for the flock; so neutrality was simply wrong.

But this didn't mean he necessarily followed the Allied line. When the Resident Commissioner ordered all natives inland, de Klerk decided this too was bad for the flock. They were coastal people who would no doubt starve in the bush. So he told them to ignore the order—stay on the coast and watch, and perhaps they could help by reporting what they saw.

He himself became increasingly involved as an informant for Snowy Rhoades. He wasn't committed to active resistance, but a steady flow of intelligence was in the flock's best interests, and he was prepared to supply it. At the same time he began taking practical precautions in case the Japanese occupied Tangarare. He was especially concerned for the safety of his three European nuns. He prepared a secret hide-out in the bush, a secret garden for food, a secret store of rice, and—one more step on the road to active resistance—a secret hiding place for a rifle and shotgun. A third gun, a relatively harmless .22, he deliberately didn't hide; he felt the Japanese would never believe him if he said he had no guns at all.

The pragmatic approach got its first test on July 10. Shortly before sunset that evening a big Japanese sampan, packed with troops, appeared around the point and headed for the anchorage. Father de Klerk rang the mission bell, told the children to stay away—go say their Rosary. Then he put on his black cassock and with Brother Michael, a visitor from Mauru down the coast, he headed for the beach. A boat soon arrived with four Japanese officers and a landing party of tough-looking marines. The leader introduced himself: He was Ishimoto and he had come to talk over the "new government."

Soon they were sitting on the mission house veran-dah—the four officers very correct in straight-back chairs, Father de Klerk and Brother Michael looking incongruously comfortable in deck chairs. Ishimoto ex-plained that the British government had ceased to exist, but the missionaries would be allowed to stay if they obeyed Japanese army law and didn't try to con-tact the enemy.

He then ordered a search of the compound for weapons. Father de Klerk assured him there was noth-ing except the .22—then almost fainted from fright when he noticed two brand-new shotgun shells sitting on a medicine cabinet in the very first building they visited. It was growing dark, and he managed to scoop them into the folds of his cassock without being caught.

Back on the verandah, Ishimoto had a few more questions. Were there any whites still on the island? Absolutely not, declared Father de Klerk. Could he supply 500 men for a native work force? Impossible—there weren't 500 healthy men in the area. (Actually, the number was far higher.) He suggested he might scrape together 300, if the Japanese would accept lepers and cases of advanced TB. Ishimoto said he'd settle for 150.

Only once did Father de Klerk resort to the truth. When asked the best place on the south coast for a radio observation post, he immediately suggested Cape Hunter. He felt this was so obvious the Japanese would pick it anyhow, and he would enhance his own credi-bility by suggesting it first.

The strategy worked. Ishimoto considered him such a good collaborator he didn't even require a parole.

The meeting ended with Father de Klerk ordering his native boys to carry the Japanese officers through the surf to their boat. This they did, with much ribald comment in the Gari dialect. "They smell like parrots!" one native cheerfully called out, as the Japanese officer thanked him for his courtesy.

It had been an evening of lies and deception, but Father de Klerk was not bothered. The Japanese were gone; the station was safe; the shepherd had protected his flock.

The next test came in the days following the American landings on August 7. Up to this point Father de Klerk had limited his activities to keeping Snowy Rhoades informed and taking protective measures at Tangarare. Now he found himself going a step or two further. On the 10th he cut an emergency landing strip behind the compound. On the 16th, when he got Rhoades's letter asking him to treat Bill Warden's arm, he decided not just to visit the cave, but to bring Warden back and hide him at Tangarare. These were far bolder steps than any he had taken before; they made him definitely an activist. But Father de Klerk's conscience was clear. Sometimes the good shepherd had to do more than look out for his flock; he must take a stick to the wolf invading the fold.

So now here he was, sitting in Snowy Rhoades's cave, urging Bill Warden to come with him to Tangarare. It would be easier to treat his arm . . . there would be more chance of rescue by passing planes . . . less chance of capture by the Japanese. Warden hesitated. Rhoades had a radio, served with the Royal Australian Navy, ran an official Allied outpost. In contrast this small, bustling missionary had no official status whatsoever. To go off with him seemed at the very least a bizarre thing to do. But Father de Klerk was a great persuader, and finally Warden agreed to go.

They reached Tangarare at 8 o'clock that night after a long, hard walk and canoe trip. Warden was still feverish and worried, but life began looking up after a shower and a pleasant supper produced by the smiling but always silent nuns. Father de Klerk dressed his arm and then—best moment of all—presented him with a toothbrush and tube of paste.

Father Emery de Klerk, the diminutive priest in charge of Tangarare mission station, Guadalcanal. He wanted to do what was best for his flock, and that meant a little Coast-watching. (Courtesy Emery de Klerk)

The days that followed were paradise. Every morning Father de Klerk trotted off on his usual rounds, while Warden loafed away the hours. He strolled the beach, played with the native children, relaxed in the verandah deck chairs, and browsed through the station's well-stocked library. Here he discovered the delights of P. G. Wodehouse. He ate well—there seemed to be a meal every five minutes—and his arm healed perfectly. Sometimes American planes passed, but always too high or too far out to see his signals. Bill Warden found he didn't mind that at all.

The spell was broken on August 28 when the missionaries stationed at Visale began stumbling in with harrowing tales of conditions up north. The fighting had spread to their end of the island, forcing them to break their parole and go to the hills. Now the Japanese were after them, and the only solution was to keep running. Down the coast they fled and into Tangarare —three priests, four white nuns, 24 black nuns, 60 school-children, and Bishop Aubin himself, wracked with dysentery and so weak he could hardly stand.

They were settled only a day or so when rumors spread that the Japanese were again hot on their heels. In a wild panic the whole crowd prepared to resume their flight. Father de Klerk tried in vain to reason with them: He had lookouts all along the coast; if any one was really coming, there would be plenty of warning. Nobody listened. Finally, he offered to make a reconnaissance himself, and the refugees hesitantly agreed to wait for the results.

Before starting out, he made a brief but important visit to Bishop Aubin's quarters. He explained he was taking a rifle—could he use it if he ran into any Japanese? Yes, said the Bishop, that would be self-defense. And now the big question: "This is war, jungle war.

If they spot me first, they'll certainly shoot me. If I spot them first, should I let them go, and destroy us?"

"No," said the Bishop, "I give you permission to attack if necessary."

To Father de Klerk nothing was more important than his Bishop's permission to bear arms in active combat. It opened the door to all sorts of possibilities for the future. Now the shepherd could really take the stick to the wolf.

At the moment it was unnecessary. There were, as he knew, no Japanese anywhere near. He returned late on September 6 to report all was well, and Tangarare enjoyed a quiet night.

But by noon on the 7th the rumors were spreading again, and Father de Klerk realized that he could never calm these frightened people. The only solution was for someone to cross the mountains to the American lines and arrange for an orderly evacuation. The trip would also offer a good opportunity to return Bill Warden, who by now was feeling quite guilty about his soft life in the tropics. It remained only to decide which missionary would make the trip, and inevitably the choice fell on Father de Klerk himself.

September 8, and they were on their way. Father de Klerk and Bill Warden took the lead, followed by four of Tangarare's most trustworthy scouts and seven bush-boys who carried the packs and presumably knew the trails. Hour after hour they struggled along, pulling themselves up the steep places by grabbing the grass along the path, then hanging on to vines to keep from falling when the trail turned down again. As usual, the jungle never seemed level and always seemed slippery. It was hard, exhausting work, and they faced 35 miles of it.

By the third day they were running out of food. They had planned to live mainly off the land, but there was almost nothing edible, and at the noon break Father de Klerk opened their last can of corned beef. Dividing half the contents between himself and Warden, he explained, "Bill, this is the last you'll get today. The rest is for tonight; so eat it slowly."

Warden downed it all in two gulps, then bet he could persuade de Klerk to give him the rest of the can too. "Go ahead and try," the Father told him, "but you'll never get a crumb before sunset."

"Well," said Warden, "it's my twenty-fourth birthday today."

His heart utterly melted, Father de Klerk gave him the beef and his last crust of bread too. Twenty-three years would pass before Bill Warden confessed to his benefactor that it wasn't his birthday at all.

Now there was nothing to eat, and that evening they were about to turn in hungry, when an old native emerged from the jungle, carrying the head of a pig. He gave it to the carriers, who graciously offered to share it. Bill Warden had seen better meals in his time, but tonight he was willing to settle for that.

The following evening, the 11th, they finally reached Nala, a major village of 200 natives in the heart of the island. Here there was plenty of food and rest, provided they could win the sympathy of the people. But this was by no means automatic. As always, the war was a mystery to the natives deep in the interior— just a fight between two sides of "whites"—and the villagers of Nala were doubly wary because they had just massacred a patrol of sixteen marauding Japanese.

How would these visitors react to that? Cautiously a native named Wiki, representing the chief, described the massacre and asked whether the district officer would punish the village. "Certainly not," Father de Klerk reassured him. "These new soldiers are enemies of all of us. You will be rewarded, not punished."

That settled, the villagers outdid themselves to make the travelers welcome. Food was produced; accommodations were arranged in the Luma, a sort of bachelors' quarters; and a runner was dispatched to Gold Ridge, only eight miles away, where Don Macfarlan was again ensconced with his teleradio. Toward midnight the runner returned with some "white-man" food and a message of welcome.

Macfarlan's note explained that the area between Nala and the American perimeter was crawling with Japanese. Why didn't de Klerk and Warden come to Gold Ridge instead and wait until it was safe for all to go down together? But Father de Klerk decided they would try to get through anyhow after a few days' rest.

All the 12th and 13th they loafed at Nala, occasionally walking to a nearby hill which gave a good view of Lunga plain and the sea. Kawaguchi's attack was on, and it was like sitting in a theater watching a show: planes dogfighting, parachutes floating down, ships maneuvering, guns blazing, and Henderson Field shrouded in smoke.

Late on the 13th a runner arrived from Macfarlan advising them to head for Belana, a village down toward the plain, about six hours away. The Gold Ridge group would join them there, and a Marine patrol would be sent to escort them all down to the perimeter.

It didn't work out. Father de Klerk and Bill Warden got through, but not the Marines or the party from Gold Ridge. There were simply too many Japanese in the area south of the perimeter. Disappointed, Father de Klerk gave up his plan to reach the coast and headed for Gold Ridge instead. Here they could all wait together until the way down was open again.

Another long, hard day of climbing, and at last, around 5:00 P.M. on September 16, Father de Klerk, Bill

Warden, and their string of scouts and carriers trudged into the Gold Ridge camp. As a final touch to the trip, their guide—a mischievous youth from Belana—slipped them by the camp's whole system of sentries, so that their actual arrival was completely unannounced. If this suggested something less than perfect security, for the moment nobody cared. The newcomers received a tumultuous welcome.

Father de Klerk was quickly introduced to the refinements of Coastwatching life, Ken Hay-style. First, a comfortable chair with a Scotch and ice. Then a hot shower, clean whites, and an excellent dinner. With the American landings and the return to Gold Ridge, many of the hidden stores had been retrieved, and Hay's Malaita cook-boy was never in better form. The dark days in the valley of the Sutakiki were over; once again the butter was served in ice.

On September 18 Father de Klerk was still relaxing on Gold Ridge, waiting for a chance to take Bill Warden safely through the lines, when two of Macfarlan's scouts burst into camp with some shattering news. The Japanese had executed two priests and two nuns at Ruavatu, a picturesque Catholic mission on the north coast. Only Sister Edmée, an elderly Belgian, had escaped. Now she lay hidden in the bush, still wearing her mud-splattered black habit, trying to care for a seven-year-old orphan.

No time to lose. Macfarlan immediately sent four of his best police to bring her up to the Ridge. To allay her fears, Father de Klerk penned a hasty note in French, assuring her that all would be well and she need fear no trap.

As the day wore on, more bad news. Snowy Rhoades came on the air to report that the Japanese were now moving down the southwest coast . . . that the bishop and missionaries were abandoning Tangarare . . . that he and Leif Schroeder were getting ready to destroy their transmitter and clear out too. Next morning the picture was even darker: The missionaries were scattering into the jungle, and Rhoades himself would head south by canoe that night. On the 20th Macfarlan radioed KEN, urging some sort of rescue operation, and a few hours later came the welcome reply: Two PBY patrol planes would be sent to Tangarare to pick up everybody—missionaries and Coastwatchers—on September 28.

Rhoades and Schroeder packed the teleradio, left the cave for good, and headed down the Hylavo River to the coast. Here they picked up Second Lieutenant E. H. Farnam, an Army fighter pilot who had been shot down off Lavoro. Then the three of them climbed into Chief Pelisse's magnificent 20-man canoe and were paddled south through a beautiful moonlit night.

They landed at Tangarare at dawn on the 24th, and Rhoades quickly set up the teleradio on Tsupuna Hill, about ten minutes' walk away. With an abundance of optimism he hoped this distance might be less embarrassing to the missionaries if the Japanese showed up.

Tuning in at Gold Ridge, Father de Klerk tried to piece together the latest developments. Contrary to earlier reports, four of the missionaries were still at Tangarare, but the rest were dangerously spread out. If they were ever to be evacuated on the 28th, there was a lot of organizing to do.

Nobody was a more energetic organizer than Emery de Klerk, and he decided to head back to Tangarare at once. Bill Warden was now in good hands . . . Sister Edmée would be safe in a day or so . . . there was really nothing to keep him here. Four of the Nala men agreed to serve as guides; and with them in front and his own scouts behind, he set out after breakfast. Macfarlan loaded him with C-rations, coffee, hash, and four packs of Lucky Strikes; while Ken Hay came through in handsome style with two bottles of dry vermouth.

Toward sunset, September 27, he arrived back in Tangarare after an astonishingly fast trip. The party rarely rested, and taking advantage of the brilliant moon, continued walking far into the night. They had one big scare when they heard a blast of rifle fire not too far away. Japanese patrols were clearly in the area, but that made them travel all the faster.

Approaching the mission, Father de Klerk sent messengers ahead, directing the various scattered parties to reassemble, and by nightfall every one was back. Now he had Snowy Rhoades radio a request that had been brewing in his mind for some time: Would Marine Division Headquarters let him stay on at Tangarare after the others left? He knew the code, could operate the transmitter, and would do far more good there than if he came along. Division Headquarters turned him down cold: "ALL, REPEAT ALL, MUST COME."

There seemed no way out; so he spent the 28th organizing for the evacuation that night. The two PBYs could take only the most essential luggage; everything else was buried or hidden in the bush. Around sunset the station's biggest canoe began ferrying the group to the embarkation point. And then the anticlimax: Lunga radioed that the evacuation was postponed until further notice.

On the 30th it was on again for that very night. This time there would be only one PBY making two trips, but that gave Father de Klerk an idea. He would hang back, sending Bishop Aubin on the first plane to argue his case with the Marines. The Bishop wanted none of it—hot words were exchanged—but calm returned when, at the last minute, once again the operation was postponed.

At Lunga, Hugh Mackenzie was thoroughly exasperated. Twice now, Division headquarters had canceled his arrangements for sending the PBYs. Presumably the planes were needed more urgently elsewhere, yet the Japanese were moving steadily down the coast. Rhoades and Schroeder would soon be trapped if something wasn't done. Division clearly recognized the value of their intelligence, but seemed to regard them as expendable—a loss to be accepted as the cost of waging war.

Mackenzie wasn't prepared to accept it at all. He was strictly "staff"—not meant to dabble in operations—but he now mounted his own rescue mission. By radio, he persuaded Malaita to send over the Resident Commissioner's ketch *Ramada,* which he then put in charge of Dick Horton, the former district officer and now a naval sub-lieutenant assigned to KEN.

At dusk on October 3, with no permission from anybody, the *Ramada* slipped out of Lunga anchorage and headed west. If all went well, she would round Cape Esperance before the nightly run of the Tokyo Express and reach Tangarare at dawn. Picking up the evacuees, she would then return by daylight, when the Marine planes could fly cover if necessary.

Tangarare was alerted, and once again everyone began packing—except Father de Klerk. He had reached a momentous secret decision. No matter what the Marines ordered—regardless of the bishop's instructions—he was not going to leave Tangarare. At this point he told only Father Brugmans, his closest confidant. Brugmans, who acted as a sort of mission treasurer, quietly handed him £20—virtually all the cash he had.

After supper that night, there was a knock on Father de Klerk's door, and ten of the mission natives filed

Major General A. A. Vandegrift, USMC, the Allied commander on Guadalcanal. His only defeat was his attempt to evacuate Father de Klerk from Tangarare. (National Archives)

in. He thought they had come to say farewell, but this was not the case. Their spokesman Teotimo Sautu, the station's chief catechist, bluntly asked, "Are you leaving too?"

"Those are the orders of the government and the Americans," Father de Klerk hedged.

Then Sautu explained they had been discussing all those sermons about the good shepherd who does not run away when the wolf comes. "Father, did you *mean* that?"

"Of course I meant it."

"Father, the wolf is here now. The Japs will take away our religion. Are you running off before the wolf?"

Father de Klerk could carry on the charade no longer. He explained that he really wasn't going to leave—"not ever"—but it must be a secret, so nobody could upset his plan. Later this evening he would slip off to a hiding place, where he would remain until the boat had picked up all the others and left. Promising to send him four scouts, the delegation quietly withdrew.

Now it was time to tell Snowy Rhoades, who responded with the practical contribution of his .303 rifle and ammunition. Next, the sisters. This was a particularly teary parting—Sister Leone had been at Tangarare since 1905—but Father de Klerk managed to make them laugh by asking Sister Reine to jot down her recipe for curing meat. Then a final farewell for Father Brugmans, and at 10:00 P.M. he vanished into the night. Left behind on his desk was a short note addressed to the bishop:

Please do not wait for me when the ship comes. I have been urgently called away and cannot possibly be back to join you. I shall be all right. Farewell and bless me.

Fr. Emery

At daybreak on October 4 the *Ramada* arrived and hovered off shore, while Dick Horton scanned the beach with binoculars. One glance at the excited people waving and running up and down convinced him that no Japanese could be around. The *Ramada* inched through a gap in the reef, anchored, and Horton came ashore to greet his passengers.

On Tsupuna Hill, half a mile behind Tangarare, Father de Klerk waited until he was sure the boat was gone. By 8:00 it seemed perfectly safe, and in the bright morning sunlight he headed back toward the mission with his four scouts proudly carrying their rifles. As he approached, a great shout went up; natives crowded around him; and a small boy ran to the little mission tower and began ringing the bell. The shepherd was back with the flock.

5

NEW EYES, NEW EARS

While the little *Ramada* was completing her rescue mission to Tangarare, a far more ambitious expedition was shaping up 1200 miles away at Brisbane, Australia. On October 6 crew members of the U.S. submarine *Grampus,* moored at New Farms Wharf, studied with curiosity the strange cargo coming aboard—cases of ration packs, folding camp chairs, four rubber boats, two collapsible canoes, a little whiskey, a great deal of radio equipment carefully wrapped in waterproofed canvas sacks. Even more curious, that night four merry strangers trooped aboard, wearing American sailors' uniforms but speaking with unmistakably English and Australian accents.

The explanation went all the way back to decisions reached in Tokyo as the Japanese struggled to cut their devastating losses in planes and pilots over Guadalcanal. The Americans always seemed to be waiting for them, yet there was so little they could do. The planes had to strike around noon in order to cover the 1120-mile round trip by daylight. They had to fly the same course, because they didn't have enough gas for fancy tactics. And they chose to fly low, hoping to cross up the Allies' radar.

Clearly the solution was to establish airfields nearer Guadalcanal. With less distance to cover, the Emperor's "sea eagles" could maneuver more freely and vary their approaches. One such field was practically ready and waiting—the nearly-completed airstrip captured at Buka Passage. This alone would shave over 300 miles off the round trip to Henderson Field.

By the end of August construction troops and native recruits swarmed over the field, lengthening the runway and digging fuel dumps. From his perch at Porapora just across the Passage, Jack Read watched the work with interest. On August 28 he radioed KEN that the strip was at last operational: FIGHTERS NOW TAKING OFF, CIRCLING, LANDING BUKA DROME. SAW FOURTEEN UP SAME TIME THIS MORNING.

The Japanese could save another 208 miles by developing a new fighter strip on the plain near the southern tip of Bougainville. On September 9 several transports began unloading off the coastal village of Kahili.

A delegation of natives hastened up Malabita Hill to Paul Mason's observation post about four miles in from the sea. Better clear out, they advised. The enemy had made brief visits before, but this time "they were bringing their beds ashore." Mason hurried to the lookout and saw a lot more than beds. Tractors, trucks, heavy guns, and war materials of every sort were being landed.

Another native appeared to report that a Japanese patrol was already working its way inland, looking for the Coastwatchers. And to show that this was no rumor—that he really knew what he was talking about

—he produced a Japanese cigarette that one of the landing party had given him.

No more delay. Mason, Otton and Wigley quickly packed their gear and headed deeper into the interior. Climbing steadily, they finally settled near the village of Barougo on a saddle of land that joined the Deuro Range to the Crown Prince Range. To the south they still had an excellent view of the Shortland anchorage, and eastward they could see across the busy Bougainville Strait all the way to Choiseul. On the debit side, a mountain spur caused a blind spot directly in front, and it was harder to pick up planes coming down from Rabaul.

It was also harder to identify Japanese shipping when the weather was bad, for they were now ten miles from the coast. References to the problem peppered Mason's neat, concise reports: September 16: VISIBILITY NIL . . . 17th: FAISI NOT VISIBLE . . . 22nd: FAISI OBSCURED . . . 28th: VISIBILITY HAZY . . . 30th: A NUMBER OF WARSHIPS BUT HEAVY GROUND MIST PREVENTED COUNT AND IDENTIFICATION.

At KEN, the Coastwatcher control center near Henderson Field on Guadalcanal, Commander Mackenzie was already worried about the gaps in his network. For nearly a month Read and Mason had been sending priceless advance information on Japanese air strikes— their warnings made the big difference—but they didn't catch them all. On August 25 and again on the 26th, for instance, both Bougainville watchers missed the enemy planes altogether, and by the time they were picked up over New Georgia by Donald Kennedy, the next Coastwatcher down the line, they were only 35 minutes out—too close to intercept. The new enemy field being built at Kahili—and the new seaplane base at Rekata Bay on Santa Isabel—would mean still more undetected flights.

Then there was the Tokyo Express. The Japanese were relying on it more and more to strengthen their hold on Guadalcanal, and they were perfecting the timetable. By carefully gauging their departures from the Shortlands, the destroyers could remain beyond the range of the Henderson Field bombers till almost dusk, then run in fast, unload at Tassafaronga on the north-west coast, and be back out of range by dawn. If the "CACTUS Air Force" (as the pilots liked to call themselves) was to get a crack at the enemy, quick, accurate information was essential.

To Mackenzie the solution called for new eyes and ears in his Coastwatching network. He must fill the gap between Mason and Kennedy—some 150 miles—with additional Coastwatchers on Vella Lavella and Choiseul, the two islands below Bougainville that marked the beginning of the Slot. It involved complicated problems of recruiting, supplying, communications and transportation, but fortunately there was high-level help at hand.

On August 30 a courtly gentleman in a Palm Beach suit and Panama hat sauntered ashore from the destroyer *Colhoun,* just in with a shipment of emergency supplies. To the gawking, sweating, grubby Marines he looked like something from another world—a guest, perhaps, at a quiet summer hotel—and they watched with amazement as he made his unperturbed way to Commander Mackenzie's headquarters.

The new arrival was Walter H. Brooksbank, the civil assistant to Australia's Director of Naval Intelligence and the closest thing to a career professional in the whole organization. "B-1," as he was called (to distinguish him from his brother "B-2," also in intelligence), had helped develop the Coastwatching operation from the start. He had been in the New Hebrides straightening out a communications tangle; now he was checking up on conditions at Guadalcanal.

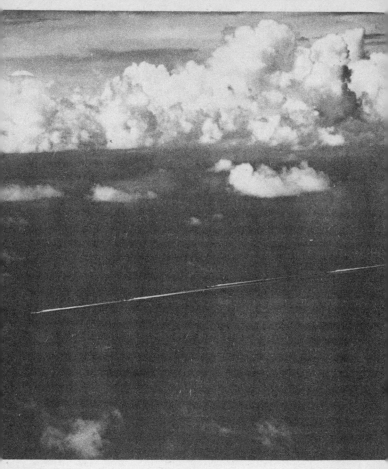

The Tokyo Express. Four Japanese destroyers return up the Slot after delivering reinforcements and supplies to Guadalcanal. Reporting these runs was an important part of the Coastwatchers' work and led to expanding the network to Vella Lavella and Choiseul. (National Archives)

He instantly took to Mackenzie's scheme for expanding the Coastwatching network, and the plan was formally approved a few days later at a meeting with Resident Commissioner Marchant and General Vandegrift's intelligence officer, Lieutenant Colonel Edmund J. Buckley. Nor was there any difficulty finding the right men. Henry Josselyn, formerly assistant district officer on Guadalcanal, had proved himself as a guide with the Marines during the Tulagi landings. Perky and resourceful, he was now "available" and volunteered for Vella Lavella. He had never been there, but he knew the Solomons, was used to working with natives, and Mackenzie was happy to have him.

Choiseul was even easier. Nick Waddell, another young district officer, had established the first formal administration there in 1941. He knew both the area and the natives better than anyone else. He too had worked with the Marines during the landings and was now recovering from a spell of malaria and aching for a new assignment. He was a natural.

So the men were chosen, but how to get them there? Brooksbank took on the assignment and headed for Espiritu Santo, the Allied advance base in the New Hebrides, hoping to pry a PBY out of Rear Admiral John McCain.

"No, Sir!" said the Admiral on hearing the request. It was an exchange made memorable to Brooksbank because it was the only time in a forty-year career that an admiral ever addressed him as "Sir." McCain went on to explain, "It would just mean the Zeros would get my plane and your personnel."

Brooksbank now went to Admiral Ghormley to beg for a submarine. This could be difficult. The submariners traditionally didn't like diverting their boats from their primary mission of sinking enemy ships. But this time there was no hitch. Ghormley's Chief of

Staff put through the request to SOWESPAC head-quarters, which controlled the subs, and back came swift approval. *Grampus* would be leaving Brisbane October 7 on her next war patrol; she would deliver the Coast-watchers to Vella Lavella and Choiseul en route to her station.

By late September Josselyn and Waddell were in Brisbane busily collecting supplies. This proved un-expectedly complicated. No one knew how much sup-port to expect from the natives; so it was hard to know how much to bring. They'd be gone at least three months; so they mustn't take too little. They'd be constantly on the move; so they mustn't take too much. They'd be landing in highly capsizable rubber boats; so the packages must be waterproof. They'd be carrying everything by hand; so nothing (except the radio) should weigh more than 50 pounds. And to top it all, whatever they brought had to be small enough to fit through the submarine's 30″ x 30″ hatch.

While Josselyn and Waddell were working out this monumental logistical puzzle, Eric Feldt came to the conclusion that each of these missions really required two men. Lists of the "talent pool" were hastily con-sulted, and for an assistant Josselyn picked a tall, dark Australian named John Keenan, who had been a Patrol Officer on Bougainville just before the war.

Waddell chose Carden Seton, a former planter from the Shortlands with an intimate knowledge of the whole area. Yet the choice wasn't that easy. A physical giant of a man and a fabled figure in the Solomons, Seton was temperamentally a person of huge extremes. Aroused, he was a man of sweeping, overwhelming passion. At other times he was gentleness itself. No one could look after a sick or injured person with more loving care. This was a volatile mixture, and Waddell wondered what would happen when the two of them were thrown together alone. He need not have worried; from the start they worked in perfect harmony.

October 6, their gear was quietly loaded on the *Grampus,* as the crew began wondering what was up. To avoid the attention that would naturally be drawn by four Australian servicemen embarking on a U.S. submarine, the Coastwatchers were now outfitted as American sailors. It was at this point that Waddell had a brilliant inspiration. Since they had to dress like gobs, why not *act* like gobs? So they spent a final, glorious evening on the town, ultimately stumbling aboard in most authentic fashion.

Awaiting them below was Australian Colonel C. G. Roberts, head of the Allied Intelligence Bureau, a sort of superagency coordinating everybody. He had come to give them a final briefing and was appalled by the frivolous chaps to whom His Majesty's affairs were about to be entrusted. It was a very grim briefing.

Next afternoon, the 7th, the *Grampus* finally cast off, slipped out of Brisbane harbor, and disappeared into the northeast. The skipper, Commander J. R. Craig, proved a good host, and for the next six days the Coastwatchers learned what submarine duty was like— the heat, the melting ice cream, the complicated "head," the intimacy, even a depth bombing by a Japanese destroyer. But for Waddell the greatest discovery was finding that his companions had never played back- gammon. He spent many lucrative hours teaching them the art.

At 5 A.M. on October 13 the *Grampus* lay submerged just off the northwest coast of Vella Lavella, and Com- mander Craig began a periscope inspection of the shore. From time to time he consulted a set of charts based on nineteenth-century German guesses and the estimates of frigate captains a hundred years earlier.

Nothing seemed to match this coastline of tangled jungle, or the solid reef that stretched before him.

He called Josselyn and Keenan to the 'scope, but they were no help. They had never been here either. The only person really familiar with the place was Carden Seton, who assured everyone that there was a break in the reef, but he certainly couldn't spot it. All day the periscope probed in vain, as the *Grampus* inched within two miles of the beach—about as close as Craig dared to go with these vague and ancient charts.

About 3 P.M. they suddenly realized they were not alone. Several miles to the north a Japanese destroyer appeared, also poking around the coast. Commander Craig turned toward the newcomer, but finally resisted the temptation to attack. There could have been no more effective way to advertise the arrival of Josselyn and Keenan.

At 6:50 the destroyer headed off to the northwest, and the *Grampus* too pulled back from the coast. Surfacing, she recharged her batteries while Craig and the Coastwatchers debated what to do. Did the Jap know they were there? Was she looking for them? Should they go on with the landing? They finally decided they should. If the destroyer knew they were coming, she would have hung around. And if she were landing a "reception committee," the sooner Josselyn and Keenan got ashore, the better their chance to avoid a meeting.

At 1:29 A.M. the *Grampus* was back again, now surfaced only a mile offshore, just south of the Mundi Mundi plantation—or where it was meant to be. There was no moon, but the tropical night blazed with stars. The sea was calm, oily calm, but the submarine rose and fell in the slow, heavy swell of the black Pacific.

The crew undogged the after hatch . . . brought up

the two rubber boats . . . inflated and launched them alongside the sub. Working as fast as possible, a sort of bucket brigade handed up the Coastwatchers' gear and stowed it in the boats. It was a tricky business on this slippery, heaving deck, and one hastily-thrown food pack punctured the side of the second boat. Some optimist covered the hole with a piece of adhesive tape.

The collapsible canoe was launched, and Josselyn jumped into it. Tying a line around his waist, he attached it to the first rubber boat, which towed the second. Taking his paddle, he dug into the water, and the little flotilla shoved off at 1:42 A.M. Keenan had planned to paddle too, but the puncture ended that. Now he sat in the second boat, his thumb pressed against the hole like the little Dutch boy at the dike.

Taking a sight on a star, Josselyn struggled painfully toward the shore. From the conning tower Commander Craig waved a silent farewell, and the *Grampus* slipped off quickly into the night.

Slowly, ever so slowly, Josselyn inched toward the shore. For a lone paddler towing two ungainly boats loaded with 2000 pounds of equipment, he did very well; but it was 4 A.M. by the time he reached the reef. Leaving Keenan with the boats, he cast off and paddled south 200 yards, still looking for an opening. No luck . . . just a solid line of white waves crashing against the coral.

Time was running out. It would be daylight in an hour, and they must be ashore and under cover by then. They had no idea whether any Japanese were stationed along the coast, but they knew they were hundreds of miles within enemy territory, and they couldn't risk being spotted. The only course left was to head straight for the reef and shoot the breakers, hoping to land safely in the quiet lagoon beyond.

For this daring maneuver both Josselyn and Keenan

transferred to the first rubber boat. Towing the other boat and canoe behind them, they paddled with all their strength. Catching a wave just right, they surged over the reef, and in a cascade of foam and spray landed safely in the lagoon. The canoe followed, but the second boat—now hopelessly waterlogged from the puncture—caught on a spur of coral, spun sideways, and capsized.

Crates and food packs swirled around in the surf, as Josselyn and Keenan scrambled back to save what they could. Scooping up everything in sight, they put it all in the undamaged boat. They had lost only three food packs and one case containing money, tobacco, a pair of binoculars, and two bottles of whiskey. Luckily, the teleradio—vulnerable to any kind of moisture— remained safe and dry in the first boat all along.

By 5 A.M. they were across the lagoon, and hauling their gear ashore. Dawn streaked the eastern sky; there was not a minute to lose. Back and forth they hurried, carrying the cases and packages into a clump of mangrove trees that sheltered the beach. By 5:45 everything was hidden—even the rubber boats—and they slipped under the trees themselves just as a big Kawanisi flying boat thundered by, examining the shore on early morning patrol.

Following a quiet breakfast, courtesy of the *Grampus* galley, they pitched a small tent and prepared for a little rest. A wave of indescribable exhaustion overwhelmed them both. After a week in the submarine they were in poor shape anyhow, and the night's work had drained them completely. They collapsed on their cots and slept as though drugged. Their clothes were still wet, but it didn't matter. Nothing mattered. At this point the whole Imperial Japanese Army could have come marching down the beach, and it wouldn't have mattered.

Henry Josselyn, in charge of the new Coastwatcher station established on Vella Lavella in October 1942. (Courtesy Henry Josselyn)

They spent the first two days mostly eating and sleeping, then cautiously began to explore the shore. There was still no sign of anyone—native or Japanese— and the war seemed very far away, except when the Kawanisis occasionally prowled by.

On October 16 they reached the Mundi Mundi plantation, about a mile down the beach. In better times it had been a busy center of the copra trade, but now it was deserted. They moved into the empty plantation house and gradually transferred their gear from the beach to a hiding place about a mile up the Mundi Mundi River.

Half a mile in from the stream they found a 300-foot hill, perfect for the teleradio. Here they built a camouflaged lean-to, covering it with sheets of galvanized iron from a plantation shed. Next the back-breaking work of bringing up the transmitter, charging engine, and all the rest. It was a job that normally took a dozen native carriers, but they still hadn't seen another human being.

October 22, and the great moment was at hand. They were ready at last to begin sending to KEN. Josselyn turned on the transmitter and felt the supreme satisfaction of making that initial contact . . . and then the supreme frustration of having the set go dead on him. Nor could they get it going again. They tried every trick they knew. Nothing worked.

Nick Waddell and Carden Seton, the team assigned to Choiseul, were having their frustrations too. The original plan was to land them the night after putting Josselyn and Keenan ashore, and at first all went well. The *Grampus* spent October 14 making a periscope reconnaissance of the coast off Nasipusi Point, drew back and charged her batteries at dusk, then began her final approach on the surface.

By 11:15 they were almost there, but that was as fas as they got. At this moment an urgent message arrived from SOWESPAC: A big Tokyo Express was expected down the Slot. They were to drop everything and take station immediately off Visu Visu Point on the northern coast of New Georgia. Naturally it was a letdown; still Nick Waddell identified with that strange exhilaration submariners always feel when closing a target.

He got his fill. Off Visu Visu the *Grampus* took on three Japanese cruisers and six destroyers. Lining up one target, Commander Craig fired a spread of four torpedoes, then dived deep to await results. He never knew whether he got a hit, but he certainly got attention. Sixteen depth charges poured down on the submarine— close enough even to throw Waddell off his backgammon game.

Four days of chasing and being chased, then new

instructions to get on with the Coastwatcher mission. On the night of October 19 the *Grampus* once again sneaked toward the northwest coast of Choiseul, and at 12:34 A.M. on the 20th Craig lay to, about a mile off Nasipusi Point.

The crew were now old hands at the game, and in twenty minutes the boats were launched and loaded. Seton would paddle the canoe, while Waddell played anchor man in the second rubber boat. At 12:54 they shoved off and watched the *Grampus* vanish into the night. Now they were alone, and as they silently paddled toward the shore, Waddell was gloomily reminded of the passage in *The Burial of Sir John Moore at Corunna:* "Not a drum was heard, not a funeral note, as his corse to the rampart we hurried."

Fortunately, there was little time for morbid meditation. About half-way to shore a strong crosscurrent caught them and began sweeping them down the coast. It took three hours of hard paddling to reach the reef, and then they couldn't find the opening. Dawn was breaking, and in desperation they finally landed directly on the reef. Soaking wet, stumbling and falling in the holes in the coral, they carried their gear the last fifty yards to shore.

By daylight everything was safely hidden except the two rubber boats. These remained wedged on the reef . . . a pair of huge yellow calling cards announcing their arrival. No time to devise a clever solution. Taking their knives and bayonets, they stabbed and slashed at the rubber until all the air was out. Then they dragged the limp carcasses to cover too, just as the inevitable Kawanisi appeared on its morning patrol.

Too tired even for breakfast, they now collapsed in the bushes that fringed the beach. Soon it began to rain, and they roused themselves long enough to build a small leaf hut. They were resting here when a native named Beni, walking along the beach, stumbled across them. In one of those happy coincidences that sometimes make life simpler, he recognized Nick Waddell from the old days when Waddell was trying to establish British authority on the island. It proved a joyous reunion, and soon Beni was telling the newcomers everything he knew about the Japanese on Choiseul. There were some, it seemed, at the northern end of the island, but few anywhere else.

Beni now went off to round up a couple of Waddell's old police boys to form the nucleus of a scouting force. This would take a couple of days; meanwhile the two Coastwatchers simply marked time, drying their clothes and cleaning their guns. While they waited, they also debated an interesting question of policy. They had come ashore with just two bottles of whiskey. Should they drink it right away, or stretch it out as long as possible, perhaps holding it to mark special occasions? They drank it right away.

A more serious question was whether to open up on the teleradio. Overhead they could see large formations of Japanese planes, tiny silver specks in the sky, winging their way down the Slot toward Guadalcanal. It looked as if a big show was brewing. On the other hand, they were dangerously exposed right there on the beach, and it would be a disaster if they were monitored and routed before they even got organized. In the end they decided to wait a few days until they had a chance to set up a lookout deeper in the interior.

On Vella Lavella Josselyn and Keenan didn't have the luxury of such an option. All day October 23 they sweated over their balky transmitter, but it was no use. It still wouldn't work. High overhead the biggest formations yet of Japanese planes rumbled by.

On the 24th they finally gave up and returned to

the Mundi Mundi plantation house in disgust. The job
clearly required a radio expert, and the nearest was
Donald Kennedy, the Coastwatcher at Segi on New
Georgia, 150 miles away. One of them would have to
take the transmitter there, while the other held the
fort. But this meant finding natives trustworthy enough
to organize a relay of canoes for the trip, and at this
point they still hadn't seen anyone, friend or foe.

Suddenly, as they were still puzzling over the problem, they spotted two natives passing by in a canoe
just offshore. Josselyn impulsively hailed them. The
natives took one look, then paddled wildly out of sight.
Fearing the worst, the Coastwatchers quickly packed
their bedrolls and prepared to head for the interior.
They were ready to leave when they spied a second
canoe approaching. Focusing his binoculars, Josselyn
made out several paddlers and a native passenger—
certainly no Japs. He decided to take a chance and
wait.

The passenger was Silas Lezatuni, chief of Paramata
village six miles to the south. Far from being hostile, he
was friendly and full of information. Yes, there were
Japanese on the island . . . with a radio . . . at Iringila
just up the coast. The natives had watched them landing from a warship (apparently the destroyer seen by
the *Grampus*), and Silas was astonished to learn
Josselyn and Keenan had been ashore ten days without
his people knowing it. How could this thing have
happened? Josselyn decided this was no time to explain
the invention of the submarine.

Silas also confirmed that the Reverend A. W. E.
Silvester, a Methodist missionary, was still on Vella
Lavella, living at Bilua on the southern end of the
island. A good man to see, Josselyn decided, before
undertaking that 150-mile trip to get the radio fixed.
He himself would go, while Keenan remained behind

to set up an observation post, recruit some scouts, and start watching the Japanese at Iringila. Silas quickly arranged a canoe, and Josselyn was off before dusk. The mounting tempo of Japanese air activity told them that there was no time to lose.

The waves of planes that poured down the Slot heralded the start of the third Japanese attempt to recapture Henderson Field and throw the Americans out of Guadalcanal. First a regiment, then a brigade had not been enough. Now Lieutenant General Harukichi Hyakutake, commanding all Japanese operations in the Solomons and New Guinea, would use a whole division. What's more, he'd lead it himself.

The build-up began October 3 with a series of air strikes. ONE BOMBER, 6 FIGHTERS NOW GOING YOURS, radioed Jack Read at 7:51 A.M., as the first planes passed over his station at the northern end of Bougainville. Then at 9:22, 6 FIGHTERS NOW GOING SOUTHEAST. And at 10:27, 28 PLANES PASSING FROM NORTH TO YOURS. FAR TO WESTWARD. MAY BE TWIN-ENGINED. And still they came: 10:42, 6 FIGHTERS GOING YOURS . . . 1:00 P.M., 6 FIGHTERS NOW ON WAY YOURS . . . 2:15, 13 FIGHTERS GOING YOURS.

Off Guadalcanal the Marine fighters were waiting. Pouncing on the Japanese, they broke up one attack after another. Ten Zeros were shot down—20% of Rabaul's long-range fighters—with the loss of only one Marine plane and no pilots. It would take a week before the Japanese air arm regained enough strength to strike again.

The CACTUS Air Force had less luck with the Tokyo Express. Fast runs were made on October 3, 5, and 8, landing not only troops but guns, trucks, tractors, even tanks. General Hyakutake himself went down with the destroyers that left on the 9th.

High in the hills behind Buin, Paul Mason on Bougainville watched them go, as he studied the ever-growing concentration of Japanese shipping that packed the Shortland anchorage. Two months ago he was pretty amateurish, sending descriptions like "one two-funneled cruiser" or "one ship with large superstructure near foremast and conspicuous tower aft." Since then he had done his homework well, mastering the penciled silhouettes sent him by Eric Feldt. Today the descriptions he radioed KEN were crisp and professional:

SHIPS VISIBLE BUIN AREA: 3 NATI, 1 KAKO, 1 SENDAI, 1 TATUTA CLASS CRUISERS, 17 DESTROYERS, 13 CARGO SHIPS, 1 TANKER, 3 MYSTERY SHIPS—COULD BE LARGE SEAPLANE CARRIERS. AT 11 A.M. 1 TATUTA CLASS CRUISER AND 5 DESTROYERS WENT SOUTHEAST.

On Guadalcanal General Vandegrift and his staff studied the message and tried to piece the picture together. Mason's report, aerial reconnaissance, captured documents, the latest CINPAC radio intercepts—all pointed to a new Japanese attack, bigger than anything that had hit the island yet.

October 11, KEN passed the word that still another Tokyo Express was heading down the Slot. This time a U.S. Navy task force was nearby—the first in these waters since Savo—and that night off Cape Esperance it gave better than it got. Yet the Japanese managed to land another load of howitzers, trucks and personnel.

On the night of the 13th the Emperor's battleships turned up. For 70 minutes they mercilessly shelled Henderson Field with 14-inch guns. Dawn found the radio station destroyed . . . the Pagoda a shambles . . . most of the aviation gas gone . . . a landscape spattered with Spam from a direct hit on some ration dump.

Casualties were light, but 85 of Henderson's 90 bombers were in no shape to fly. For the next several days the Tokyo Express would face little opposition.

Hugh Mackenzie came through the bombardment without a scratch, but he had a close call in the morning's first air raid. Normally he never took cover on such occasions and seemed to live a charmed life. This time, however, he squeezed into a dugout, and inevitably a bomb landed right on top of it. Miraculously, he suffered only a "dirty neck" and emerged as nonchalant as ever.

On October 24 the big blow finally fell. After several postponements, General Hyakutake launched his all-out attack on Henderson Field. It was another of those complicated Japanese plans, calling for perfect timing and coordination, and once again the jungle made that impossible. For two days Vandegrift's Marines, now bolstered by Army units, threw every charge back. By dawn on the 26th it was clear that the third Japanese attempt to retake Henderson Field had failed.

For the weary victors—relief. Relief that they had come through again, and better still, a feeling that they had survived the worst the Japanese could do. At sea, too, the feeling was relief. The rejuvenated fleet came off well in several night engagements—the Japanese specialty—and now boasted a new, exciting leader: Vice Admiral William F. Halsey, who replaced the competent but lackluster Ghormley.

At KEN, Hugh Mackenzie also felt a surge of relief. On October 28, after more than a week of tense waiting, Nick Waddell's familiar voice came on the air. He and Carden Seton were now established at the little village of Tagatagera on northern Choiseul. They were about two miles in from the west coast and had a magnificent view of Bougainville Strait, the Shortlands, and down the Slot all the way to Vella Lavella. Station

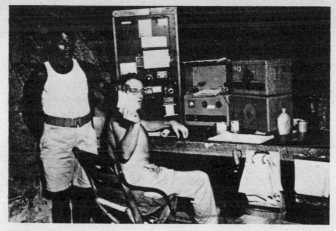

KEN, *control station for all the Coastwatchers in the Solomons, moved to this new dugout near Henderson Field in October 1942.* (Australian War Memorial)

DEL, as they called it, should be of tremendous value in filling the information gap south of Bougainville.

Josselyn and Keenan were not operating yet, but from that single brief message before their transmitter broke down, Mackenzie knew that at least they had landed safely on Vella Lavella. Meanwhile conditions were improving daily at KEN. A new dugout 200 yards farther north from the airfield—meaning 200 yards closer to safety—boasted such amenities as battery-powered lights and packing crates for seats.

Not exactly the soft life, but all in all, the pressure did seem to be easing these last days of October. Yet this was illusory, for as it turned out, the Japanese were far from finished on Guadalcanal. Starving, ill-equipped, often in desperate need of medical attention, they remained tough, brave warriors, steeped in the Bushido spirit of their homeland. Totaling some 23,000, they fully expected to make another try and were prepared to wait until the Tokyo Express brought reinforcements and opened up the supply lines again. Meanwhile they still controlled the island and were in every sense a dangerous enemy to any Allied fighting man rash enough—or unlucky enough—to be caught outside the perimeter.

6

TAKING THE STICK
TO THE WOLF

One man unlucky enough to be outside the perimeter
was Second Lieutenant Dale M. Leslie, a rangy young
pilot with Marine Scout Bombing Squadron 231. Returning from a routine reconnaissance mission on September 28, Leslie had been caught flat-footed by a Zero
off Cape Esperance. His gunner killed, his cockpit blazing, he managed to bail out at about 700 feet and
splashed into the sea several hundred yards from land.

That evening he came ashore near Tabea, about
three miles south of Cape Esperance and deep in Japanese territory. He started for the interior but almost
immediately ran into an enemy patrol coming along
the trail. He fell flat and watched them go by. He
went a few yards deeper into the jungle, but he was too
tired to go very far. It was pouring rain and the ants
had a field day at his expense, but he lay down and
slept the sleep of exhaustion.

The next eleven days he moved gradually down the
southwest coast of Guadalcanal, living on coconuts,
sleeping where he could. He had heard there were

friendly natives down this way, but all he ever saw were Japanese.

On October 10 he was still working his way down the coast when he came across an unguarded native canoe near a Japanese camp. Stealing a paddle from an empty hut, he then hid under a log to wait for the night. Hearing a rustling he looked up, and there stood a Japanese soldier staring down at him. Leslie jumped from the log . . . the soldier yelled in alarm . . . and both of them ran.

When things calmed down a little, Leslie returned to the beach to find a new hiding place until dark. He finally picked a fallen coconut palm that lay so its roots and the dirt clinging to them formed a sort of cave. He crawled in there and began to wait.

Soon he had a curious feeling someone was near, and when sand began trickling down on him, he peeked out to see what was happening. A Japanese was sitting on the fallen palm—right on top of him—eating supper. Leslie could hardly believe it: The Japanese even had thick glasses and buck teeth, the way they did in American cartoons.

Leslie ducked back into his hollow and continued waiting. But now a new danger developed. The palm began sagging under the weight of the soldier, gradually caving in on Leslie. At first he tried to brace it with his hands and prop the Japanese up, but he was too weak to do this for long. Finally he hit upon the ingenious expedient of gradually letting the soldier down, until the man grew so uncomfortable he moved to a better log to finish his supper.

Darkness at last, and Leslie sneaked down to his canoe while other Japanese relaxed on the beach, smoking and chatting under the stars. He tried to keep a tree between himself and the troops, but just as he was about to shove off, they saw him and began shouting.

He jumped in and paddled away, calling back an answering shout that must have convinced them he was a native, since they soon went back to their smoking.

Now three more days of hide-and-seek as he slowly paddled south along the shore. Then, on the morning of the 14th, he reached a sunny, tranquil coast with no trace of the Japanese. A whole new world seemed to dawn: plenty of oysters, papaya, bananas and sweet potatoes. Leslie left his canoe at this point and began walking again. His heart surged with the feeling that help was near.

Next day about noon he began to see tracks and came at last to a village full of natives. They took one look and, deciding he was Japanese, the entire population fled for the hills. He shouted as loud as he could, "American!" This didn't convince them, but they turned and came cautiously toward him, inspecting him from a distance with the greatest care.

Persuaded at last, they swarmed around him, laughing and shaking hands. In fact, he had to shake hands with every single member of the group—about 150 altogether—down to the smallest child.

He completely collapsed at this point, and the natives took him to a hut, where they put him on a reed cot and fed him some fish and potatoes. One of the villagers spoke a little English, and he explained that a white missionary lived nearby, and they would take Leslie there next morning.

It was, of course, Father de Klerk, the Marist priest and occasional Coastwatcher on the south side of Guadalcanal. Two weeks had passed since his decision to remain behind when the *Ramada* rescued the little group of Westerners stranded at Tangarare. He was now the only European on the south coast. He still liked to picture himself as just a shepherd looking after the flock, but his unique position made him far more than that.

"I will take the place of the Bishop and the government to give you advice," he told the natives in a short sermon just after the *Ramada* left. "Follow my advice always. Don't show lights at night. Keep away from the Japanese at Cape Hunter and Maravovo. Never help the enemy of our country."

He was, in short, becoming more and more a war leader. It was inevitable. Outwardly life returned to normal at Tangarare, but the major problem facing the people was not medical, or educational, or even spiritual; it was the problem of survival. The great struggle for the island dominated everything, and Father de Klerk found himself increasingly concerned with such matters as anticipating shortages, protecting the mission, and maintaining discipline.

Almost immediately, in fact, he faced a possible revolt. A local chief named Kesa was reported to be conspiring with four other natives to kill him and divide up the mission property. In a face-to-face confrontation Kesa backed down—said he meant no harm—but Father de Klerk cut him short: "You know I have a rifle, and Mistu Roti (Snowy Rhoades) left me *his* rifle. I can kill at a mile's distance. Now I want you five to leave right away, and on the run. . . . I'll walk up to my house, get my gun, and start shooting, and I shall shoot to kill!" Strange words for a missionary, but effective. Kesa ran off, and Father de Klerk had no more trouble with his people.

The arrival of Dale Leslie involved him still more deeply in the war. Leslie was, in fact, the second Marine aviator now on his hands. Another downed fighter pilot, Second Lieutenant Douglas Grow, had been brought in a few days earlier.

Like everyone else at Tangarare, Leslie was immediately captivated by the sensuous loveliness of the place—the rustling palms, the sparkling Coral Sea, the distant crash of the surf on the reef. Those tiny silver specks of planes wheeling back and forth across the sky seemed light-years away. "You know," he remarked one day to Father de Klerk, "I wouldn't mind staying here till the war is over, if only I could let my mother know I'm still alive."

While the flyers loafed and browsed through Wodehouse, a new drama was completing the metamorphosis of Emery de Klerk from priest to warrior. On Sunday, October 18, a delegation of natives called on him and asked him to lead them in combat against Japan. They explained they were tired of living away from their villages while the Japanese plundered their homes and gardens . . . weary of being on the run, afraid even to go fishing for fear of being strafed.

De Klerk dodged the request, pointing out that they were already perfectly free to fight and kill the marauders.

But how? asked the village chief. They had only machetes and knew nothing of modern war. They needed some one to instruct them in its ways, and who better than the Father? He knew them, and they knew him . . . trusted him . . . would follow him.

De Klerk still hesitated. Until now it could be argued he had acted only in self-defense, for the safety of the natives, the missionaries, and a few U.S. pilots. He had shouldered a gun, all right, but he had not gone looking for a target.

Then he thought again of the shepherd and his flock. The truly good shepherd should not be content simply to use the stick when the wolf attacks. Then it might be too late. If he knows the wolf is on the prowl, the truly good shepherd will go after him before he strikes.

And—most important—he had the sanction of the

Church. The Bishop himself had given him permission
to shoot first during the big scare in September. The
danger was far greater now. What was permissible then
must be doubly so today.

"All right," Father de Klerk told the delegation, "I'll
lead you, but I must have the authority of all the
chiefs." Then, without waiting for this formality, he immediately began issuing his orders: a call for 20 volunteers "to start our army" . . . all refugees to be fed,
work to continue in the gardens . . . anyone working
for the Japanese to be killed . . . all possible aid for
downed Allied airmen . . . only those selected for the
"army" to bear arms . . . no fires anywhere at night . . .
a system of runners to be established . . . penalty for
desertion—death. And finally, a simple restatement of
his role as he saw it: "I am now your leader and your
government—but I remain your Father and priest and
doctor just as always."

The first objective was to wipe out the Japanese post
at Cape Hunter. This consisted of nine men equipped
with rifles, two machine guns, and a radio transmitter.
They were said to be short of food, so Father de Klerk
planned an ambush built around a decoy pig. He then
wrote two local chiefs in the area, inviting their cooperation. One turned him down, but the other, Joe
Turukaia, promised to help.

It was Father de Klerk's intention, when all arrangements were set, to go down to Cape Hunter and personally lead the ambush, but the next message from Joe
Turukaia announced that the job had already been
done. Eight of the nine Japanese were killed, their
transmitter dumped into the sea. The radio operator
somehow escaped, but a lone Japanese hiding out in the
jungle posed little threat. He was, in fact, never seen
again.

Meanwhile there were other promising developments

on the Tangarare front. On October 24, after months of inattention, two U.S. planes unexpectedly appeared, circling low over the mission compound. Father de Klerk and Doug Grow were not on hand at the moment, but Dale Leslie began waving wildly. A pause, and then the plane dropped a message wrapped around a flashlight battery: "Who are you? Where is the missionary? If you are a pilot, show rubber dinghy and Mae West."

Leslie had no dinghy, but a spare one at the station served the purpose. The plane then dropped a second message, this one addressed to Father de Klerk, who by now had arrived on the scene. It was from General Vandegrift's intelligence officer Lieutenant Colonel Buckley, and it sought the Father's help on future operations. "If you accept, wave arms over head; if not, stand still, arms down."

It was an easy decision. The pilot acknowledged de Klerk's wave by dipping his wings, and then both planes flew off. They were back that afternoon with a longer message asking whether de Klerk could supply guides and carriers for a Marine landing on the south side of Guadalcanal. "If yes, show a white cross." The mission hospital was quickly raided for enough bandages to make the white cross.

A busy week followed. Father de Klerk visited the neighboring villages, lining up carriers. Planes from Henderson came and went with messages. The 20-man "army" drilled and drilled. Tangarare took on a new air of bustle and excitement, which reached a climax on November 2, when a native police sergeant named Tsaku—one of Snowy Rhoades's old scouts—arrived with a contingent of 40 armed men from Nala. They had just killed 55 Japanese soldiers, Tsaku explained, and now wanted to join Father de Klerk's army. He accepted them gladly, turned the boys' dormitory into a barracks, and Tangarare looked more than ever like an armed camp.

This was the situation on November 4 when, without any advance notice, Dick Horton unexpectedly appeared with the *Ramada*. He had been picking up pilots stranded on Isabel and the Russells and was now here for Grow and Leslie.

Would Father de Klerk come too? Horton could only ask—he had no actual authority over this valuable informant—but he did emphasize that this was what General Vandegrift wanted. The Father politely declined. "Tell the General I'll come later; I'm still too busy here." So the *Ramada* left without him, and the good shepherd continued to take his stick to the wolf.

7

DERAILING THE TOKYO EXPRESS

Hunting down the Japanese was the last thing on Jack Read's mind this same 4th of November. His main concern was how to elude them. For weeks he had heard rumors that Rabaul was sending a force of picked troops to get him at his hideout at Porapora in northern Bougainville; now it looked as though they were here.

Focusing his binoculars on the little village of Soraken, 2500 feet below, he counted 100 men coming ashore from a Japanese schooner that had just anchored. Taken alone, there was nothing so unusual about that. Landing parties often poked about Buka Passage, and Read never worried because they always dressed in their whites. No one in his right mind would wear whites very far into the Bougainville jungle. But this particular group had black uniforms, and they were loaded down with gear. Each man shouldered a pack and a rifle, and they were followed by a line of natives carrying supplies.

Read hung on for two days. The Porapora lookout was too good to abandon until he had to. But as the

Japanese patrols fanned out, he finally signaled headquarters on the 6th that he was pulling back to the
mountain village of Aravia.

Eric Feldt understood. The head of the Coastwatching organization not only approved the move; he immediately ordered Read off the air. The Japanese might
be using radio direction-finding equipment.

November 7, and Read's party moved ever higher
and deeper into the interior. It was a hot, muggy morning—terrible for climbing—and worse in the afternoon.
It began to rain, and it came down in torrents, the
patented way it did in the Solomons. Read, Corporal
Sly, the police boys and carriers continued on, pulling
themselves up the slippery trail by roots and vines.
Finally they reached a ridge where Read decided to
spend the night. Visibility was nil—the rain, the clouds,
the steaming jungle took care of that—and they sank
down exhausted, too miserable to care really where
they were.

Then the rain stopped, suddenly as it often did. The
sun broke through; the clouds vanished; the air cleared.
Below them stretched a breathtaking expanse of sea
to the east. Read looked—and looked again—for there
on the horizon was a convoy of twelve big Japanese
transports majestically steaming southeast.

The orders might say radio silence, but they never
contemplated a scene like this. Read immediately
hooked up the teleradio, strung out an aerial, and began sending. No risk was too great. A convoy like that
could be carrying a whole division to Guadalcanal.

He was right. Aboard were 12,000 Japanese troops
—the main body of the 38th Division, which would
spearhead General Hyakutake's fourth attempt to retake
Henderson Field. It would be his biggest effort yet—
and the simplest. Instead of complicated feints and

Rear Admiral Raizo Tanaka, mastermind behind the Tokyo Express. He had the task of delivering to Guadalcanal the troops and supplies designated for the November Japanese attack. (Naval Photographic Center)

flanking attacks, the Imperial Navy would first knock out American air power by bombarding the field; then the troops would land and smash their way to victory by frontal assault.

When the convoy reached the Shortlands on November 8, the preliminaries were already under way. Some 1300 men had gone down on the 7th; another 600 would be leaving on the 10th; the main body would start on the 12th. And this time, instead of feeding them in piecemeal via furtive destroyer runs, Admiral Tanaka would shepherd them down in one big convoy—eleven transports guarded by twelve destroyers.

The anchorage teemed with the traffic of a major operation. Destroyers raced in and out . . . tankers moved wherever needed . . . supply vessels hovered near the transports . . . the covering cruisers and support ships awaited their assignments . . . patrol boats and harbor craft scurried about like water bugs.

From his lookout near Barougo in southern Bougainville, Paul Mason calmly studied the Japanese anchorage. He noted that the buildup was bigger than ever. November 6, he counted 33 vessels; by the 10th the number had increased to 61. He was now equipped with pages from *Jane's Fighting Ships,* and he was marvelously precise in the summary he radioed that day. It was the largest concentration of Japanese shipping he had ever seen:

AT LEAST 61 SHIPS THIS AREA, VIZ: 2 NATI, 1 AOBAI, 1 MOGAMI, 1 KISO, 1 TATUTA, 2 SLOOPS, 33 DESTROYERS, 17 CARGOES, 2 TANKERS, AND 1 PASSENGER LINER OF 8,000 TONS.

At Lunga General Vandegrift pieced Read's and Mason's reports together with the other information flowing in. The latest radio intercepts, patrol plane reports, submarine sightings—everything pointed to an all-out Japanese attack in the immediate future. Once again the Marines hunkered down inside the perimeter.

But with a difference. They were much stronger. The Navy had finally made up its losses in the early battles. It could now keep the sea lanes open, and a steady stream of reinforcements and supplies flowed in: October 30, some heavy artillery . . . November 4, a fresh regiment of Marines . . . November 11, more Marines, ammunition, and provisions . . . November 12, the 182nd Infantry.

Responding to the Coastwatcher alerts, the CACTUS Air Force did its best to intercept the Tokyo Express. But Admiral Tanaka had his timing down pat. Some ships were hit, but most got through—65 destroyer runs between November 2 and 10. Now the big convoy at Faisi was ready to try its luck too.

On the 11th the planes from Rabaul began bombing Henderson again. Admiral Yamamoto's Combined Fleet edged south from Truk, and on the 12th two battleships, a cruiser, and fourteen destroyers moved in to soften up the field for the big attack.

Thanks again to CINCPAC's code breakers, Halsey knew they were coming. For three nights the U.S. fleet slugged it out with the Japanese in what became known as the Naval Battle of Guadalcanal. American losses were greater, but the Japanese were stopped. They failed to knock out Henderson Field.

While the battle raged, Admiral Tanaka's big convoy started down the Slot, returned to Faisi on hearing the bad news from the south, and then set out again on the evening of the 13th. The weather was too thick for Paul Mason to see them go, but when the fog lifted early on the 14th, he flashed word that the anchorage was empty.

All day, November 14, American planes pounded Tanaka's eleven transports and twelve destroyers. Strike after strike took off from Henderson Field, joined by B-17s from Espiritu Santo and dive bombers from the carrier *Enterprise*. By evening six of the eleven transports were sunk, another so battered that it limped back to the Shortlands. The remaining four steamed doggedly on, reaching Guadalcanal at dawn on the 14th. Tanaka drove them hard on the beach and commenced unloading, as the air strikes began again.

When it was all over, the Japanese had managed to land just 2000 of the 15,000 that set out from the Shortlands. Of 10,000 tons of supplies, only 260 cases of ammunition and 1500 bags of rice ever reached shore. General Hyakutake did the only thing he could do—he canceled the great attack.

War can be a parochial business, and as the bombs rained down on Tanaka's transports and the warships battled it out, the big excitement at KEN on November 14 was the sound of a single voice through the crackling static of the station's receiver. After 23 days' silence, NRY—Henry Josselyn and Jack Keenan's Coastwatching station on Vella Lavella—was back on the air. The biggest gap in Commander Mackenzie's network was filled at last.

Josselyn had been anything but idle during those 23 days. After leaving Keenan on the evening of October 25, he had taken the faulty transmitter by canoe to the Methodist mission at Bilua, where the Reverend A. W. E. Silvester was still carrying on. It was an all-night paddle, interrupted at one point when a Japanese patrol plane spotted the canoe. As it swooped down for a closer look, Josselyn hid under some palm leaves. Seeing nothing unusual, the plane flew on.

When he reached Bilua early the following morning, the Reverend Silvester greeted him with astonished delight. A small, energetic, immensely precise man, Silvester had been here since 1935. He was extremely efficient, and the mission station with its neat church, outbuildings, and airy residence was a real showplace. To the natives he was appropriately pious, but not above occasionally swatting anyone who got out of line. But it was a brand of paternalism that worked, for there were no natives in the Solomons more loyal or devoted than those on Vella Lavella.

This was just as well, for the danger was growing. No Japanese had visited Bilua yet, but they were now on the island, and a few days earlier a Zero float plane had shot up the mission launch. Preaching the gospel some 200 miles inside enemy-held territory, the Reverend Silvester was very isolated indeed.

But he was not alone. Working with him was a slender, tousle-haired trained nurse from New Zealand. Thirty-six-year-old Merle Farland had switched from piano teaching to nursing during the depression. She came out to the Solomons in 1938 and insisted on staying when most of the other missionaries fled before the advancing Japanese. As she wrote a friend, "It is surely not consistent with Christian service that our medical work should be completely dropped because things are a little difficult. I am the only medical person left: Therefore I stay. There is no other course."

She had the right temperament, too. She was humorous, adventuresome, and a bit brisk, the way experienced trained nurses sometimes are. She presided over the mission hospital, which had its own compound complete with operating theater, wards, and a little outpatient clinic. The days were always busy—injections, setting broken bones, dentistry (which she loathed), maternity cases. The evenings were usually spent trouncing the Reverend Silvester at Chinese Checkers.

This morning, the 26th, she was still in her quarters when Silvester burst in to announce he had a visitor— an American he said. Josselyn was, of course, English, but the confusion was understandable. He was the first Westerner Silvester had seen in six months. Josselyn, in turn, was amazed to find Merle Farland—he had no idea there was a white woman on the island.

He explained his problem, and the Reverend Silvester understood perfectly. He himself was part of the network run by Donald Kennedy, the Coastwatcher at Segi on New Georgia. Silvester meticulously recorded all ship and aircraft sightings, planted native spies on nearby islands, sent regular reports to Segi by canoe. He couldn't transmit, but he could receive coded messages on his short-wave radio, and he even had his own call letters—MSF, Merle Farland's initials.

Now he immediately dispatched a canoe to Segi with a message from Josselyn requesting a new transmitter. The message had to be relayed to KEN, and while they waited for an answer, Josselyn fitted easily into the life of the mission. He attended evening services and, Merle Farland noted approvingly in her diary, "made quite a good attempt at the hymns too."

On October 29 KEN radioed that it was impossible to send a new transmitter. Josselyn should take the defective set to Donald Kennedy for repairs.

There was no question that Kennedy was up to the job. The radio hadn't been built that he couldn't fix. The problem was getting it to him. Even from Bilua, the trip was 130 miles through enemy waters. The natives could do it without arousing too much suspicion, but a white man with a radio transmitter was a different matter.

Josselyn left at 7:00 P.M. on the 30th. He traveled only at night, moving from village to village. At each stop, he was handed over to a new set of paddlers and a new canoe—always the best the village had. The Reverend Silvester's connections seemed miraculous.

The first night they paddled across Vella Gulf, down Blackett Strait, and into Wana Wana Lagoon. At Mandou village he holed up for the day and lay watching the Japanese camp fires on the beach at Rendova.

Then it was dusk, and on again. Soon they were dodging a steady stream of Japanese barges ferrying men and supplies to various posts. Their engines gave them away, but it was hard to judge sound in the dark, and one barge chugged by within twenty yards. Now they were in the Roviana Lagoon, and here they were met by a 30-man canoe sent up by Kennedy.

On down the lagoon, with only one hurdle left. The

Japanese were building an advance base at Viru Harbor, near the southeast tip of New Georgia, and it was just too dangerous to pass. So the canoe landed a little to the west, and Josselyn crossed New Georgia on foot, coming out on the north coast by the Marovo Lagoon. By this time it was daylight, so he holed up again until dark.

Nightfall, and still another canoe picked him up. On down the coast they paddled, around the eastern end of the island, and into the sheltered passage that separated New Georgia from the island of Vangunu. The passage gradually narrowed, and finally, just before dawn on November 2, Josselyn and his transmitter were landed on Kennedy's dock at Segi.

Donald Kennedy was far more than the best radio repairman in the Solomons. As district officer for the western islands, he knew the area perfectly. Originally on Santa Isabel when the Japanese came, he instantly saw the greater advantages of Segi, with its central location and protected approaches. The charts might say "foul ground" and warn mariners to keep away, but he knew where the channels were. He was also a superb organizer. He took the old Markham plantation and made it a perfectly run base, complete with mess facilities, arsenal, and even a prisoner-of-war compound. Finally, he was a tough warrior—a resourceful commander and relentless disciplinarian. As one of his natives later confessed, only half-jokingly, they were more afraid of him than they were of the Japanese.

At the moment these impressive credentials were underutilized. The big action was to the west toward Bougainville, and to the east on Guadalcanal. Segi was neither here nor there. It was in a dead calm—or was it the eye of the hurricane?

In any event, Josselyn provided a welcome change, and as Kennedy puttered over the transmitter, the two

The Markham plantation house at Segi Point, headquarters for Donald Kennedy's Coastwatching operations on New Georgia. (National Archives)

men divided up their areas of responsibility. Josselyn would take everything west of Kula Gulf; Kennedy everything east.

As for the transmitter, Kennedy diagnosed the problem as a bad transformer. He radioed KEN for a new one, then had the frustration of seeing it broken in the air-drop. Disgusted, he gave Josselyn his own transmitter. He could always patch up the smashed set he had just salvaged from a downed Japanese bomber.

November 11, Josselyn headed back for Vella Lavella. It was far easier than the trip down, for Kennedy lent him a launch, and by taking the long way home via the Slot, he avoided the Japanese barges. By dawn on the 14th he was again at Bilua, where the Reverend Silvester had gathered all the local chiefs and headmen to be organized for intelligence work. Working out assignments would take an extra day; so the new transmitter was sent ahead to Keenan, and it was his voice that Hugh Mackenzie heard when NRY finally came on the air that evening.

Josselyn himself reached NRY on the 15th and found that his partner had been far from idle in his absence. Keenan had established the station at a place called Deneo, about three miles inland from Mundi Mundi and a thousand feet above the coast. There was a ridge here, and he had a lookout built in a tree atop the ridge. It commanded a broad view of the north and the west. On the reverse side of the ridge, about 400 yards to the south, he then prepared a leaf house for Josselyn, himself, and the teleradio. The intervening hill, he hoped, would interfere with any Japanese attempts to use direction-finding equipment.

Far below the lookout—but in clear sight—lay the Japanese post at Iringila, about three miles to the northwest. On one of his reconnaissance trips, Keenan had crept within 500 yards of it, carefully studying the setup: a large building with red corrugated iron roof . . . a smaller store house . . . an observation platform built between two coconut palms. Permanently mounted on a swivel on the platform was a fine pair of telescopic binoculars, which Keenan noted with envy.

So far the Japanese hadn't been very active, but whatever they did could be watched and reported from Deneo. Events elsewhere on the island should be well-covered by Josselyn's network of natives, for his meeting with the chiefs had been a great success. They all agreed to help; sentry posts would be established at fourteen different points along the coast; duty shifts were arranged so that the posts could always be manned without interrupting work in the fields. The sentries were to report all air and ship movements, enemy landings, any downed aircraft.

The first test came on November 18, when Colonel LaVerne Saunders led eighteen B-17s up the Slot in a bombing attack on Buin. A swarm of Zeros caught the Colonel's plane, killed the pilot, badly wounded the co-pilot, knocked out the left engines, and set the wing tanks on fire. Saunders scrambled into the pilot's seat, and picking the nearest island, he smacked down off-shore in a plume of spray.

Scrambling into two rubber rafts, the crew shoved off as the bomber sank. Saunders managed to get every-body out except the pilot, who went down with the plane. By the time they reached shore, the co-pilot was dead too, and the navigator, Lieutenant Nelson Levi, suffered from a badly wounded thigh. Saunders himself had a severe head-gash. Once on the beach, the sur-vivors did their best to make Levi comfortable, buried the co-pilot, and began to wonder where they were.

Soon they noticed a native canoe approaching from a much larger island two miles away. Friendly or un-friendly? There was no way to tell, but "Blondie" Saunders knew all too well that he was deep in Japanese-controlled territory. Taking no chances, he stationed his men behind various trees and bushes with the few pistols they had, prepared to fight to the end. Then he went alone to the shore to negotiate.

None of the natives could speak English. But when he indicated he was thirsty, one of them ran up a tree like a squirrel and shook down some coconuts. Then they piled back into their canoe, and were gone again.

Another hour, another canoe. Again Saunders sta-tioned his men for a last stand, but as it drew closer, the Colonel saw to his immense relief that it contained a white man.

Jack Keenan stepped ashore, introduced himself, and in what surely must have been a high in Coastwatching etiquette gave Blondie Saunders his card. Keenan had been on duty in the observation post that morning when one of the new native sentries rushed up to report that a big American plane was down, with survivors on nearby Bagga Island. While Josselyn stood by the tele-radio, Keenan hurried to the scene with first-aid kit, and now—only three hours after the crash—was on hand distributing K-rations and bandage rolls.

Next step was to get everybody over to Vella Lavella, where food, medical help, communications, and ultimate rescue would be easier. There were too many Japanese patrol planes to risk the trip in bright daylight, but as soon as dusk came, the survivors were paddled across. They landed at Paramata, Silas Lezatuni's village, and this always-resourceful chief outdid himself. From somewhere he came up with blankets, a cooked meal, even knives and forks.

Meanwhile more messengers fanned out. One runner hurried up to the lookout, bringing Josselyn up to date, so he could contact KEN and arrange for a pickup. Another runner headed down the coast and across the island to Bilua to alert the Reverend Silvester.

It was 3:30 A.M. on the 19th when the messenger panted up the path to the missionary's house. Taking in the situation, Silvester rushed over to Merle Farland's quarters. He explained that he had better head for Paramata with some medical aid, while she prepared the mission to receive possible survivors. That wouldn't do at all, she told him in her nicest brisk way: She was the one with medical training. She would go, and he could get out the sheets and blankets.

She quickly pulled together an emergency kit, re-cruited four native guides, gulped a cup of tea, and was off by 6 A.M. At first it was cross-country on a rough but well-cleared path. Then the trail petered out, and she walked mile after mile along the rocks that lined the shore. A fine rain was falling, and all the stones were round and slippery.

Coming to a river she climbed on the shoulders of

one of her guides, and with the others ready to help if needed, they all crossed together. Then on again, now going harder than ever, leaving three of her guides far behind. When she finally reached the little village of Supato at noon, she had walked more than fourteen miles.

Here she shifted to a canoe and continued up the coast. Planes were prowling overhead. They sounded American—she was becoming quite an expert—but playing it safe, she pulled a native umbrella over herself.

Henry Josselyn was waiting on the shore when she reached Paramata at 3 P.M. During the night he had come down from the lookout, trading places with Keenan. Josselyn quickly briefed her on the injuries as she walked up to Silas's house, where the flyers were waiting. A PBY was expected any minute, so she decided not to touch Lieutenant Levi's thigh. With any luck he could have real hospital treatment in a few

Merle Farland, Methodist nurse on Vella Lavella, aided Coastwatchers in rescue of fallen U.S. bomber crew. She was later evacuated to Guadalcanal, where her presence started rumor that Amelia Earhart had been found alive.
(Courtesy Merle Farland)

hours. Turning to Blondie Saunders, she was just starting to unwind a bandage on his head, when they heard the sound of approaching planes. The patient dashed out to investigate.

It was the PBY, escorted by three Grumman Wildcats. While the fighters circled above, the big flying boat glided down to a perfect landing a hundred yards off the beach. No time to lose—Japanese planes might turn up any minute. A canoe was launched, and the flyers loaded in. Seeing Lieutenant Levi in obvious pain, Merle Farland—always quick with her needle—managed to give him a shot of morphine in the buttocks as the party shoved off.

It was a long way to go just to give a shot in the buttocks, but far more important, the episode proved that Josselyn's setup worked. The downed plane had been promptly reported. Help was immediate. KEN was notified. The pick-up was carried out. Everything went off exactly as planned.

Six days later, and 80 miles to the east, an unexpected Japanese move gave NRY a new chance to prove its usefulness. On the afternoon of November 24 several enemy warships approached Munda Point on the southwestern coast of New Georgia, as a couple of Methodist mission schoolboys excitedly watched from the shore. Alesasa Bisili and Solomon Hitu were two of the very few natives left in the village. Nearly everybody else had fled to the hills when some trigger-happy American fighter pilots strafed the settlement a few weeks earlier.

The warships anchored off the mission around 5 P.M., and it must have been nearly 7:00 when one of them fired a rocket. Landing operations began, and all night long the two boys watched a flotilla of small boats ferry in troops and supplies. They were so fascinated that they failed to notice an approaching patrol until too late.

They were seized and taken to an officer who spoke a little English. Did they know where the white men were? The boys said all were gone. The officer then released them, but told them to report back the following morning, adding, "If you lie, we'll cut your neck off."

He never had the chance. Alesasa and Solomon ran into the bush and joined their families in the hills. The refugees were, of course, in touch with Donald Kennedy's scouts, and word was quickly passed to Segi that the Japanese had landed in strength at Munda.

At this point, that was all Kennedy knew. His best man in western New Georgia, Willie Paia, was completely in the dark. Operating from a small island in the Roviana Lagoon, Paia controlled some 30 scouts, but none of them could find out exactly what was going on. For once Japanese security was just too good; this time they weren't even using native labor. Creeping as close as they dared, the scouts could only report that more ships were arriving and unloading equipment . . . that construction troops were working with picks and shovels . . . that others were busy chopping down trees.

It was NRY that caught the first clue. Japanese barges en route to Munda made a habit of hiding out along the Vella Lavella coast during daylight hours, and Josselyn's natives were watching them closely. Based on their descriptions of the cargos carried, he radioed KEN about December 1: SUGGEST THAT JAPS ARE LANDING HEAVY GEAR, CEMENT, ETC., MUNDA POINT, POSSIBLE AIRFIELD MATERIALS.

Airfield was right. The destruction of Admiral Tanaka's big convoy didn't end Japanese hopes of recapturing Guadalcanal, but it convinced Tokyo that nothing could be done until Japan could hold its own in the air.

More planes were available through a new agreement of cooperation between the Army and the Navy, but there remained the problem of distance.

The new fields at Buka and Kahili—the new seaplane base at Rekata Bay—all helped, but they were not enough. A base still closer to Guadalcanal was needed, and careful reconnaissance indicated that the big Lambeti plantation at Munda Point might be the answer. It would shave another 240 miles off the round trip to Guadalcanal, saving enough fuel to provide real fighter protection for future convoys.

The problem was how to get the field built before it was destroyed by the very planes it was meant to counter. One way, as Willie Paia had discovered, was better security. But the real stroke of genius was a brilliant job of camouflage. Instead of clearing away the coconut palms that were chopped down for the runway, the tops were left suspended on wires while work on the strip continued below. To the American photo reconnaissance pilots poking about overhead, the plantation's neat rows of trees appeared absolutely normal. It was not until December 5 that some sharp-eyed photo interpreters detected the truth, and by then the strip was virtually complete.

For Donald Kennedy at Segi it was one more headache in a growing list—all indicating that the war on New Georgia, after a long lull, was definitely heating up. Besides Munda, he had to keep an eye on new Japanese landings at Wickham Anchorage to the east ... at Ramada Island to the North ... at Vila, a plantation on Kolombangara, far to the west. He had to cope with aggressive enemy patrols that were now fanning out from Viru, only nine miles away. He had to run a hotel for the American flyers his natives had rescued—and a jail for the Japanese pilots they had captured.

He felt so shorthanded that he decided to try a dar-

Munda Point, New Georgia, November 1942. This early U.S. reconnaissance photo suggests nothing amiss, but clever Japanese camouflage conceals new airstrip already being built under the palms at right. (National Archives)

ing experiment. Recalling that Merle Farland had once offered to do "anything anywhere," he wrote her and very hesitantly suggested she might shift from Vella Lavella to Segi and relieve him on the teleradio. It would release him from the base, giving him more time to keep on top of these new, fast-breaking developments.

Merle knew the area, knew the native dialects, knew the codes, and loved the challenge. She was a little worried about leaving her medical work at Bilua, but there would also be plenty of that at Segi.

At 1 A.M., December 3, she was on her way. It was another of those hair-raising canoe journeys, made all the more dangerous by the increased Japanese traffic off the western end of New Georgia. To avoid Munda, they curled north through Hawthorne Sound, then east into the Marovo Lagoon, dodging enemy barges and once gliding right by a Japanese outpost on Bukobuko Island. A mildly curious sentry emerged from his hut to watch them pass; then, satisfied, he ducked back in as Merle lay flat in the canoe.

Dawn, December 6, they reached Segi, and Donald Kennedy was soon indoctrinating his new assistant. She scored 22 out of 25 on her first target practice with a rifle—not bad for a missionary nurse—and proved a skillful radio operator. But one of the very first messages she decoded brought disastrous news. Sent by Resident Commissioner Marchant, a "raj" of the old school, it said simply: ARRANGEMENTS BEING MADE TO EVACUATE SISTER FARLAND. HAVE YOU ANY NEWS OF OTHER MEMBERS OF THE MISSION?

The irony of it. For nearly a year she had worked on Vella Lavella, completely overlooked by the powers that be. Now, by coming to Segi in order to make an even greater contribution, she had apparently reminded them of her presence, and they would have none of it. For a week she parried with officialdom, trying to get the decision reversed, but it was no use: She was violating "present restrictions on white women remaining in the Protectorate"—she would have to go.

She did have the consolation of one last fling. On December 16 word came that a B-17 was down at sea, and Donald Kennedy rushed off in a boat to the rescue. Handing Merle a loaded automatic, he left her virtually in charge of the station. For three days, she handled all the radio traffic, received reports from the scouts, and even concocted a signal recommending bombing targets for Henderson Field.

Then it was over. On December 21, while no less than seventeen U.S. fighters flew cover overhead, a PBY landed off Segi Point; picked up Kennedy's fourteen Japanese prisoners; and plucked Merle Farland out of the Solomons campaign.

At Tulagi and later on Guadalcanal, where she stayed overnight awaiting transportation to Noumea, she caused something of a stir. She was, after all, the only woman among 30,000 troops, and it was quite understandable when one malaria-wracked boy glanced up from his stretcher and declared, "Now I *know* I am delirious." As others caught a glimpse of her pert look and tousled hair, a new rumor swept the island: Amelia Earhart had been found alive.

Despite the sensation that Merle Farland caused, life on Guadalcanal was far more normal than six weeks before, when the Marines were grimly waiting for the fourth and greatest Japanese attack.

General Hyakutake still had 25,000 men on the island, but they had lost much of their punch. Naval losses had been high—particularly in destroyers—and the Tokyo Express just couldn't deliver supplies on the scale needed. The troops were now ragged scarecrows, weak from starvation, living on berries, roots and leaves.

In contrast, the American strength mushroomed. Army units were pouring in, relieving Vandegrift's battle-worn Marines; the new commander, Major General Alexander M. Patch, would soon have 35,000 fresh troops at his disposal. The CACTUS Air Force now had 200 planes, including 100 fighters operating from a new airstrip beyond the range of "Pistol Pete," as the Japanese guns that shelled Henderson Field were called.

The Americans were no longer penned up in their hard-won perimeter. For one thing, the eastern end of the island was finally cleared completely of the Japanese by Lieutenant Colonel Evans Carlson's 2nd Marine Raiders. Originally the Raiders had been landed at Aola to guard the construction of a reserve airstrip. When the ground proved too swampy, Carlson's men headed back for Lunga on November 3 . . . cutting through the jungle, living off the land, mopping up stray enemy units.

Guided by Sergeant Major Vouza's scouts, they wiped out over 400 Japanese, losing only sixteen Marines in the process. Finally on December 3 they reached the hills overlooking Henderson Field. Here they had the satisfaction of destroying two of the Pistol Petes that plagued the airstrip. Surrounded by the carnage of this last fight, Colonel Carlson called his men together, explained they would be entering the American lines next morning, and led them all in singing the "Marine Corps Hymn." The natives were so moved they persuaded the Marines to add, so that every one might join in, a chorus of "Onward, Christian Soldiers."

Meanwhile, other American troops began probing south and west. On November 19 a U.S. plane dropped a message to Father de Klerk at Tangarare asking if he could provide guides for a patrol of 20 men, to be landed the following night. Of course he could—it was what the "commander-in-chief" of the south coast had been longing for—and on the evening of the 20th they arrived on the faithful *Ramada*.

At last Father de Klerk and his native troops were part of the big show. Tangarare even acquired a code name, PINEAPPLE, with the Father serving as "base commander." On the 21st he guided the patrol up the coast for a reconnaissance behind the Japanese lines at Maravovo and Lavoro, and on the 30th he returned to

Lunga with them, to get supplies and hold conferences on future operations.

He arrived just as the Army was taking over from the Marines, and General Patch took to him right away. When de Klerk returned to Tangarare on December 5, he had ample stocks of food, rifles, ammunition, a case of hand grenades, and a complete U.S. uniform bequeathed him by some departing Marine. The shepherd could now take the stick to the wolf in earnest.

As the Americans steadily consolidated and expanded their hold on Guadalcanal, the Coastwatcher station on Gold Ridge became less important. Don Macfarlan had been relieved in October, leaving Ken Hay in charge. By December 7th it was safe enough to send down the elderly Sister Edmée, who had been marooned there since the Ruavatu massacre. Hay himself remained a month longer, fretting over his "deadly boredom."

The big action was now 300 miles to the northwest. Here the Coastwatchers on southern Bougainville, Choiseul, and Vella Lavella vied to be first in reporting the Tokyo Express starting down the Slot on its regular runs from the Shortlands to Guadalcanal. Their messages were often received at KEN within five minutes of the actual sighting, and within another five minutes the information was in the hands of the air command. By cutting the time lag to an absolute minimum, the CACTUS Air Force began getting in some hard blows before darkness swallowed the approaching destroyers.

More and more often the Express was "derailed," and Admiral Yamamoto turned to desperate measures to keep the supplies flowing. Submarines were tried, but they carried little, and the risks were great. Air drops were attempted, but the planes were torn to bits by the American fighters. Then Admiral Tanaka came up with a scheme to cut the turnaround time of the Tokyo Express. He would load his destroyers with drums of supplies, linked together by rope like a string of beads. Reaching Tassafaronga, the destroyers were to jettison these "necklaces," and troops waiting on the beach would haul them ashore. This should cut to an absolute minimum the amount of time his destroyers would be within range of those devastating Henderson Field bombers.

It never really worked. On their best night the destroyers managed to cast loose 1500 drums, but only 300 ever reached shore.

The lesson was clear. Stopgap measures would do no good. The solution lay in new bases like Munda, near enough to give Japan a reasonable chance in the air. Only then could she hope to retake Guadalcanal, or at the very least, seal it off as a springboard for any American advance.

All this focused Japanese attention on the other islands in the Solomons. They began establishing supply dumps for food and materials . . . hideouts for barges during the daylight . . . outposts to protect the new flow of traffic.

At KEN, Hugh Mackenzies caught the drift and further expanded his network of Coastwatchers. As early as November 18 he sent Andy Andresen, recruited from the Gold Ridge miners, with a U.S. team to Rennell Island, 120 miles south of Guadalcanal. They found plenty of Polynesian girls, but few Japanese ever came that way, and the station was soon closed.

He decided to put another new station on Ontong Java, about 300 miles north of Guadalcanal. This flat coral atoll was ideal for observing traffic coming down from the great Japanese base at Truk, but it was also highly exposed. None of the islets forming the atoll were more than a few feet high or a few hundred yards wide. There was literally no place to hide.

It might be supposed that the Coastwatcher selected

The Coastwatcher staff at KEN relaxing. Hugh Mackenzie is seated; Snowy Rhoades, fourth from left. (Australian War Memorial)

for such a strategic, vulnerable spot would be one of Commander Feldt's most experienced hands. Actually, Sub-Lieutenant William McCasker had never even been to the South Pacific islands before the war. He was a bright, breezy young intelligence officer who had been sent to New Caledonia because of his knowledge of French. As the fighting moved north, this was no longer so important, and he was shipped up to Guadalcanal and told to report to Mackenzie. He was selected for Ontong Java because, as so often happens in war, he was available.

On December 1 he arrived by PBY, accompanied by two equally bewildered U.S. Army privates named Robbins and Guillette. Fortunately some excellent groundwork had been laid by Dick Horton. He had managed to visit the atoll a few days earlier, and when the three neophytes reached shore, a royal welcome was waiting.

The island king, an enormous Polynesian named Isea, waddled down to meet them, followed by his chief constable, Billy. Then, with great ceremony, Isea formally declared war on Japan and put McCasker in charge of defense.

It turned out that there was nothing to do. Instead of Truk, the Japanese used Rabaul as their base for mounting operations against the Solomons, and Ontong Java was far off the beaten track. Through rare good fortune, or truly great insight, McCasker was remarkably well prepared for this state of affairs. He had brought along an entire set of Gibbon's *Decline and Fall of the Roman Empire;* and when that ran out, he had a Latin edition of Ovid's *Metamorphoses.*

The months rolled by. His assistants changed, and changed again, but still no one at headquarters could bring himself to believe that Ontong Java wouldn't somehow become important. McCasker finished Gibbon and Ovid, then passed away the time compiling a dictionary of the native language. Nine months went by before he was finally recalled—the Coastwatcher stationed where nothing ever happened.

Lastly, on December 21 Mackenzie sent Dick Horton, one of his most trusted assistants, to New Georgia to set up a new station for the express purpose of watching Munda. Flying to Segi on the same PBY that picked up Merle Farland, Horton checked in with Donald Kennedy, then headed west on the Marovo Lagoon to a little village called Alalu. Here on the 23rd he met a half-caste trader and plantation manager named Harry Wickham, who he hoped would be the key to his whole operation. Member of New Georgia's most famous family—his half-brother had been a world champion swimmer—Wickham was married to a Roviana Lagoon girl and knew every foot of the area. Only time would tell, but if anybody could find the right spot for watching the Japanese at Munda, he would be the one.

As a base for exploring the possibilities, Wickham had prepared a leaf hut hidden deep in a jungle ravine. Horton set up his teleradio here, and the following night —Christmas Eve—he caught the distant signal of a San Francisco station. Bing Crosby was singing "White Christmas."

The other Coastwatchers, too, had their reminders. In the mountains of southern Bougainville Paul Mason was on the run again. The local Japanese political officer, Tashira, had won over many of the natives, and they were chasing him. Mason led his party still deeper into the interior, and just before Christmas a playful message arrived from Tashira indicating that his move was none too soon: "Come in and spend Christmas dinner with us, and bring your friends. If you don't, we'll shoot you on sight."

Instead, Mason had Christmas dinner with Tom Ebery, a European planter also hiding in the hills. It was nothing special and ended abruptly when a scout rushed up to report that the Japanese and their native friends were closing in.

At Tangarare, Father de Klerk took time out from patrol work and returned to the little mission church to hold midnight mass. Some 400 people packed the place. It seemed like the old days, until, near the end, the distant rumble of guns reminded them how different it really was.

At Noumea, the teeming Allied base 800 miles to the south, Merle Farland went to Major General "Miff" Harmon's big Christmas party. Everybody was there— Admiral Halsey, all the brass, Allied liaison officers, French colonial wives, a few self-conscious American Red Cross girls. It was one of those parties where the ceilings are too low and the voices too high. Merle had a good time—especially when she had a brief re-union with Blondie Saunders—but there was something superficial about this babbling headquarters world. She thought of Vella Lavella and knew that was where she really wanted to be.

8

THE STRANGEST
NEW YEAR'S EVE

There's not much room in a submarine, so Christmas was a matter of small pleasures for the crew of the USS *Nautilus*, patrolling off the east coast of Bougainville. For Ensign George Davis, it meant filling his pipe with the deliciously aromatic "79 Mixture" tobacco his wife had sent him. Then he lit up for a quiet smoke in the forward torpedo room.

He was just settling down when the *Nautilus*'s skipper Lieutenant Commander William H. Brockman, Jr., happened by. "Davis," he remarked, "let this be the last time I ever find you smoking a pipe while we're running submerged." Since Brockman said nothing to Chief Red Porterfield and an old torpedoman, who were also in the compartment smoking their pipes, the incident confirmed Davis's hunch that young ensigns survived only by keeping a low profile.

It also showed the blunt, unpredictable side of Bill Brockman. He was a passionate, exasperatingly stubborn man, but he knew no fear, would try anything, and had the complete confidence of his men. Alone among the submarine commanders at Midway, he had mixed it up with the Japanese carriers; later he carried a detachment of Carlson's Marines in their commando raid on Makin. Now he was bringing the *Nautilus* from Pearl Harbor to Brisbane for whatever new exploits lay ahead.

There was no hurry, and on December 29 he was still hovering off Bougainville, hoping for some fat target, when at 4:00 A.M. he received an unexpected radio message from COMSOPAC, Admiral Halsey's headquarters at Noumea. It ordered him to proceed immediately to Teop Bay on the northeastern coast of the island, where some stranded personnel were waiting to be rescued.

"How many women can you take care of?" the *Nautilus*'s communications officer, Lieutenant Phil Eckert, asked the commissary officer, young Ensign Davis, as more information about the refugees trickled in.

"Any number, Sir!" brightly answered Davis.

But the "women" Eckert referred to were a far cry from those Davis had in mind. Sister Mary Isabelle Aubin, for instance, was a fifty-year-old nun from Newport, Vermont, who taught school, spoke fluent French, and played either violin or trumpet as the occasion required. A born organizer, she was the natural choice as Superior when the Sisters of Saint Joseph of Orange, California, decided to send four missionary "pioneers" to Bougainville in 1940. Under her wing were another teacher, Sister M. Celestine Belanger of Lowell, Massachusetts, and two registered nurses, Sister M. Hedda Jaeger of Saskatchewan and Sister M. Irene Alton of Huntington Beach, California.

They were stationed at Hanahan, a remote mission on the eastern coast of Buka Island. None of them had ever been to the South Pacific before; all were middle-aged; and war was raging over half the globe. In the face of what others might consider handicaps, they plunged into their work with good cheer and boundless optimism. To cover more territory, they even learned to ride bicycles and could be seen scorching along the jungle trails, their white habits flowing out behind them.

December 8, 1941, and their lives were changed more than they had ever dreamed. At first, like most of the Catholic missionaries in the Solomons, they thought they could be above it all. Expecting Japanese occupation, Sister Hedda noted in her diary, "We wonder if the new officials will be staying at Buka Passage, and just what we are meant to do to fulfill our role as neutrals." Seeing their bicycle tires wearing thin, she hoped they would last "until we can order some from Sydney or Tokyo."

Jack Read knew better. He urged them to leave while they could still get out, but they wouldn't hear of it. Then, early in March 1942, the Japanese began landing on Buka, and on the 16th they executed Australian planter Percy Good and carried off Father James T. Hennessy, a Boston priest stationed at the northern end of the island.

The news shook Hanahan, only 17 miles away. Father Lamarre, the missionary in charge, immediately ordered the sisters south. On March 22 they crossed over to Bougainville, and by the 30th they were at Asitavi, 90 miles down the east coast. But the Japanese were moving south too, and Bishop Tom Wade, the American-born prelate who was personally escorting the nuns, decided to disperse them. Sisters Hedda and Celestine remained at Asitavi; while Sisters Isabelle and Irene were sent to Monetai, a small inland mission still farther south.

Here they found a lone German priest named Father Mueller living in the most primitive conditions. He gallantly gave them his own leaf hut, but this was no treat.

BOUGAINVILLE

Hanahan

BUKA

BUKA PASSAGE

Tarlena

SOHANO
Porapora
Soraken
Aravia
Lumsis
Namatoa
Dariai
Kunua
Kiakara
Sikoriapaia
Kereaka
Rugen
Tinputz
Teop
Tsipatavai
Teopasina
Inus
Aita R.
Asitavi
Numa Numa
Aita
▲ Mt. Balbi

PACIFIC OCEAN

EMPEROR RANGE

ATSINIMA BAY

Laruma R.

Monetai

Kieta

Torokina

CROWN

Mom
Koro
Dubonami
Moru
Soveli

EMPRESS AUGUSTA BAY

Puruata

PRINCE

Luluai R.

RANGE

Barougo
Malabita Hill
Kahili
Buin

SOLOMON SEA

BALLALE

SHORTLAND ISLANDS
Faisi

FAURO ISLAND

0   10   20   30   40 miles
0 10 20 30 40 50 60 kilometers

TREASURY ISLANDS
MONO
Falamai
STIRLING

It swarmed with mosquitoes, roaches, and a family of precocious rats. The two nuns gamely carried on. Sister Isabelle began teaching school and was soon giving trumpet lessons to Father Mueller. Sister Irene resumed her medical work, eventually visiting inland villages where no white woman had ever been seen before.

July 5, the war once again came closer. The Japanese occupied Kieta and seized Bishop Wade, who happened to be visiting a nearby mission. They held him for an anxious month, then released him on August 2 and left Kieta as suddenly as they had come. The bishop made his way on foot to Monetai, greeting the sisters with a little song, "Just Released from Jail."

He now faced an ordeal far worse, in its way, than the entire Japanese army. He had a horrendous toothache. Knowing that Sister Irene had a set of dental instruments among her supplies, he asked her to pull the offending molar. She politely demurred, explaining that she had seen dentistry performed but had never actually done this sort of thing. The bishop told her that now was the time to start, or he would have to do the job himself. She finally agreed to try her skill the following morning and asked the bishop to say a mass for the success of the operation.

More tangible help was on the way. Sister Isabelle found a French textbook on dentistry, and translated the chapter on extracting molars. That night the two sisters studied the diagrams together, trying to match the instruments they had with those illustrated in the book.

Wednesday, August 18, Bishop Wade said the mass as promised, and appeared promptly at 8:30 for his dentist appointment. Sister Irene gave him a Seconal, added a shot of novacaine, and seated her patient in a deck chair on Father Mueller's porch. Then, while the entire village gathered around in a huge semicircle, she went to work. Sister Isabelle held a spoon as a retractor,

The Sisters of Saint Joseph who were trapped on Bougainville. Left to right: Sister M. Irene Alton, Mother M. Francis (not on the island), Sister M. Hedda Jaeger, Sister M. Celestine Belanger, Sister M. Isabelle Aubin. Taken at Orange, California, in 1940, just before their departure for the Solomons. (Courtesy Sister M. Irene Alton)

and Father Mueller stood by for "emergencies." But his services were never needed. After a few twists with the forceps, Sister Irene triumphantly held the tooth aloft. The crowd broke into wild applause, and the bishop said it didn't hurt at all.

Minus a molar but free from pain, Bishop Wade headed north to learn how the other missions had fared during his month in Japanese custody. It was now clear that whatever long-run benefits might result from the American landings on Guadalcanal, for the short run they meant even harder days for the missionaries on

Bougainville. The five priests on Buka were rounded up, their missions closed and pillaged. At Turiburi three priests and seven nuns were seized and locked up in a small metal shed near Buin. And from Guadalcanal came the shattering news of the execution of the four missionaries at Ruavatu.

October 10, the bishop discussed the situation with Father Albert Lebel, the priest in charge of Timputz Mission. In the course of their talk the bishop formally gave Lebel full authority to act in his name on the evacuation of all the sisters still on Bougainville.

He couldn't have made a better choice. Born and raised in Brunswick, Maine, Father Lebel had been in the Solomons for thirteen years, the last ten on Bougainville. He knew every trail and short-cut. He was now about 40—old enough to have a backlog of experience, yet young enough to take the physical beating of living in the bush, always on the move. He had boundless energy. Even on Sundays at Tinputz, as soon as mass was over he would immediately open his clinic and start treating cases.

Most important, Father Lebel could get along with anybody. Bougainville had more than its share of eccentric Europeans, and there was always the latent clash of interests between missionaries, planters, and government officials. Getting things done required enormous tact and patience and the ability to adjust to other people's whims. Albert Lebel learned this early in life. He had to. He was the fourteenth child in a family of seventeen.

Diving into his assignment, he decided that the first step was to prepare a safe, convenient place where the nuns could be collected until rescue was arranged. There were at least a dozen sisters involved, and at the moment they were scattered among five different mission stations, as much as 90 miles apart. Here his in-

Bishop Thomas Wade, the American-born prelate on Bougainville. Shown here with some of his flock, he hoped in vain that the Church could remain aloof from the war. (Courtesy Sister M. Irene Alton)

timate knowledge of the island came in handy. About 90 minutes' walk from Tinputz was a little village high in the hills called Tsipatavai. The natives were trustworthy, and he knew the chief well. Best of all, it was near Teop Harbor, sheltered water, free of the Japanese, and ideal for evacuation whether by boat or PBY.

A quick visit to his friend the chief produced immediate results. The entire village went to work, building a leaf dormitory some 50 feet long which would help house the refugees.

Now to get them there. Farthest away were four Marist sisters at Soveli, deep in the interior, 90 miles

to the south. Father Richard O'Sullivan, a priest who
had escaped from the Buin area, escorted them up.
Meanwhile Sisters Isabelle and Irene headed north
from Monetai, rejoining Sisters Hedda and Celestine at
Asitavi. By November 13 all eight nuns were assembled there awaiting Father Lebel's next instructions.

At the moment he was busy taking the most daring
gamble in his whole rescue scheme. Near Buka Passage,
and completely under the thumb of the Japanese, was
the mission of Tarlena. Two priests and three nuns were
confined here. Two of the sisters were so ill they could
barely walk, and all five were under strict orders from
Captain Ito, the local commander, to stay put. A guard
was posted to see that his orders were obeyed. Nevertheless, Father Lebel was determined to save them all.

November 24, he set out for the beleaguered mission
with seven of his huskiest natives. It was a 30-mile walk,
and to make it more difficult, he didn't dare take the
well-beaten coastal track. Reaching Rugen, a former
coffee plantation, he found Jack Read there with his
teleradio. The place had been chosen for a supply drop,
and the plane was expected that night.

It was Father Lebel's first chance to tell Read what
he intended to do, and surprisingly Read was less than
enthusiastic. The plan was a long shot at best, and if it
failed, the Japanese would crack down hard. "It's a big
risk, Father."

"Yes, I know. I've weighed the pros and cons, and
the pros have it."

Read pointed out that the Church would no longer
be able to argue that it stood apart from the war. *"Now*
you are on *this* side of the fence."

Father Lebel said he knew that too.

Read finally gave up and did the only thing possible:
He asked how he could help. A good police boy would

be useful, Father Lebel suggested, so Read lent him Corporal Sali, one of his best.

The expedition continued on across the island, reaching the village of Chabai at dusk. Now they were on the northwest coast, just five miles below Tarlena. Here the natives went to work, cutting poles and lashing them onto two cane chairs, which would be used for carrying the ailing sisters. Then they ate and rested for what was bound to be a long, hard night.

After dark two of the natives sneaked through the bush to Tarlena and made contact with Father McConville, the priest in charge. They quickly reported that Father Lebel was waiting nearby, and a brief meeting was held where the arrangements were explained. Luckily the sentries had taken the night off, and the coast was clear.

But there was no time to lose. Once the Japanese learned they were gone, the chase would begin, and the missionaries must get as big a lead as possible. Father McConville agreed to have everyone ready in an hour and rushed off to alert the other priest, Father Morel, and the three sisters, who were just getting ready for bed.

By 9:00 P.M. they were on their way, silently hurrying through a moonlit night. In the lead were the natives carrying the cane chairs with the two nuns who couldn't walk—Sister Claire, old and worn out, and Sister Remy, who had a bad knee. Just behind was Sister Henrietta, who could get along on her own. Then came a large half-caste family—Bobby Pitt, his wife and five children . . . then a blind native girl and her companions . . . and finally Fathers Morel and Lebel. The departure was so sudden that Father McConville lingered behind to attend to a few details. He caught up with the party later.

They had to keep moving, and it was an exasperating moment when Father Morel fell into a deep mud hole and lost his pipe. The entire caravan ground to a halt, while he sloshed around on his hands and knees trying to recover it. In desperation Father Lebel promised to give him another, but Morel would have none of it—this was his favorite, and for long minutes he continued to hunt, while Father Lebel pleaded and even tugged at him in vain. The search was fruitless, and the procession continued, with Father Morel now brooding in resentful silence.

November 26, they finally reached Tsipatavai, and it turned out that Father Lebel's faith in the mountain villagers had not been misplaced. The dormitory, another smaller bamboo house on stilts, various outbuildings, even a small church stood ready for the refugees.

Now to get the eight sisters waiting at Asitavi. Led by Father O'Sullivan, they headed up the coast on December 5 in a small motor launch lent by a Chinese trader. Around noon on the 6th they staggered into Tsipatavai—weary, bedraggled, but still proudly wearing their white habits. They compromised their standards only to the extent of substituting navy-blue veils to make them less conspicuous from the air.

At last Father Lebel had all his nuns collected together: eleven at Tsipatavai plus three more at Tinputz, less than two hours away. Anticipating this day, he had for some time been working on Jack Read, trying to get the Coastwatcher to arrange an evacuation. Read would have liked nothing better. He considered the nuns on Bougainville a weight around his neck, but it was no simple matter to get a plane or a ship.

Several times during November he had queried Eric Feldt about the chances of evacuation, but nothing materialized. At Lebel's urging, he again tried on December 16. The answer was the most discouraging yet:

no planes or ships available, nor were any likely in the future. Read felt the only course left was to move the nuns deeper into the bush, plant food, and sit out the war.

Impossible, said Father Lebel. He continued his prodding, while he tried to think of some new argument—some new approach—that might yield better results.

Meanwhile the group at Tsipatavai was growing. Mrs. Edie Huson, a planter's widow who had fled from her holding on Buka, suddenly turned up. Then came Mr. and Mrs. Claude I. H. Campbell, who owned a magnificent 7000-acre plantation at Raua on the north coast about three hours away.

Like most Bougainville planters, Campbell was fiercely independent and had resisted all Jack Read's efforts to get him and his wife to safety when the war broke out. The plantation was his life, and since it was isolated and without military significance, he hoped the Japanese wouldn't notice the place. It worked out that way for nearly nine months, but his luck ran out in the early hours of December 22. At 2:45 A.M. an enemy schooner and some landing barges appeared without warning; a raiding party stormed ashore; and the Campbells barely managed to clear out before their house was seized.

They fled to a hideout they had prepared, but the Japanese were hot on their heels, and they escaped only by tumbling into the gorge of the Ramoizan River. Climbing the opposite side, they found temporary shelter in a leaf hut. While here they learned the Japanese had burned their house and told the natives they would be back in a few days to kill the Campbells and "all the English." Taking a scrap of paper Claude Campbell scribbled a hasty note to Father Lebel: "We are distressed and stranded at this place. Appreciate you come to see us immediately. Please come, Father."

The results were immediate. Within a few hours

Father Lebel was on the scene, persuading the Campbells to join the group at Tsipatavai.

The episode showed clearly that Japanese pressure was growing, and that harsh treatment awaited any Westerners caught. On December 23 Father Lebel visited Jack Read at Porapora to press once more for evacuation. Read said there wasn't a chance; Eric Feldt had made that clear again and again.

At this point Lebel had an inspiration. Would Read bypass the whole command structure and let him send an appeal in the bishop's name direct to Admiral Halsey? After all, most of the nuns were American.

Jack Read had no fondness for red tape, but this seemed to be going too far. Well, how about asking Feldt for *permission* to send such a message? Read still seemed reluctant.

"Jack, this is an American bishop asking an American commander for the evacuation of American women!"

As usual, Father Lebel got his way in the end. Jack Read radioed Townsville, asking permission to send an appeal direct to Halsey. Then began the long wait that inevitably occurs when a military headquarters, faced with an unusual request, tries to crank itself up for an answer.

Christmas Eve, and time was running out. That morning the Japanese raiders struck Tinputz itself. Father Allotte, temporarily in charge; Brother Gregor, who ran the sawmill; and the mission's three nuns barely escaped. While the two priests hid in the bush, peeking at the invaders, the nuns joined the group at Tsipatavai—making fourteen sisters altogether.

The Japanese left during the afternoon, but that night word reached Tsipatavai that they were back again . . . maybe heading for the hideout. Father Lebel interrupted midnight mass to announce that the refugees must head deeper into the hills at once. "Be prepared to be cold,

wet, and hungry. I want you to cooperate with everything I ask you to do. Move quickly and be ready for
anything."

Half an hour later—1:30 A.M. Christmas morning—
they were on their way. A native scout took the lead,
with Sister Henrietta close behind, holding up a flickering lantern. The others trailed along in single file, each
nun carrying a blanket roll with a few necessities across
her shoulders. A bright moon helped light their way.

Soon they came to a terrifyingly steep gorge, which
the nuns descended on their hands and knees, clinging
to roots and bits of rock. Then across a shallow stream
and up the other side. It was an almost vertical climb,
with very little to cling to for support. No one ever
knew how the natives made it who were carrying the
two sisters who couldn't walk.

They continued—faster now, but tripping, stumbling,
slipping, always out of breath. At 3:00 A.M. they rested
briefly at a mountain village, where the natives—awakened by this strange intrusion—stared at them in frightened bewilderment. Then on again, with Sister Elie
from Tinputz handing out biscuits in hopes they would
give the group fresh energy.

The first rays of dawn began to brighten the sky,
and everyone took new heart. They were now so high
they could see the ocean through the trees. Surely their
ordeal must be just about over. But Father Lebel
wanted one more gorge between his party and the
Japanese, so they made yet another harrowing descent
and climb. Now at last he was satisfied, and they sank
down on logs, resting their heads on their knapsacks.

Father Lebel himself continued for a few yards, until
he found a good, level spot suitable for a camp. The
rest then joined him, except the independent Campbells,
who decided to go on to the Australian commando post
at Mutahai, still higher in the mountains.

Father Albert Lebel, who collected and hid the nuns stranded on Bougainville. It was his radio message, direct to Admiral Halsey, that led to their successful evacuation. (Courtesy Sister M. Irene Alton)

When the others reached the campsite, it was a very different Father Lebel they found waiting for them. During the long flight he had set the perfect example— always in good spirits, always full of energy—but now that they had reached their goal, the strain was telling. He slumped on the ground, shoes and stockings off, trying to ease the pain of his bleeding feet. He had deep circles under his eyes, three days' growth of beard. He hadn't slept for 52 hours and looked it.

The nuns tried to make him comfortable. One of them bathed his feet . . . another made him a hot drink, spiking it with a shot of rum . . . another spread some banana leaves over the ground. Then they wrapped him in a blanket and "put him to bed."

The natives began clearing the bush and building a lean-to out of branches and vines. They worked fast, but most of the nuns were too tired to wait. Finding some huge taro leaves—literally six feet long by four feet wide—they laid these on the ground, curled up on them, and went to sleep.

During the afternoon three of the Australian commandos arrived to report that the Japanese had reembarked and everyone could safely go back to Tsipatavai. But Father Lebel decided they had traveled enough this Christmas Day; so they spent the night in camp, sitting under the stars, singing all the carols they knew and ending with the "Magnificat."

It was a day late, but next morning Father Lebel got the best Christmas present he could have wanted. A runner arrived from Jack Read with permission from headquarters to send a message direct to Admiral Halsey, requesting evacuation. There was just one condition: It couldn't be over 200 letters long.

Lebel lay down in the thick jungle grass to think the matter out. This was his one chance to go straight to the top; he must make the most of it. There were, it seemed, three points to stress: first, that American women were involved; second, that they were in deadly danger; and third, that rescue was practical. But how to say all that in 200 letters: In the end he beat his quota, using only 171:

URGENTLY REQUEST IMMEDIATE EVACUATION OF AMERICAN WOMEN FROM BOUGAINVILLE STOP FEAR REPETITION OF CRIMES ON GUADALCANAL STOP TEOP AND TINPUTZ HARBORS SAFE AND CONVENIENT STOP ETERNALLY GRATEFUL

                                                    WADE

He shrewdly decided that Bishop Wade's name would carry more weight than his own, and felt no qualms in using it, since he had full authority to act in the bishop's name.

The message worked. December 28, Jack Read received word that a submarine would probably be sent, and on the 29th he was told it would be coming to Teop that night. This was moving too fast. Father Lebel's party was now back at Tsipatavai, but it would take Read himself two days to get over from Porapora. Since all communications depended on his teleradio, he persuaded headquarters to hold everything until he could reach the scene.

He started off early on the morning of the 30th, after sending a runner to Tsipatavai, alerting the group there to be ready to move at a moment's notice. At the same time he sent messages to several other people he hoped to get out, even though they hadn't been mentioned in Father Lebel's appeal. There were, of course, the Campbells and Mrs. Huson. Another spunky widow who had stayed on for a year was Mrs. Chris Falkner, who had a plantation right at Teop Harbor. Then there were several other planters still hanging on, like Alf Long and Max Babbage down near Numa Numa. With luck he could get them out too.

Finally, there was Fred Urban, the Austrian manager of Hakau plantation near Tinputz. He not only was an enemy alien but had been in touch with the Japanese when they first landed. They let him remain on his plantation, and there were rumors of further contact. To Jack Read it all smacked of collaboration, and he had held what amounted to a court martial. Father Lebel, who had great faith in Urban, rushed to his defense. In the end, Read allowed him to go back to Hakau on condition that he have no further contact with the Japanese. Urban obeyed to the letter, but Read remained suspicious. This looked like a good opportunity to get rid of him, and he was told to start packing.

All parties had been alerted by the time Jack Read reached the village of Tasku at noon on December 31. He was about an hour inland from Teop Harbor, as close as he dared bring the teleradio. Hooking up the set, he alerted KEN that he was in position, and was told the submarine would probably come that night. Lieutenant Mackie, who was now on hand with some of his Australian commandos, hurried down to the beach to collect canoes, prepare signal fires, and hoist a white sheet in the trees—a prearranged signal to the submarine that all was well.

Now it was 1:00 P.M., and at Tsipatavai Father Lebel checked to make sure everyone was ready. The big problem at the moment was footwear—all that tramping over Christmas had taken its toll. Sister Irene was clomping about in Bishop Wade's tennis shoes, and Sisters Hedda and Henrietta had nothing at all. Father Lebel quickly gave them his own last two pairs of sneakers.

At 2:00 P.M. the caravan started, single file as usual, with Sisters Remy and Claire being carried on stretchers. Father McConville was in charge; Father Lebel himself stayed behind to help the Campbells, who had to come all the way from Mutahai and were bound to be late.

All afternoon they trudged along the slippery trail. Downhill was always slow going, and to make matters worse, a heavy rain set in, soaking them to the skin. At 5:00 they reached Tasku, where they found Jack Read, earphones on his head, trying to get the latest word from KEN. They waited a while, but there was nothing new. "Probably tonight," but still not definite.

Read ordered them to continue on to Fred Urban's place and wait for further orders. Urban himself would join the party there. He emphatically didn't want to go, but there was no sign of friction when the refugees reached Hakau around 7:00. He graciously welcomed them and served everyone supper on his verandah.

It was 8:00 P.M. when Jack Read finally got the signal he was waiting for. KEN radioed that the operation was definitely on for tonight. He was to light his signal fires at 10:00, and everyone was to be on the beach ready for immediate embarkation.

He hurried over to Hakau. There must be no slips or miscalculations. He himself would lead the party on this last leg. As they fell in at 8:30, word spread that they would be going by submarine. The nuns were utterly astonished. Visualizing their rescue, they had pictured planes, speed boats, island coasters, but in all their speculations, the possibility of a submarine never entered their minds.

No time now to wonder what it would be like. With Jack Read leading, they started off. Close behind came Sister Irene with a lantern, and behind her the other nuns, the three priests, Mrs. Huson, and Bobby Pitt's three young daughters. Pitt himself stayed behind with his wife and two boys. As half-castes, they hoped to stick it out in the bush but didn't dare take a chance with the little girls. Bringing up the rear were a few of the A.I.F. commandos, who had magically turned up to help them.

Here and there other lanterns and an occasional worn-down flashlight dotted the line of march, but it was really a game of follow-the-leader as they hurried through the night, tripping over roots, stumbling into mud holes, slipping on the wet leaves and grass. Holding her lantern high, Sister Irene found it impossible to please anybody. One minute Sister Elie would beg her to slow down—she had lost her glasses—then Jack Read would call out, "Faster, faster, we have to be there by 10:00!"

Somehow they made it. Drenched and dishevelled, splattered with mud, the party finally pushed through to the beach, where the mood was more like a family reunion than an evacuation. Jack Read's system of alerts had worked perfectly. Alf Long, Max Babbage, three or four other planters were on hand. Father Fluett had come up from Asitavi to see the sisters off. The rest of Lieutenant Mackie's men were there too, organizing the canoes and paddlers. Many of these people had not seen each other for weeks, even months. There were quiet greetings, embraces, exchanges of news.

Shortly after 10:00 Read's favorite scout, Sergeant Yauwika, touched off two signal fires, one behind the other. The flames roared up, casting a flickering light on the group milling around. All eyes scanned the sea, but there was no sign of the submarine. The four Sisters of St. Joseph decided they had time to wash up and change to dry clothes at Mrs. Falkner's plantation house, right on the edge of the beach.

They walked into a different world. Not a cushion was out of place in the beautifully furnished living room. Bowls of sweet-scented frangipani graced the polished tables. Here and there a handsome lamp cast a soft glow, picked up and reflected by the carefully waxed hardwood floor. Servants glided in and out, going about their normal duties.

Dressed in exquisite black lace, Mrs. Falkner graciously received the sisters. Having assumed she would be in the last stages of packing for the evacuation, they looked at her in astonishment. "I'm not joining your party to Australia," she explained pleasantly.

Outside, Jack Read was seething. After all the difficulty of arranging for the submarine—after all the work of collecting everyone together—it was just too much to have this impossible woman suddenly balk at going. Nor did he intend to have her on his hands just when the Japanese were increasing their pressure and he needed all the mobility he could muster. Dropping by the house from time to time, he begged, pleaded, argued, threatened. Mrs. Falkner remained adamant: She wouldn't go. He finally told her she was going even if he had to use force. She seemed unmoved.

Meanwhile a new problem was boiling up. There was still no sign of the Campbells. True, they had to come all the way from Mutahai, but they were now far behind schedule. Finally Father Lebel, who had stayed behind to help them along, appeared on the beach to report that they were on the way, but lagging badly. They had been on the road for nearly 20 hours and were just about all in.

Jack Read had the perfect man for this crisis. Sergeant Bill Dolby was one of Lieutenant Mackie's best commandos, combining great physical strength with rare determination and resourcefulness. Read quickly sent him up the trail with Private Waterhouse and a team of natives. If anybody could get the Campbells moving, Dolby would do it.

Back on the beach, all eyes continued to search the sea. It was now after 11:00—Sergeant Yauwika's signal fires blazed ever higher into the night—but still no sign of the submarine. The nuns, again in clean white habits, stood around in little groups, talking to pass the time. Some of the commandos had messages for home, and notes were scribbled by the light of the fires. In her beautiful house Mrs. Falkner continued to play the gracious hostess. Jack Read wondered what he would do when the ultimate confrontation came. But where was the submarine? How could it take this long?

Bill Brockman was doing his best. All day the *Nautilus* had been submerged ten miles off Teop Harbor, most of the time examining the shore with her periscope.

Sergeant Bill Dolby, one of the Australian Commandos who worked closely with Coastwatcher Jack Read on the evacuation of the Bougainville refugees. (Courtesy Bill Dolby)

There was no sign of the sheets that were meant to be displayed if the coast was clear; on the other hand, a periscope at ten miles wasn't the ideal way to check this out.

Brockman designated a three-man shore party for the night's work. All were "volunteers," but that was a bit of a euphemism. CBM Red Porterfield, for instance, had to go because he was the only man on board who really knew how to handle small boats. He decided that the most important person to have along was a good motor man. The *Nautilus* had three, but one was a little slow, another too meek. That left only CMM Moe Killgore, who moved fast and wasn't meek at all. In fact, his mastery of four-letter words stood out among a crew not known for its restraint in language. So Killgore "volunteered" too.

Lieutenant Richard B. Lynch, the *Nautilus*'s torpedo and gunnery officer, would be in charge. Ozzie Lynch was a rangy six-footer of great charm and brilliance. Like many academically inclined people, he sometimes seemed a little removed from the practical world, but he balanced the other two men nicely.

At 7:39 the *Nautilus* surfaced and began edging toward the harbor entrance. She was always a clumsy boat, and the charts as usual were awful. The night was pitch black, and it was hard to see anything ahead. Brockman took her in as close as he dared, and finally hove to about three miles offshore.

Crew members scrambled onto the deck and immediately began rigging the boom to hoist out the *Nautilus*'s whaleboat. A slow business even in daylight, it took all the more time in the dark. Finally they got the boat into the water only to discover the motor was hopelessly flooded. So they hoisted it back and broke out the ship's launch instead, as more minutes ticked by.

Now the loading began. Tommy guns, flashlights, binoculars, rubber raft, a walkie-talkie, emergency rations—everything the shore party could conceivably need was dumped in. Then supplies for the Coastwatcher: cans of boneless chicken, corned beef hash, spaghetti, pork and beans, brandy miniatures—things Jack Read hadn't seen for a year.

The U.S. submarine Nautilus, *which staged the New Year's Eve rescue.* (National Archives)

Caught in the spirit of the affair, the crew below began sending up presents for him too—soap, cigarettes, a scout knife, toothpaste, sewing kit, pipes, tobacco pouch. Perhaps it was the tobacco pouch that gave Bill Brockman an inspiration. He still hadn't forgotten Ensign Davis and the overwhelming aroma of that Christmas tobacco. He sent a sailor down who announced to Davis: "Captain says you have some pipe tobacco you want to give to the Coastwatcher."

George Davis knew when he was licked. He surrendered unconditionally and handed over the tobacco.

It was almost 10:00 by the time Lynch started off, and almost immediately he was back with a broken rudder. Forty minutes more while the rudder was repaired, and then off again around 10:30. By now the two signal fires were blazing on the shore, and the launch was meant to take its bearing by lining them up. For some reason Lynch didn't do this and instead aimed directly at one of the fires. The boat veered off course, ran onto a reef, and capsized.

The three men tumbled out into the shallow water that surged around the reef. Scrambling to their feet, they began the slow process of righting the launch and bailing it out with their helmets. Killgore was furious—sure they would be taken by the Japanese—and his language was never more picturesque. He saved his choicest comments for Lieutenant Lynch, who silently took it all, but Porterfield got his share too.

On the beach Jack Read and the others continued to wait. Thanks to Bill Dolby's efforts, the Campbells had now arrived, and Father Lebel had taken on the job of trying to persuade Mrs. Falkner to come voluntarily. It was now nearly midnight, and still no sign of the submarine.

Then suddenly Dolby's sharp ears picked up the sound of voices out on the water. Read listened, heard something too, and took a native canoe to investigate. Several hundred yards out, he came to the *Nautilus*'s launch. Lynch, Porterfield and Killgore had just finished their bailing and were trying to push the boat off the reef.

Read and his native crew pitched in, and the launch was soon refloated. The culmination of this joint effort came when one of the Americans reminded Read that it was New Year's Eve and handed him a brandy miniature from the supplies they were bringing in. All hands paused for a moment to toast the occasion.

With the launch refloated, Read and Lynch quickly worked out the mechanics of the evacuation. They decided Lynch would remain offshore and get the rubber boat ready, while Read went into the beach, loaded the evacuees into the canoes, and brought them out to be transferred. At some point Read broke the news that there were not only the nuns, but a number of other refugees—29 altogether. This was far more than Brockman expected—far more than could be carried out to the submarine on one trip. It was agreed to take out the women and the Pitt children first, then if Brockman approved, bring out the men on a second lift.

Read paddled back to the beach, calling out that the submarine had come, it was time to leave. Sister Irene was still at Mrs. Falkner's house chatting with some of the commandos when an excited native rushed up: "Boat he come! Boat he come!" Inside, Father Lebel was talking with Mrs. Falkner. She poured out her worries—her property, her house, all the reasons she should stay. Lebel listened patiently, then gently explained why it would be best for all if she left . . . and he felt sure she would want to help if she could.

Finally she broke into tears and said, "Yes, Father, I will go." In minutes she had a small bag packed and was on the beach with the others.

Lieutenant Mackie had his canoes launched, paddlers standing by, and the loading was now in full swing. Jack Read was losing an argument with the Campbells over how much luggage they could bring. A few steps away the fourteen sisters knelt in the sand to receive Father Lebel's final blessing.

"What if I fall in?" Sister Irene asked the native paddling her out toward the *Nautilus*'s launch. The harbor was choppy, and it did not seem a silly question. Don't worry, he answered, he'd pull her out. Somewhat reassured, she nevertheless took the precaution of saying her Rosary.

Reaching the launch, the canoes clustered around, while Red Porterfield finished pumping up the rubber boat. He made some joke about the amount of air "these things" took, and to Sister Hedda his Oklahoma drawl was the most welcome sound in the world.

At last all was ready. While the supplies for Jack Read were shifted to the canoes, the refugees piled into the launch and rubber boat. Some 21 were transferred altogether—seventeen women, the three Pitt girls, and Mr. Campbell, who had managed to squeeze in with his wife. When Mrs. Huson's turn came, Lieutenant Lynch made some remark about excess baggage. Without a word she tossed one of her two suitcases overboard.

Slowly the launch headed out of the harbor, towing the rubber boat in its wake. A native pilot guided them safely through the reef. From time to time Lynch flicked on a pencil flashlight, and occasionally there was an answering flash in the distance. No one said much. Moe Killgore, perhaps awed by the presence of fourteen nuns, used impeccable language.

On the *Nautilus* Bill Brockman was anxiously waiting. Over four hours had passed since the launch shoved off—a far longer time than expected—and everyone's nerves were on edge. The submarine lay flooded down to reduce its silhouette; the 20-mm. guns were manned; the 6-inch gun crews were standing by. Finally, at 3:00 A.M. the launch and rubber boat loomed alongside to everyone's relief.

Relief and surprise. SOPAC had said "a few" nuns had to be evacuated, but here were fourteen . . . plus six more women and children . . . plus a man. Nor was that all. Ozzie Lynch was already requesting permission to gas up and go back for eight more people.

Fortunately Bill Brockman loved challenges and enjoyed the unusual. Here was a full share of both. The only thing that worried him was time. He was determined not to be caught here on the surface at daylight. He approved the trip, stressing that the launch was to be back by 4:30.

The nuns were now scrambling aboard the *Nautilus,* aided by outstretched hands from the deck. Sailors guided them to the forward escape hatch and down into the forward battery compartment, which also served as wardroom. Here Ensign Davis was ready with coffee and sandwiches. Sister Hedda couldn't get over her first sight of the table. *"Real* sugar! *Real* salt!" she gasped in an awed whisper.

Topside, the launch cast off and headed back to the harbor entrance, where the eight remaining evacuees were waiting in canoes. They were deeper inside the harbor than Lieutenant Lynch anticipated, and getting back to the ship was a race with the dawn. Bill Brockman's deadline of 4:30 slipped by, but he was still there at 4:41, when the launch finally eased alongside. More-than-willing hands hauled aboard Fathers Allotte and Morel, five planters, and the Austrian Fred Urban. There was good reason for all to feel relieved, but planter Fred Archer was particularly pleased. He was a great Jules Verne fan, and it seemed especially fitting that the submarine was called the *Nautilus.*

Lieutenant Commander William H. Brockman, Jr., skipper of the Nautilus, *gave up his quarters to a nun and three children.*
(National Archives)

The crew quickly hauled in the launch, drained the oil, and stowed the gear. At 5:37 the claxons sounded, the *Nautilus* submerged to 100 feet, and crept away from Teop.

"Make the submarine your home," said Bill Brockman, sensing the bewilderment of the nuns sitting in the wardroom. And he really meant it. He turned over his own stateroom to one of the Marist Sisters and the three Pitt children. The other women moved into the wardroom, an officer's stateroom, and the Chief Petty Officer's quarters. Various members of the crew gave their bunks to the priests and planters. Father Allotte lay much of the time on a cot in the forward torpedo room, praying with his beads. "Nothing can happen to this ship," said a young crewman watching him.

The refugees enjoyed a New Year's Day dinner that

seemed simply incredible after months of taro and pau
pau. Soup, fried chicken, vegetables (even buttered
asparagus), peach pie, and fruitcake appeared in miraculous succession. A neatly typed menu cheerfully proclaimed, "Happy New Year to All Hands and Guests."

After spending the day submerged, the *Nautilus* as
usual surfaced at night. Now was the time for recharg-
ing batteries, gulping fresh air, picking up radio traffic.
Tonight a message came in from SOPAC that meant a
lot to Brockman, even more to his guests: "CONGRATU-
LATIONS, NAUTILUS. YOU WERE JUST AHEAD OF THE
SHERIFF. JAP DESTROYER ENTERED TEOP HARBOR
SHORTLY AFTER YOU LEFT."

The *Nautilus* was always a happy ship, but never
more so than during the next two days. The nuns
quickly adapted themselves to submarine life. The heat
was stifling—it averaged 94°—and they had only their
long white habits, but they endured this new world of
sweat and skivvy shirts with vast good humor.

In only one respect did they fall short—they never
learned how to work the "head." Flushing the toilet on
a submerged submarine was an immensely complicated
business in 1943, and the facilities on the *Nautilus*
seemed invented by Rube Goldberg. The process involved separate steps—mostly opening and closing various valves—which had to be done in exactly the right
sequence, or nothing would work at all. Bill Brockman
knew this would be a problem and gave Sister Isabelle
a special course, so she could teach the others. But
it was hopeless. He finally put his steward Billy Fer-
nandez in charge of what became known as the "head
watch."

Otherwise the nuns proved perfect shipmates. They
showed an interest in everything, never got in the way,
and soon were learning to play cribbage and that peren-
nial Navy favorite, acey-deucy. In return, the crew

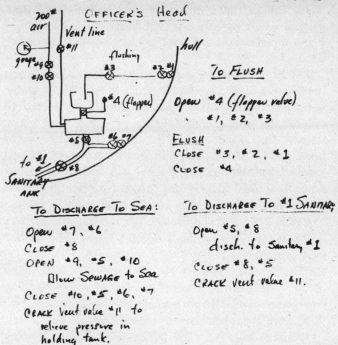

U.S.S. NAUTILUS (SS168)

circa 1942-45

OFFICER'S Head

200# air

Vent line #11

gauge #9

#10

flushing #3   #2 #1

#4 (flapper)

hull

#5   #6 #7

to #1 #8

SANITARY TANK

TO FLUSH

Open #4 (flapper valve)
    " #1, #2, #3

FLUSH
CLOSE #3, #2, #1
CLOSE #4

TO DISCHARGE TO SEA:

Open #7, #6
CLOSE #8
OPEN #9, #5, #10
    Blow Sewage to Sea
CLOSE #10, #5, #6, #7
CRACK Vent valve #11 to
    relieve pressure in
    holding tank.

TO DISCHARGE TO #1 SANITARY

Open #5, #8
    disch. to Sanitary #1
CLOSE #8, #5
CRACK Vent valve #11.

Flushing the officers' head on the Nautilus *normally required nineteen separate steps, done in exactly the right sequence. The nuns never mastered the art. The proper procedure, sketched by a member of the crew, suggests the complexity of the problem.* (Courtesy Hal M. Winner)

showered them with gifts—toothbrushes, candy, cake from home. They even threw a children's party for the Pitt girls, complete with wrapped presents. These turned out to be socks, sweaters, souvenirs and knick-knacks drawn from the crew's personal possessions.

There were serious moments too, as Brockman's officers pumped the planters for useful information.

They picked up a good deal that should come in handy later: Tanker traffic heavy off the north coast of Bougainville . . . ships usually kept about ten miles out . . . a patrol plane passed down the east coast every morning about 7:00. . . .

January 3, and the ship's company learned that their improbable idyll was drawing to a close. The *Nautilus* —heading southeast for three days—was ordered to rendezvous with a Patrol Craft off Tulagi that night, transfer the evacuees, and resume her regular operations. Late in the evening Bill Brockman issued a typed sheet of instructions. Everything was spelled out: Passengers would leave by the forward hatch, Lieutenant Eckert in charge; baggage via the after hatch.

It was 2:47 A.M. on the 4th when radar contact was made. A minute later the *Nautilus*'s signal lamp flashed its challenge . . . and got the correct response. At 3:00 the dim outline of the *PC 476* could be seen, lying about 900 yards off. The refugees were ordered up and emerged on deck. Now it was time to say good-bye, and there were even, Brockman noted, a few farewell kisses.

A rubber boat from the PC came alongside, bobbing in the choppy sea. "Don't drop anybody," Brockman called as the first nuns were lowered. It was Red Porterfield who came up with the practical answer: "We won't drop them now after going way out there to get them."

The boat took them in batches of six to the PC, where sailors helped them up a rope ladder thrown over the side. Other crew members lined the rail, peering into the dark, trying to figure what was up. Catching a glimpse of the white habits of the nuns, one mystified sailor asked, "What are we taking aboard, sacks of flour?"

By 3:49 all the *Nautilus*'s guests had left, and the

*Before departing, the refugees drew up this testimonial to
Bill Brockman and his crew.* (Courtesy William H. Brockman, Jr.)

submarine vanished into the night. Watching her go,
Sister Hedda felt her eyes fill with tears.

December 31, 1942, proved an eventful New Year's
Eve in Tokyo too. After weeks of soul-searching and
buck-passing, Imperial General Headquarters had come

to the reluctant conclusion that indeed Guadalcanal could not be held. The garrison was starving and support impossible. Any further investment of the national treasure would be throwing good money after bad.

Resplendent in full-dress uniform, the Army Chief of Staff, Lieutenant General Gen Sugiyama, and his Navy counterpart, Vice Admiral Osami Nagano, called on the Emperor during the day. They reviewed the problem and formally recommended withdrawal. His Majesty gave his approval.

On January 4—the same day the *Nautilus* evacuees reached Tulagi—a staff officer, Major General Ayabe, arrived in Rabaul from GHQ. He brought with him a set of top-secret orders implementing the decision. The troops were to be withdrawn in late January and early February, but this did not mean, he stressed, the end of the Japanese effort in the Solomons. On the contrary, operations on Santa Isabel, New Georgia, and the northern Solomons were to be pushed more vigorously than ever.

The effect would be a whole new chapter in the air war over the Islands . . . and another opportunity for the Coastwatchers to prove their unique value to the Allied cause.

9

FRIENDS IN NEED

It looked like any other Tokyo Express to Marine fighter pilot Captain Jack R. Moore in the early morning light of January 15. Actually, the purpose this time was not to land troops for some new offense, but to put fresh men ashore to cover the Japanese evacuation of Guadalcanal. Now the nine destroyers were scurrying back up the Slot, and the CACTUS Air Force was trying to stop them from getting home.

The results were disappointing. No hits, and Moore's Grumman caught a burst from a covering Zero. His oil pressure fell . . . the engine froze . . . and he splashed heavily into the Slot.

Breaking out his rubber boat, he found himself midway between New Georgia and Santa Isabel. It was a toss-up, but he chose Isabel and began paddling east. The distance was perhaps 30 miles, but he hadn't reckoned on the current. It took three days to get there.

On the afternoon of the 18th he was offshore looking for some sign of life, when two natives in a canoe paddled alongside. They spoke no English but seemed to know what they were doing. With reassuring smiles they escorted Moore to their village, bathed and fed him, and lashed together a leaf shelter where he could rest.

Next morning they put him in a canoe and took him down the coast to another village. Here too everyone seemed to know what they were doing. Early on the 20th guides and carriers appeared and took Moore over the mountains to the eastern side of the island. Now another group of equally efficient natives took over, and the canoe trip resumed.

At last they came to a village called Tataba near the southeastern tip of Isabel. Here they were met by a good-looking, well-proportioned young man with dark skin and European features. He too had an air of self-assurance, partly because Moore was no less than his fourteenth visitor from the sky.

Geoffrey Kuper was the only Coastwatcher in charge of a station who was born in the Islands. His father, Henry Kuper, was a German trader-planter who had come out before World War I, settled on Santa Ana off the eastern end of San Cristobal, and built up a splendid plantation. Like many European planters in the Solomons, he was lonely and found a native girl; unlike most of the others, he married her.

Born in 1917, Geoffrey developed into a bright, personable boy, but given the colonial world of the time, with its rigid racial barriers, there was no place for him in the white planter society of his father. For a young man of mixed blood, there was only one route open to a good education and some semblance of professional status. This was to become a "native medical practitioner." The NMPs, as they were called, were trained in the Fijis and came back to serve the district officers as medical assistants. While not technically a doctor, an NMP was about the closest thing to a doctor that most natives ever saw.

When the Pacific war began, Geoffrey Kuper was NMP on Rennell Island south of Guadalcanal, working under Donald Kennedy, district officer for the whole Western Solomons. Brought back to Tulagi as the Japanese tide swept south, Kuper continued his medical work for a time at Aola and later on San Cristobal.

Mid-February 1942, Kennedy recruited him for a new job. By now most of the European planters had fled, often leaving their workers—migrants from other islands—stranded without food or money. The only solution was for the government to repatriate them back to their own islands, and Kennedy undertook to do this with Kuper as his assistant.

Using the District sloop *Waiai,* they first cleared Rennell, then New Georgia, and early in March headed for the Shortlands. Here they visited Faisi . . . back to Gizo . . . and finally down to Ranongga Island, just below Vella Lavella. Life wasn't all work, and on Ranongga Kuper met Linda Martin, daughter of a leading local family of mixed blood. In a week they were engaged.

On March 28 the Reverend Silvester came over from Vella Lavella and married them, with Merle Farland in attendance. There were the usual toasts and refreshments, but when the newlyweds sailed away next morning, it was the Japanese who provided the big send-off.

As the *Waiai* headed north for the Shortlands again, a Zero float plane swooped down from nowhere, machine gun blazing. Geoffrey, Linda, Donald Kennedy, the whole crew dived for cover as the plane flashed by at masthead height. It circled and made another run—in fact, five runs altogether—but the pilot must have been a poor shot indeed, for he failed to score a single hit.

Continuing on, they reached Faisi that night, where two Catholic fathers invited them to stay at the mission.

Kennedy toyed with the idea but finally decided to head for Choiseul Bay, their next stop, without further delay. It was just as well. Early the following morning the Japanese stormed ashore in a surprise landing on Faisi. It was the start of Japan's big advance down the Solomons that culminated in the capture of Tulagi and Guadalcanal. Had the *Waiai* remained, the whole group would have been trapped.

Kennedy and Kuper knew none of this at the time. Reaching New Georgia a few days later, they assumed Faisi was still safe, and two young half-castes, John Klaucke and Hugh Wheatley, were sent there with a teleradio. The Japanese snapped them up as they landed, and the ominous silence that followed was the first clue that the Shortlands were gone.

The *Waiai* now headed for the southeast coast of Santa Isabel, where Kennedy had established a base at a village called Mahaga overlooking Thousand Ships Bay. Next, a quick visit to Rennell; then back to Mahaga around the end of April. On all these trips Linda went along, quickly adjusting to the peripatetic life of a Coastwatcher's bride.

May, and they were caught in the tide of the Japanese offensive. With the capture of Tulagi, they were now deep in enemy territory; and with the submission of George Bogese, the native medical practitioner on Savo Island, they were suddenly in deadly danger. He knew all about the Coastwatchers. Worse, he came from Santa Isabel himself, had plenty of contacts there, and knew the best hiding places.

Early on May 17 Kennedy's party sighted two Japanese barges with about 100 troops landing at Kolare, a small island directly below Mahaga on the southeastern coast of Isabel. Scouts soon confirmed their worst fears. Bogese was with the force and was now recruiting his relatives to serve as guides in an assault on the camp.

The District vessel Waiai, *used by Donald Kennedy and Geoffrey Kuper in their early Coastwatching work. She was later trapped and burned by the Japanese.* (Courtesy D. C. Horton)

There was little to do but wait. Besides Kennedy and Kuper, the defenders included only five police boys and six Rennell Islanders brought north on the *Waiai*'s last trip. Between them all, they had only five Lee-Enfield rifles. It looked like a last stand, and Kennedy prepared to destroy the teleradio and burn the fuel and provisions.

Then a reprieve. A Japanese float plane appeared, dropped a message to the force, recalling it immediately to Tulagi. No one ever knew why, but whatever the cause, the result was clear. Kennedy, Kuper, and all the rest lived to fight again another day.

But they didn't get off scot-free. One of Bogese's relatives showed the Japanese a creek where Kuper had hidden the *Waiai,* and as the barges retired they opened fire on the little sloop. The boat burst into flames and sank at her moorings.

Clearly Mahaga was no place to linger. Kennedy put every one aboard his only other boat, an ungainly auxiliary ketch called the *Marara,* and sailed northwest up the coast. They had no particular objective—just some good observation point as far away as possible from Bogese and his relatives.

For the next month they were pretty much on the move, but Kennedy managed to keep up a steady flow of radio traffic on Japanese movements, and he also had a chance to see Geoffrey Kuper under pressure. He liked very much what he saw.

Around the middle of June he decided that Kuper should operate independently. There was an extra boat now—a scavenging party had brought in an 8-ton auxiliary cutter called the *Joan*—and with his genius at radio, Kennedy put together an extra set from spare parts lying around. Kuper, with Linda and a three-man crew, took off for New Georgia. Soon he was radioing regular reports to Kennedy, using the rather odd call-sign, "Unattached K."

The arrangement didn't last long. Toward the end of the month Kuper ran aground in heavy weather and had to bring the *Joan* back to Isabel for repairs. This left New Georgia uncovered, and Kennedy decided to move into the breach. It was now clear that most of the Japanese convoys from Rabaul were coming down west of the Slot, and New Georgia would offer a far better spot for observing them. On July 8 he established himself at Segi—that perfect example of site selection—and left "Unattached K" to cover Isabel.

By August the *Joan* was repaired, and Kuper started down the northwest coast, planning to recruit some natives to cut a new trail across the island. Early on the 7th he was well on his way when the boat's engine conked out, leaving her drifting and rolling in the off-shore swell. At 8 A.M. he was still struggling with repairs when a fighter plane with stubby wings roared down from the clouds without warning. It held its fire, but buzzed the *Joan* twice and flew off. Later Kuper would recognize this sort of plane as a Grumman Wildcat, but this morning he didn't know what it was. It happened so suddenly, he didn't even notice the white stars on the wings.

The American landings in the Solomons had begun.

Geoffrey Kuper didn't know this either. He only knew that the helmsman had fled the wheel, and the *Joan* was now stuck hard on a reef. No way to get her off till high tide; so he let go the anchor and ordered abandon ship. Loading the teleradio into the dinghy, he led the crew to a nearby beach.

He was still there around noon when he spotted 27 Japanese bombers flying southeast. Two hours later he watched them fly back—far fewer now and chased by American fighters. Some Zeros turned up, and dogfights erupted all over the sky. Three . . . four planes careened into the Slot.

Around 4 P.M. the *Joan* floated free of the reef on a rising tide, and Kuper completed his repairs. He then chugged out to look for survivors of the great air battle, but saw no one. As dusk fell, he headed back down the coast and into an ever-narrowing creek. Huge cypress-like trees lined the banks and almost touched overhead. As far as he knew, it had no name, but he called it the "Kilokaka hiding place" after the name of a nearby village.

On August 9 he learned there was a survivor from the great air battle after all. A native runner arrived to report that a flyer had been picked up on the beach and was now resting at a village near Mufu Point. American or Japanese? The native said he couldn't tell the difference. Well, what did he look like? Short and rather stocky, answered the native. This sounded too much like a Japanese for comfort, and before going to the scene, Kuper dashed off a note asking the stranger to identify himself:

To the aviator shot down: Whether you be ally or otherwise, report to me immediately. Geoffrey Kuper, Base Defense Officer, Santa Isabel.

In a couple of hours the runner reappeared with an answer: "I am unable to travel. Gordon E. Firebaugh, Lt. (j.g.), USN."

Kuper now hurried to the village, somewhat reassured —but not completely. His hand was on his pistol as he entered the leaf hut where the flyer was staying. One glance was enough to dispel all doubts, but it seemed that Lieutenant Firebaugh too had his worries. "What are you going to do with me?" he asked. "I don't know whether you are a British or Japanese agent."

Kuper said, "British," and the alliance was formally sealed with a handshake. Firebaugh, it turned out, was a fighter pilot from the carrier *Enterprise,* covering the landings at Tulagi and Guadalcanal. Shot down during the dogfight on the 7th, he had bailed out of his burning plane and landed in the sea. Although his legs were burned and his Mae West leaked, he somehow managed to swim first to a tiny offshore island and later to Isabel itself. Here he was quickly found by the natives, and since then his only problem had been the local witch doctor, who wanted to treat his legs. "Perhaps tomorrow," Firebaugh tactfully suggested.

Now he was put aboard a huge dugout canoe—nearly 50 feet long—and with Geoffrey Kuper steering and six paddlers at work, they raced down the coast. Entering the bay that led to the Kilokaka hiding place, Kuper covered Firebaugh with a tarpaulin—even friends were not allowed to see the exact location of the creek—and it was over an hour before he let the lieutenant sit in the open again. It was dark when they finally drew alongside the *Joan,* moored beneath the trees and lighted by a single lantern.

Helped aboard, Firebaugh was introduced to Linda, given a meal of rice and yams, and treated to a roll-your-own cigarette that was so strong it made his head spin. His quarters proved to be a mattress on top of the after cabin. The Kupers slept below, while the crew kept to the bow of the boat.

Early next morning "Unattached K" went on the air, reporting Firebaugh's rescue and requesting a plane to pick him up. It seemed a reasonable request—the Americans always had plenty of everything—but this was 30 hours after Savo, and headquarters truthfully replied that they had no planes; would Kuper bring him to Tulagi? Understandably, they didn't add that the whole Allied fleet had been destroyed or dispersed, and the trip would be entirely through enemy waters.

As dusk fell on the 14th, the *Joan* cast off, glided down the creek into the bay, and turned southeast along the coast. The tide was low, and they ran aground countless times during the night. Kuper would then wade the anchor to deeper water, giving something to pull on as they pushed with poles and rocked the ship loose. At sunrise they turned up a tributary and hid for the day under some trees. They were far behind schedule.

During the morning Kuper vanished into the jungle to visit a "friend." Later the friend himself appeared, paddling alongside the *Joan* in a canoe. To Firebaugh's surprise he turned out to be Chinese. Chan Cheong had been a prosperous storekeeper in Tulagi. When the Japanese approached, he didn't flee south with the rest of the Chinese community but moved his family into the jungle and was now determined to sit out the war. There wasn't much he could do to help the Allied cause, but he contributed whatever he could. This afternoon his contribution was a small rooster, which he gravely presented to Geoffrey Kuper.

It was as tough a bird as Firebaugh ever tasted, but that evening it did vary the monotony of yams at every meal. With darkness they continued on, through Thousand Ships Bay and into the open sea that separated Isabel from the Florida Islands. Engine trouble put them still further behind schedule, meaning that they must finish the trip by daylight—an inviting target for either the Japanese or trigger-happy American gunners.

It was a B-17, patrolling from Espiritu Santo, that first spotted them shortly after sunrise on the 16th. It circled them low, guns bristling, and the *Joan* had no colors to hoist. Firebaugh desperately signaled "U.S. Navy" by semaphore, and to everyone's relief the plane apparently understood. It flew off, and an LST appeared, which escorted the *Joan* to a pier in Tulagi harbor.

As a Marine inspection party came aboard, Geoffrey Kuper emerged from his cabin. For the past week he had been barefoot, usually wearing only an old pair of shorts. Now he was resplendent in a beautiful green shirt, spotless tan military trousers, tan shoes, and an Aussie hat with one brim turned up. A small automatic pistol in a black leather holster hung from his waist. He looked splendid, and no one would suspect that he had not slept in 48 hours.

Back on Isabel August 18, Kuper received a radio message from Resident Commissioner Marchant (probably inspired by Donald Kennedy) to establish a permanent Coastwatching post at Tataba. He was now formally incorporated into the Coastwatcher network and given the official call-sign ZGJ-6.

At Tataba he moved into a leaf house with Linda and the teleradio and gradually built up a staff of twelve native assistants. Two natives were always on watch, the rest used as needed. Linda cooked for them all.

At the same time he established a network of scouts and contacts all over the island. He divided the coast into sectors and assigned each sector to a nearby village. Natives in canoes covered the entire shoreline at least once a day. He had no trouble getting volunteers; they poured in, and soon (as he later put it) "the whole island was scouting."

The timing was perfect. Henderson Field began operating on the 20th, and the great aerial battles for its control were largely fought above Isabel. A whole new Coastwatcher "industry" sprang up—the rescue of downed American flyers—and in these early days no one played a more important role than Geoffrey Kuper.

His first "customers" arrived on September 17, when Marine pilot Second Lieutenant Archie M. Smith, Jr.— lost while returning from a bombing mission up the Slot —crash-landed his SBD a few yards off the coast. Smith and his gunner, PFC Tommy Costello, came ashore on San Jorge, a small island virtually contiguous to Santa Isabel. After a harrowing night when every firefly looked like the glowing tip of a cigarette held by some Japanese, they swam to Isabel itself and spent the next night in a deserted house near a native village. A Japanese calendar on the wall was not reassuring.

On the 19th they awoke to the sound of native drums, and Smith had visions of cannibals, a large pot, and himself as the entrée. But they couldn't hide forever; so they took a chance and revealed themselves.

Several of the natives spoke pidgin English, and they made it clear that the Americans must go to "the Chinaman." This led to a series of canoe rides into the interior. Finally they came to a European-type sloop hidden in the bush. Up in the rigging, wearing a western shirt and shorts, was "the Chinaman."

It was, of course, Chan Cheong. He escorted Smith and Costello to his leaf house, and for the next two days they relaxed in style. Even though a fugitive, Chan Cheong saw no reason to live like one. His beds were comfortable, the meals delicious—especially breakfast, which featured pancakes wrapped around apricot preserves.

Meanwhile Chan made use of the network of scouts and runners to alert Geoffrey Kuper. ZGJ-6 immediately contacted Henderson, and arrangements were made for a small amphibian to pick up the flyers on the 22nd.

Everything went off so smoothly that it wasn't even necessary for Kuper to be on hand. He felt a little bad about this, and along with his final instructions, he sent Smith a brief message of apology: "I am sorry it has not been my pleasure to meet you two and have you as my guests, but I have no doubt Mr. Chan Cheong has been a good host, better than I could have been in these hard times."

Two weeks passed, and Kuper's network was tested again. On October 5 Lieutenant Commander John Eldridge, skipper of dive-bombing squadron VS-71, was forced down off the southwest coast while returning from a strike on Japanese shipping. Reaching shore,

Eldridge and his gunner, ACRM L. A. Powers, Jr., were almost immediately found by Kuper's scouts and brought to Tataba. They were evacuated by amphibian that very afternoon—the quiet, competent Eldridge was desperately needed to lead his squadron at Henderson Field.

Another two weeks, and two more members of VS-71 turned up. While flying a search mission over Rekata Bay on October 17, Lieutenant (j.g.) C. H. Mester was shot down and his gunner, ARM/2c E. L. Forwood, badly wounded. Picked up by the scouting network, they were brought to Tataba, and Kuper radioed for an urgent pickup. But this was right after the devastating Japanese bombardment of the 14th, and Henderson simply had no planes available. Kuper must cope with the situation as best he could. Falling back on his medical training, he successfully extracted several bullets from Forwood's legs and left arm.

"Say, he's just got another bullet out!" Forwood observed at one point in the operation.

"You must be getting lighter," said Mester encouragingly.

Mester and Forwood were still at Tataba on October 25 when Marine fighter pilot Second Lieutenant John Henry King ran out of gas, splashed down just offshore, and was added to the group. King's plane was almost intact, and Kuper hauled it up on the beach. Proud to have saved the U.S. government the cost of a new fighter, he notified Henderson and waited for some one to retrieve it. He was still waiting 34 years later.

These were trying days for the stranded flyers. General Kawaguchi's attack—the third great offensive to recapture Guadalcanal—was in full swing, and there was evidence of hard fighting everywhere: air battles in the sky, warships knifing through the Slot, and on the 25th a big display of fireworks practically on Geoffrey

Kuper's doorstep. Late that afternoon Henderson Field bombers caught the Japanese cruiser *Yura* about seven miles offshore and sent her blazing to the bottom. The airmen at Tataba took turns watching the show through Kuper's binoculars . . . and longed to be a part of it. When Kawaguchi's last assault had finally been crushed, a landing barge arrived from Lunga on the 29th and picked the flyers up.

They were hardly gone when Kuper's organization brought in still another flyer—First Lieutenant Wallace L. Dinn, an Army Air Force fighter pilot based at Henderson. Like others before him, he had fallen afoul of the Japanese anti-aircraft gunners at Rekata Bay, who seem to have been among the best in the business. The fighting on Guadalcanal had simmered down now, and on November 3 Dick Horton brought over the *Ramada* with a load of supplies and picked him up.

Kuper's next customer was already on the way. On the 1st Marine fighter pilot Second Lieutenant Michael R. Yunck had also been clipped by the AA gunners at Rekata Bay. Splashing off the northwest coast near Austria Sound, he paddled southeast in his rubber boat. On the fourth day he finally met a party of three natives roasting a pig on the beach. Using a combination of pantomime and pidgin English, he tried to explain that he was an American aviator. He put on, he felt, a very good show: spreading his arms like wings . . . "flying" up and down the beach . . . pointing his fingers like machine guns . . . and adding sound effects. The natives watched for about 30 seconds, then the youngest spoke up with flawless British accent: "I understand. You are an American aviator. We work for Mr. Geoffrey Kuper, who is the Coastwatcher on the island, and we will take care of you."

The organization sprang into action. Relays of canoes moved Yunck down the coast for three days . . . then guides escorted him inland for another day . . . and finally around noon on November 9 he reached Tataba. Having been fooled once, Yunck expected to meet a typical Britisher—"a Cooper spelled with a C"—and was somewhat nonplussed by the dark, lithe young man who came forward to greet him.

Like the others before him, Mike Yunck fretted to get back to Henderson Field. But once more the fighting had heated up—the Japanese were mounting their fourth great attack—and again, there just wasn't any transportation available. In his impatience, Yunck even suggested going up to Rekata Bay and hijacking a Zero float plane.

This struck Kuper as an appalling idea—a good Coastwatcher survived by being inconspicuous—and he made a mental note to send this eager warrior on his way as soon as possible. A big canoe was obtained, and on the 16th Mike Yunck headed back to the wars.

And so it went. After Yunck there was Lieutenant Joe Murdoch . . . then a Marine pilot named Kovaks, who bailed out so high his face was bruised by hail-stones . . . then Corporal J. E. Hartman, tail gunner of a B-17 and the only survivor when his plane was rammed by a Zero. Hartman was initially picked up by Seton and Waddell on Choiseul; they slipped him to Isabel, and Kuper's network took over.

After the Japanese defeat in November, the air battles tapered off, and for the first time in weeks Geoffrey Kuper had no flyers on his hands. But this didn't mean he was idle. Twenty-six survivors from a sunken Japanese barge had formed an outpost on nearby San Jorge Island and posed a growing threat. On December 18 Kuper's scouts caught the party by surprise, routed them from their camp, and wiped them out completely.

The Japanese seaplane base at Rekata Bay was another problem. Fortunately Kuper's chief scout in the

area, a native named Mostyn, had won the confidence
of Lieutenant Yoneda, the Japanese commander, with
gifts of fish and fruit. He soon had the run of the base,
and his information was regularly used by the Henderson Field bombers. After every raid Mostyn would turn
up to commiserate with Yoneda—and assess the latest
damage.

Despite the bombings, the Japanese continued to develop Rekata Bay, and at KEN Hugh Mackenzie decided to establish a second Coastwatching station on
Isabel to give the enemy base full-time coverage. On
January 8, 1943, RAAF Flying Officer J. A. Corrigan,
formerly a New Guinea gold miner, took over Kuper's
northern network of scouts and spies, including the ingenious Mostyn.

With January, Japanese ships and planes began reap-
pearing in large numbers, and the great air war flared
up with new intensity. Once again Geoffrey Kuper found
himself in the air-rescue business: It was his network
that brought in Captain Jack Moore on the 20th. As
usual in times of crisis, headquarters could provide no
transportation, and after waiting thirteen days, Kuper
sent Moore to Tulagi by canoe.

As the CACTUS Air Force ranged far up the Slot
harassing the Japanese planes and convoys, for the first
time the other Coastwatchers too began playing a major
role in these rescue operations. On Vella Lavella Henry
Josselyn and Jack Keenan got word from KEN to keep
a sharp lookout for two fighter pilots seen to bail out
over the island of Kolombangara during a strike on
January 31.

The scouts were alerted, and two days later a canoe
arrived at Bilua with Staff Sergeant James A. Feliton
of VMF-121. He had parachuted into a mammoth tree
on Kolombangara and was badly shaken up when he
fell to the ground. Discovered by Josselyn's men some

24 hours later, he could shed no light on the other missing pilot.

But he was very much alive. During the strike First Lieutenant Jefferson J. de Blanc had single-handedly shot down five Zeros, before a sixth got him. Bailing out, he landed in the water off Kolombangara, swam ashore, and was picked up by natives a couple of days later. They then looked up one of Josselyn's scouts and exchanged him for a sack of rice—a deal that still makes de Blanc wonder how much a fighter pilot is really worth.

Reaching Vella, he was greeted by name by the Reverend Silvester and was soon reunited with Feliton. Escorted by Keenan to Paramata, they were both evacuated by PBY on the 12th. Boarding the plane, de Blanc presented a memorable sight: He was now wearing a complete Japanese uniform and carried, as a souvenir, a nine-foot native spear.

On New Georgia Donald Kennedy was getting his share of flyers too. On February 4, American fighters and bombers caught some 20 Japanese destroyers coming down the Slot. They were covered by Zeros, and a wild dogfight developed off Visu Visu Point. Navy Lieutenant Bob Sorensen, flying an F4F, found himself chased by four of the Zeros. He sent one down smoking, but the other three got him, and he splashed in the Marovo Lagoon off Batuna Mission.

Encountering some natives next morning, he was paddled over to Segi, where Kennedy greeted him with a very reserved British "Howjado." Four other flyers from the battle soon joined him—a Marine fighter pilot named Leeds . . . two gunners from a downed TBF . . . and a captured Zero pilot. They were taken out in a week by a PBY.

On Choiseul Nick Waddell and Carden Seton played host to four more participants. Ensign Keith Hollands-

First Lieutenant Jeff de Blanc at the time of his rescue from Vella Lavella. He has on the Japanese uniform he wore off the island. (Courtesy Jeff de Blanc)

Jeff de Blanc and his rescuer, Henry Josselyn, meet again for tea 33 years later. (Courtesy Jeff de Blanc)

worth's TBF was knocked out by A.A. fire, then harassed all the way down by Zeros. They got the turret gunner as he swam away from the plane, but Hollandsworth and the radio gunner, Adcock, managed to escape. Heading for shore in their rubber boat, they were picked up by natives and taken to a village called Boe-Boe.

Next morning the natives reported two Japanese were down too and not far away—what should be done? Hollandsworth recommended wiping them out, and a war canoe set off full of natives with hatchets and clubs. Closing in, some one realized at the last second that the "Japs" were actually Americans—Marine SBD pilot H. J. Murphy and his rear seat man, Corporal G. W. Williamson. They had been shot down in the same battle and made shore during the night.

Soon all four flyers were at Boe-Boe together, and on the 8th Hollandsworth and Murphy accompanied a party of natives to the Coastwatcher hideout up the coast. A pickup was arranged for the 12th, and Nick Waddell suggested a feast to celebrate. This unfortunately had to be aborted when the flyers discovered they had a day less than they thought to get back to Boe-Boe. It seemed Waddell was still operating on a 1942 calendar.

The PBY arrived exactly on schedule, scooping up the castaways while fifteen fighters flew cover above. It was the first pickup in the Solomons by VP-44, a squadron that would become famous for its "Dumbo" missions, as these rescue flights came to be called.

The early days of February were especially rough on the flyers who operated out of Henderson Field. The Tokyo Express was more active than at any time since the November offensive—big runs of about 20 destroyers on the 1st, 4th, and 7th. Ominously, Yamamoto was again at sea—two carriers, two battleships, more than a dozen cruisers and destroyers hovering about 200 miles north of Choiseul.

To the American command on Guadalcanal it all looked like preparations for a new Japanese offensive. General Patch had launched a cautious push west of the Matanikau River; now he suspended the drive and recalled the 25th Division to defend Henderson Field. From the looks of things, the Japanese were bringing in thousands of troops.

Actually, they were taking them out. In a masterpiece of deception called Operation KE, Lieutenant General Hitoshi Imamura and Vice Admiral Jinichi Kusaka, the commanders at Rabaul, were evacuating the 13,000 Japanese remaining on Guadalcanal. In a series of leapfrogging tactics, the starving remnants of the Imperial Army were pulled back, while a sprinkling

PBY at Segi Point on a typical "Dumbo" mission. Coast-watcher Donald Kennedy's scouts are bringing out to the plane Second Lieutenant Milton M. Vedder, shot down off New Georgia, April 25, 1943. (National Archives)

of fresh troops held the line against any American advance. Even the men themselves didn't know what was up; they were told they were being redeployed for a new attack.

Gradually the force was concentrated at the coastal village of Komimbo on the extreme western tip of the island. Here they were ferried out to the destroyers in the blackness of night. Only the occasional flash of blue signal lights indicated that anything unusual was going on. February 1, 5424 men were taken out . . . on the 4th, another 4977 . . . on the 7th, Colonel Matsuda's rear guard of 2639. General Hyakutake went with the last contingent. Boarding the destroyer *Hamikaze,* he went straight to his cabin, never looking back at the lost island.

The Americans still didn't catch on. Planning a classic pincers movement, Patch had landed a well-equipped force southwest of the Japanese position on February 1. The spot was picked by Father de Klerk, now wearing a U.S. Army second lieutenant's bars, pinned on him by General Patch himself. On the 7th this force began moving toward Cape Esperance, as the main body of U.S. troops advanced from the east. The pincers snapped shut on the 9th, but caught nothing. The Japanese were gone.

The spotlight shifted to the Central Solomons, as Tokyo moved to strengthen its hold on the other islands. Occasional cargo ships and an ever-increasing number of diesel barges headed down from Faisi, pouring men and supplies into the seaplane base at Rekata Bay . . . the airfield at Munda . . . a supporting strip at Vila on Kolombangara . . . the advanced base at Viru . . . a dozen other outposts along the way.

Paul Mason was gone now—driven out of Buin and trying to join Jack Read in northern Bougainville—but from their lookout on Choiseul Nick Waddell and

Carden Seton usually caught the traffic as it left the Shortlands. Then Henry Josselyn would pick it up as it passed Vella Lavella—either to the east down Vella Gulf; or to the west, hugging the coast and hiding out during the day near Bagga Island. Finally Dick Horton —now established on a ridge high in the hills of Rendova Island—would catch the shipping as it unloaded at Munda, or headed on for some other point. Using his 10-power artillery binoculars, Horton could even see trucks and individual Japanese working on the runway.

Back on Guadalcanal KEN would receive their reports and pass them on to the Air Strike Command. It was all very routine now, and everything seemed in order when Eric Feldt arrived on an inspection tour in mid-March. Then, without a hint of warning, on the 20th he suffered a coronary stroke. He survived but was sidelined for good and replaced by Lieutenant Commander J. C. McManus, a wiry Australian with long experience in both intelligence and the South Seas. It might have been a disaster—Feldt had such close ties with so many of his men—but McManus proved a skillful, tactful replacement.

Through all these weeks Waddell, Josselyn and Horton continued to radio their ship and barge sightings, generating new business for the flyers at Henderson Field. On February 27, for instance, Nick Waddell reported a large freighter escorted by two corvettes leaving Faisi at 1:00 P.M. At 6:40 the CACTUS Air Force struck, sinking all three ships within sight of Choiseul. For the first time Waddell had the satisfaction of personally seeing the results of his reporting.

Another time, acting on a message from Josselyn on Vella Lavella, SBDs delivered a devastating attack on the cargo liner *Toa Maru*. They left her in sinking condition, and the crew abandoned ship. But she did not go down. Instead she stranded on a reef off Gizo Island.

Josselyn's scouts soon boarded her and salvaged not only a great deal of military equipment but also the ship's supply of cutlery and linen. From then on, the Coastwatchers at station NRY dined with Japanese silver.

But these triumphs had their cost. The air battles were now taking place deep in enemy territory, and the downed American flyers were in greater danger than ever. Even with the Coastwatchers on the lookout, the way home could be long and hard. . . .

On April 13 Staff Sergeant William I. Coffeen of Marine Fighter Squadron 213 was escorting some TBFs on a strike against Munda when his engine failed and he bailed out over the Slot. Landing halfway between Kolombangara and Choiseul, he managed to scramble into his rubber boat just as two sharks flashed by.

Wind and current carried him into the maze of small islands that make up the southeastern tip of Choiseul, and soon he was hopelessly lost in a labyrinth of inlets and channels. For a week he aimlessly paddled from island to island, often retracing his steps, misguided by whim and fancy. He had no food except coconuts, and sleep was next to impossible. If it wasn't the mosquitoes that droned "like a flight of four-engined bombers," it was the inquisitive rats that nibbled at his fingers.

About the tenth night he heard something walking toward him that sounded very much like a man. He jumped into his boat, ready to flee, but it turned out to be a giant iguana.

Three weeks must have passed when he stumbled on an island that boasted a European house. A sign proclaimed it to be the "Salikana Plantation Estate— Solomon Development Co.," but the proprietors were long since gone. The only sign of life was a crafty old hen, which he pursued in vain for nearly two days. He did find about a dozen eggs in the hen house. All were rotten but went down surprisingly well.

Back in the boat, he continued his aimless paddling, vaguely hoping that if he could once reach the mainland of Choiseul, life would somehow improve. He grew steadily weaker; his body was covered with sores; his teeth were loose, and his mind began to wander.

On the 32nd day a great storm swamped the boat. Somehow he got it ashore and dumped it. By now he was raving and screaming, completely delirious, and shortly after he shoved off again, he collapsed in exhaustion.

A native in a canoe eased alongside. Attracted by the commotion, he had been discreetly following the boat for some minutes. Now he politely inquired whether Coffeen was American or Japanese. "Me American," said Coffeen and passed out.

After resting at the native's hut a couple of days, Coffeen was taken to Boe-Boe on Choiseul, and here Nick Waddell's scouts took over. They relayed him up the coast by canoe, dodging several Japanese barges and on one occasion paddling right by the campfire of an enemy outpost.

On the 23rd of May, 41 days after he bailed out, Bill Coffeen finally reached Waddell and Seton's station DEL, now located on Mount Vasau, about five miles inland from the coast. Coffeen was little more than skin and bones, and he almost immediately came down with malaria. Carden Seton patiently nursed him back to health, while Waddell once again marveled at the way this huge man, so ferocious in a fight, could magically turn into the tenderest of human beings when caring for the sick.

As Coffeen slowly regained his health and strength, he learned that DEL had a jauntiness all its own in looking after flyers. Waddell kept a "visitors' book" and

> The Ancient Order of
> the Rubber Rafters of Choiseul
>
> ~~This is to certify that~~
>
> John R. Stott: A.R.M. U.S.N
>
> has qualified as a member of this
> distinguished order having saved his
> life by Rubber Raft and suffered
> diverse adventures on this island.
>
> He is ~~required~~ to get intoxicated
> every year on ~~this~~ date and to make
> as many ~~others~~ ~~as possible~~ ~~equally~~
> drunk
>
> Frn. F W addell
> 24th July 1943. Lieut. Royal Aust. Navy
> Chief Rubber Raffer

"Certificate" awarded flyers rescued by the Coastwatchers on Choiseul. (Courtesy John R. Stott)

also organized a club called the "Rubber Rafters Association." Every rescued airman got a "certificate" saying he belonged, and the only condition of membership was that the candidate had to promise he would get drunk every year on the anniversary of his rescue.

Mid-June, and Coffeen was at last strong enough for the long walk across the island to Nanango Point, where he would be picked up by PBY. This was the first evacuation from the eastern side of the island, but it was no longer safe to use the more convenient west coast. The Japanese seemed to be planting outposts everywhere.

All went off without a hitch. When Seton and Coffeen reached Nanango early on the morning of June 25, they found no less than 30 canoes and 100 natives waiting to help. At 9:35 two PBYs landed and discharged supplies for DEL, while 16 fighters flew cover overhead. Twenty minutes later Bill Coffeen said his good-byes, boarded one of the planes, and headed home—exactly 73 days after his odyssey began.

These dangerous days a flight in the Solomons could wind up with a rescue ten weeks later—or it could just as easily end in the towering clouds with murderous abruptness. Early on the morning of April 18, only five days after Bill Coffeen went down, Admiral Isoroku Yamamoto, Commander-in-Chief, Imperial Combined Fleet, took off from Rabaul for a brief inspection of the Navy's advanced bases at Ballale, Shortland, and Buin. Yamamoto and his staff flew in a pair of medium bombers, while six Zeros provided cover above. At 9:34 they were over the west coast of Bougainville, just letting down for the landing at Ballale, when four P-38s tore into them, chopping both bombers to pieces before the Zeros could intervene. Yamamoto's plane plunged into the jungle and exploded, while the second bomber smashed into the sea. A crash boat picked up three dazed survivors, but there were none from the plane that fell in the jungle. Isoroku Yamamoto, Japan's brilliant and indispensable naval leader, had been killed with a single lightninglike stroke.

The P-38s—appropriately nicknamed "Lightnings" —were doing triumphant barrel rolls as they returned to Guadalcanal from this most fateful of missions. Catching the meaning, ground crews ran up to the planes whooping and shouting as they landed. Off-duty pilots crowded around, laughing and slapping backs.

They had good cause to celebrate. Major John W. Mitchell's 339th Fighter Squadron had just completed the longest planned interception of the war—a 750-mile round trip. Thanks to another coup by CINCPAC's dazzling code-breakers, Yamamoto's exact schedule had been learned. With the approval of Navy Secretary Knox and President Roosevelt himself, Nimitz authorized Halsey to stage an assassination mission if feasible. Even with special belly tanks, the P-38s were the only planes with range enough to do the job; and even then, Major Mitchell's flight plan allowed virtually no margin of error. He based all his calculations on an estimate that Yamamoto would reach the interception point at 9:35. He was one minute off.

By nightfall just about everybody in the CACTUS Air Force knew about the 339th's spectacular kill. Those who missed the excitement at the field couldn't escape the boisterous celebration that night, as the squadron took care of a case of I. W. Harper supplied by Vice Admiral Marc Mitscher. But the source of the remarkable information that made it all possible—the decoding of Yamamoto's schedule—remained a dark secret. The rumor spread, encouraged by headquarters, that the Coastwatchers were responsible; and most of the flyers, who by now believed these guardian angels could do anything, were happy to give them credit for one more miracle.

Actually, the Coastwatchers knew nothing about Yamamoto's inspection trip and were among the last to learn of the ambush. Geoffrey Kuper got the word on May 7 from another P-38 pilot, Second Lieutenant A. L. Weckel, who ran out of gas returning from a photo mission to Buka and was brought in by the scouts. Weckel's own squadron played no part in hunting down the admiral, but all the P-38 pilots took a proprietary interest in the feat.

Weckel was Kuper's seventeenth rescued flyer—and more would follow. His smoothly functioning network of scouts and guides ultimately saved 28 Allied airmen. Not that success was automatic. There was the harrowing day, for instance, when a fighter plane crashed into Rekata Bay, and the pilot bobbed to the surface as Kuper's scouts and a Japanese launch raced for the scene from opposite directions. It was a toss-up, until the launch opened fire on the scouts, forcing them back. In bitter anguish they watched as the Japanese scooped up the flyer in triumph.

Or there was the time on Vella Lavella, when Henry Josselyn's natives had to bring some aviators right by

The only Coastwatching family: Geoffrey, Linda, and Gordon Kuper, photographed at their home on the island of Santa Ana 30 years later. (Author's collection)

the enemy base at Iringila to reach safety. A fight developed, and in the confusion a Navy gunner named Evans vanished—no one ever knew whether he was shot or captured. But these were the exceptions. Altogether, the Coastwatchers in the Solomons saved over 100 flyers.

It was quite different when a Japanese pilot fell into the hands of a Coastwatcher. In this grim behind-the-lines struggle neither side paid much attention to the Geneva Convention. To the Japanese, the Coastwatchers were spies, and that was that. To the Coastwatcher, Japanese prisoners were a deadly liability. There was no place to keep them, and they knew too much to be turned loose. Very few escaped with their lives.

Geoffrey Kuper played this dangerous game like the others, but the authorities never treated him in quite the same way. Of the fourteen Coastwatchers who ran tele-radio stations in the Solomons, he was the only one never given a commission. He remained a private in the local defense force the entire time. The prewar attitudes lingered on: Commissions were for "Europeans," and in the euphemism of the South Pacific, Kuper was a "local" . . . a person of mixed blood.

Yet this attitude had its compensations. As Merle Farland found out, the colonial government was shocked by the very thought of a white woman in the war zone. But nobody cared about Linda. The great air battles raged in the skies . . . the aviators came and went . . . and on three different occasions Japanese planes found and attacked the Tataba hideout. Through it all, she remained at her husband's side, and on May 3, 1943, she bore him a son, later christened Gordon Henry Kuper. Whatever distinctions he missed, Geoffrey Kuper now had one that made him unique—he was the head of the Solomons' only Coastwatching family.

10

DRIVEN OUT

Compared to the birth of a baby, a supply drop was a comparatively minor complication in the life of a Coastwatcher, and Jack Read was not unduly worried about the drop scheduled for northern Bougainville on the night of April 26.

After some wildly inaccurate drops in the early days, these affairs were now almost routine. Guided by the signal fires, the plane—usually an RAAF Catalina of 11 or 20 Squadron—would circle down to about 500 feet and begin a series of runs over the drop site. Each time it passed, crew members would toss out some containers: fragile things like radio parts would float down by parachute; bulk items like rice and sugar would hurtle to the ground double-packed in jute bags. Never too much on any one pass, so as to concentrate the drop in the area bounded by the fires. When the last container had been jettisoned, the plane would usually waggle its wings, sometimes flash "good luck" on its signal lamp, and disappear again into the night.

On the ground the Coastwatchers would gather in

the containers, smother the fires, and vanish as quickly as possible.

Back at camp the containers would be opened, and along with the supplies the Coastwatchers would almost invariably find little presents tucked in by the "delivery boys": cigarettes, candy, sometimes a bottle of whiskey, and once for Slim Otton, who religiously followed the races, the latest Australian pink sheet giving the results of the Caulfield Cup.

Only occasionally was there a complication, like the time on the Abia River when Paul Mason scheduled a supply drop just a few hours after the local chief planned a funeral pyre. Worried that the plane would confuse the pyre with his signal fires, Mason asked rather indelicately, "Can you cook him before the moon comes up?" The Chief assured him that this could be done, and it was.

There were no funeral pyres on the night of the 26th. The only problem was the shift to a new drop site. For months Read had used the abandoned coffee plantation called Rugen near the north coast, but in December mounting Japanese pressure forced him to move the site south to the Inus area. Now that was dangerous too, and tonight would be the first time for using Aita, a small village deep in the mountainous interior of the island. It would be unfamiliar ground, but the pilot had all the necessary bearings, and there shouldn't be any trouble.

By 11 P.M. everything was ready. Four stacks of branches soaked with kerosene marked off a rough rectangle in the clearing. Natives stood by, ready to light the stacks. A group of bearers hovered in the rear. Two of the Australian commandos working closely with Read—Sergeant Walter Radimey and Sergeant H. J. Broadfoot—cast a practiced eye over the scene, making doubly sure all was in order.

At 11:59 they heard the distant hum of the Catalina's engines. That was the signal to light the fires, and all four stacks were soon blazing. The hum grew louder, and soon in the glare of the flames the Coastwatchers could make out the plane itself, circling down to make the first run.

On the Catalina, Flight Lieutenant W. J. Clark peered down at the signal fires mushrooming up below. Behind him the plane snapped to life. The monotony of the eight-hour flight from Australia was over now, and the crew took their posts for the drop. The navigator, Flying Officer C. S. Dunn, asked whether Clark wanted him in the bombardier's compartment; the skipper said no, he could see quite well. The moon wasn't up yet, but the sky was clear.

Corporal H. Yates removed the gun from the port blister, and Pilot Officer C. J. Twist crawled in with the headphones. They would be making the drops from here, and Corporal J. Fenwick squeezed into the blister compartment to help.

About 12:15 the drops began. Circling to the left, Clark swung low over the fires. The men in the blister pushed out the first container, watched the parachute open and float lazily down. Still circling to the left, Clark came by on his second run; another parachute floated down. Clark asked if the third chute was ready, and Pilot Officer Twist said not yet. Instead of continuing his left-hand circles, Clark now swung to the right, planning to fly a sort of "figure 8" to use up time.

Perhaps it was a downdraft . . . or a miscalculation . . . or the unfamiliar terrain—whatever the reason, the plane clipped some trees near the top of a ridge, sliced off its starboard wing, and ploughed on through the bush for 300 yards in a long, tearing crash.

Then silence, except for the trickle of gasoline as it leaked from the ruptured tanks. But men still lived in the wreckage and were soon calling to one another. Flying Officer Dunn and Sergeant F. G. Thompson managed to crawl free. Others were moving around, but trapped in the tangle of metal. No one could find a flashlight, and since it was obviously too dangerous to strike a match, they decided to stay as they were until dawn.

At the drop site Sergeants Broadfoot and Radimey didn't see the crash, but they heard it all too clearly. They immediately doused the signal fires and divided their men into two search parties. It was Broadfoot who finally located the wreckage at 6:00 A.M. and summoned the others by firing his pistol.

One by one they freed four survivors still trapped in the plane: Twist, Fenwick, and Yates, who had been handling the chutes; and Corporal R. H. Wettenhall, one of the helpers. Flight Lieutenant Clark, his co-pilot, and the engineer were all dead and left in the wreckage.

Most of the survivors were too badly injured to walk; so the plane's bunks were used as stretchers to carry them to the Australian commandos' camp at Aita. Here they were given first aid plus the good news that they might be evacuated almost at once. A U.S. submarine was due tomorrow to land and pick up some personnel at Teopasina, just 15 miles away. That operation would be rescheduled for April 29. With luck they could make it.

But luck was something they didn't have. After an early start on the 28th, a heavy rain set in, turning the trail to grease and at some points blocking it with flash floods. It was the 30th before the last of the party even got to Dariai—and that was only halfway to the coast. The sub had come and gone.

Jack Read decided the airmen should remain for the time being at Dariai. Here they were as safe as anywhere and could be treated by Sergeant Radimey, who had good medical training. Once they were mobile again, they could be taken out when the next opportunity came.

And the opportunity *would* come, Read felt sure, because his situation was steadily improving. Things had progressed a long way from those dark days in December and January, when the Japanese had Paul Mason and himself on the run. First, Mason managed to join him on January 28, and the two men were now operating together. In addition, the Army agreed to replace Lieutenant Mackie's commandos, worn out after eighteen months in the bush, with fresh men reporting directly to Read.

The first 12 replacements came at the end of March on the U.S. submarine *Gato,* landing at Teop, where Bill Brockman had picked up his nuns on New Year's Eve. Creeping into the harbor submerged on the 28th, Lieutenant Commander Robert J. Foley raised his periscope to find a Japanese schooner sitting at anchor a few yards away. Evening, and it was still there. A radio message from Jack Read put off the landing until the following night.

At dusk on the 29th the *Gato* was back, this time approaching cautiously on the surface. The schooner was gone, and signal fires blazed on the beach. The submarine hove to only 100 yards offshore, and a canoe appeared alongside with Jack Read. He welcomed the new arrivals and presented Foley with a small problem in arithmetic. The orders said the *Gato* would be taking out 12 of the original commandos plus another 12 refugees. But waiting to go were the commandos, three elderly Belgian nuns just rescued from Buin; nine island women, and 27 children—51 altogether. How many could Foley fit into his submarine?

All of them, said Foley, who evidently believed the *Gato* wasn't full as long as he could dog down the hatches. A swarm of native canoes now went to work, ferrying the replacements in and the evacuees out. In an hour the job was done, and the *Gato* stood to sea, her forward torpedo room turned into a nursery. Until she transferred her charges two days later, one 10-month-old baby would sleep nowhere except in the arms of a giant, bearded torpedoman named Phillips.

Back at Teop Jack Read began clearing the beach even before the *Gato* was out of sight. The canoes were hidden in the bush, the new supplies and equipment carried inland. By dawn everything was gone, so that when a Japanese coaster and two barges poked into the harbor later that day, there was no sign that anything unusual had happened.

Lieutenant Mackie, still on the island with the remaining 12 men of his company, escorted the new commandos to his camp at Namatoa. Leading them was Lieutenant Douglas M. Bedkober, an intensely dedicated young officer, although without experience in the South Pacific.

But there was plenty of experience packed into another new officer, also landed by the *Gato*. This was Australian Navy Lieutenant Jack Keenan, transferred from Vella Lavella. He not only had five months of Coastwatching under his belt, but he knew Bougainville like a book. In pre-war days he had served on the island as a patrol officer.

April 29, the *Gato* was back again with the last of the commando replacements. This was the trip rescheduled in hopes she could take out the injured airmen. The rendezvous was also moved south to Teopasino Plantation, which seemed safer from the Japanese.

Lieutenant Charles McGivern, the *Gato*'s young navigator, regarded the change with some misgivings. His chart showed just a dotted line for this stretch of coast. "Nothing to it, Pilot," skipper Foley cheerfully assured him, "just follow directions."

Somehow the *Gato* threaded the reefs and inched into the harbor, guided by the usual signal fires. Once again dozens of native canoes shuttled back and forth, landing 16 fresh commandos and taking out Lieutenant Mackie with the remainder of the original group. Also evacuated were the last of the missionaries, including a tired and discouraged Bishop Wade and a perky Father Lebel, already plotting how he could get back to the island.

It was now obvious that the six survivors of the Catalina could never arrive in time; so around midnight the *Gato* headed back to sea. Jack Read was so anxious to clear the beach that he doused the signal fires before the submarine was by the reef, leaving her to feel her way out. "Hell of a time to turn off the lighthouse," remarked Bob Foley, but once again navigator McGivern proved up to the challenge.

On Bougainville the new arrivals included two more thoroughly experienced officers. Lieutenant George Stevenson, who had been married just before leaving Brisbane, had been a patrol officer before the war. He was a slender young man, quiet and rather serious.

Captain Eric Robinson was just the opposite—a jolly, roly-poly Sydney pubkeeper, who had once been a public health official on the island. He was universally known as "Wobbie" because, as he put it, "I have twouble wolling my r's."

In assigning Robinson, Stevenson, and Keenan to Bougainville, Eric Feldt originally hoped they would spell Read and Mason, who had been behind the lines for over a year and surely needed a rest. Read and Mason saw it differently. They had been routed from the south, were barely hanging on in the north. They simply couldn't walk out on their natives at such a

Eric ("Wobbie") Robinson with five of the natives who worked with him. Taken on Guadalcanal shortly after their evacuation from Bougainville, July 1943. (Courtesy John R. Hubbard)

crucial time. Instead, this new manpower should be used to reestablish the Coastwatchers' position. Feldt finally agreed; it was one of his last decisions before his coronary.

Read quickly organized a new network designed to cover the whole island. Jack Keenan took on the north coast, basing himself near a village called Lumsis, with an observation post at Read's old lookout, Porapora. Sergeant G. J. McPhee, one of the new commandos, was put in charge of the isolated west coast, where not much action was expected. Read himself—assisted by "Wobbie"—took the central east coast, where the Japanese were currently most active. Mason and Stevenson headed south with a large party, hoping to cover Kieta and, with luck, Buin.

All four bases not only had teleradios but several new "midget" radio sets brought in by the *Gato*. These had a range of about 30 miles and would be used by outposts reporting to the main stations.

Supporting this network, Lieutenant Bedkober had commando units stationed at Namatoa, Dariai, and Aita. Bedkober himself was at the Dariai camp, where the six injured airmen still awaited evacuation. A second plan to get them out by PBY had to be abandoned when the Japanese occupied the rest of the east coast.

Dawn, May 26, and every one was finally in position, except for Mason's station in the south, which wasn't expected to open up for some days. Surveying the setup, Jack Read felt the glow of pride that often comes when an ambitious plan actually works.

Then, a little after 9 A.M. the roof fell in. At the Porapora lookout Sergeant W. V. Florance and Corporal N. L. MacLeod were just finishing breakfast when one of their scouts dashed by their hut shouting, "The Japs are here!" MacLeod grabbed his rifle, rushed to the doorway, and saw several Japanese soldiers standing about ten yards away with guns at the ready. He got off one shot . . . then bolted into the bush and down the mountain side, losing both his rifle and revolver in the process.

Sergeant Florance stayed behind long enough to smash the radio on the floor. Then, seizing his Tommy gun, he too plunged down the mountain. Like MacLeod, he lost his revolver, and in addition his shoes. The Japanese made no attempt to follow either man. They were content to loot the camp and lob grenades in the general direction the fugitive fled.

At Lumsis, the main Coastwatching station for the north, Jack Keenan knew from his native contacts that the enemy was on the prowl. Early on May 26 he tried to warn Porapora but couldn't get through in time. Around noon on the 27th it was clear his turn would come next. His scouts reported an enemy patrol scrambling up the trail that led to his camp.

No time to lose. Keenan and his commando assistant, Corporal A. R. Little, hastily hid the teleradio and went bush. An hour or so later they could hear the snapping and crackle of blazing bamboo as the Japanese burned their camp.

May 29, they returned to the ruins, recovered the hidden teleradio, and set off to find a new camp site. Just after leaving they met Sergeant Florance stumbling through the jungle, and he told them what he knew of Porapora. For three days he had been thrashing around alone in the bush, his flesh torn by vines, his bare feet cut to ribbons. He was in no shape for duty; Keenan packed him off to Dariai to join the convalescent airmen.

Two days later Keenan got the rest of the Porapora river valley who had come to barter fruit and tara for wandering aimlessly through the jungle. He had been six days without food, and for shelter had only the banana leaves he covered himself with at night.

Reconstructing the events that led to these disasters, Jack Read learned that both camps were betrayed by the natives of Tetakots, a small village near the northern coast. Nor was this an isolated case. As the Japanese expanded their hold on Bougainville, an ever-growing number of natives were shedding their loyalty to the old government. At first, Read had sounded plausible when he assured them the Allies would be back, but the Japanese had been in control for more than a year, and there was no sign of deliverance yet. Tashira, Tokyo's clever spokesman, was the one who sounded plausible now. He insisted that the old days were gone forever, pointing to the number of Japanese bases and airstrips multiplying on the island. And with his military arguments he mixed in allusions to white exploitation, while suggesting that the Japanese were really like cousins. As he talked, more and more natives were listening.

Read sensed he was losing his grip and took a desperate step. He radioed KEN urging heavy strafing and bombing of the coastal areas occupied by the Japanese, including the native villages friendly to them. On May 31, and for the next several days, American fighters and bombers swept in, chewing up piers, storehouses, gun positions, barges—and countless native huts as well.

The benefits were questionable. Read understandably could never see anything wrong about bombing the villages that were supplying the Japanese with scouts and carriers. Others felt such measures would never win back the disaffected natives, and would only drive others into the enemy camp.

In any case, it did no good. The Japanese moved steadily down the east coast, while their patrols— guided and supported by natives—probed ever deeper into the interior. Soon they had the commando base at Namatoa and were threatening Dariai, where the injured airmen lay.

Read had them moved back first to Aita, then still farther back to a little village called Sikoriapaia. They were now more than halfway across the island, and

Lieutenant Bedkober, in charge of the camp, began searching for a spot on the west coast where they might be rescued. Meanwhile they missed another chance for evacuation, when KEN radioed on June 8 that a submarine had unexpectedly become available and could pick them up in three days at Empress Augusta Bay. This was much too short notice—it would take a week to get them there—so a third chance was lost to get the flyers out.

June 11 was a quiet day at Read's camp, high above the Aita River and overlooking Numa Numa. The only visitor was an old chief from a village across the river valley who had come to barter fruit and tara for newsprint (used by the natives as cigarette paper) and a few strips of parachute cloth. Negotiations were successful, and toward evening he headed back for his village.

At dusk the scouts brought word of a Japanese patrol, accompanied by many natives, heading up the river below. There were some tense moments, but it passed the turnoff to Read's camp, and with a feeling of relief he sent a couple of runners to alert the commando camp about five miles farther up the Aita valley.

To be on the safe side, he also hid the teleradio and strengthened the guard at his own camp. Constable Ena, one of his best men, took charge of the sentry post on the path leading up from the river; then a second post was established on the path just fifty yards in front of the camp. Here the three Europeans—Signalman Alan Falls, "Wobbie," and himself—would take turns standing guard with the natives all night. As a final touch, dry bamboo sticks were planted across the path for several yards in front of this inner post. Any one clever enough to get by Sergeant Ena would still give himself away the instant he stepped on those sticks.

At 9 P.M. Signalman Falls relieved "Wobbie" and

began standing guard with the giant, bearded Sergeant Yauwika and Read's servant Womaru. Each of them had a rifle and a couple of grenades, but there was not the slightest hint of trouble. All was quiet, except for the occasional rustling and small stirring sounds that are so much a part of the jungle at night.

Suddenly, the crackle of bamboo. Thinking it might be a friendly scout who didn't know about the warning system, Sergeant Yauwika challenged. No reply. Falls then fired a tentative shot in the direction of the sound. He was answered by a roar of gunfire that split the night. The three guards emptied their magazines, threw their grenades, then ran for it as two light machine guns joined the barrage.

At the camp Read and Robinson grabbed their guns, dived through the thatched side of their hut, and plunged into the bush. The scouts were scrambling for cover too. Only Constable Iamulu hung back briefly. He remembered Read's repeated warning to the natives that any traitor who led the enemy to his camp would be the Coastwatchers' prime target. Now Iamulu paused long enough to shoot the first native he saw with the Japanese. It was the old chief who had visited them that afternoon.

For a few minutes Read and Robinson lay in the bush watching the Japanese storm the camp. Grenades and automatic fire cleared the way, and a horde of yelling natives followed them in. Long after the camp was taken they continued to rake the bush with submachine guns, but never the narrow area where the two men lay. It seemed so strange that Read began to wonder whether a second force of Japanese might be approaching from their own direction.

In any case it seemed wise to clear out as fast as possible. Hoping to reach the Aita River far below, they now headed down the mountainside together. It was too steep to stand; so they slid feet first, grabbing occasional roots to slow their speed . . . starting small avalanches of rock and gravel . . . hoping, praying that the Japanese were too busy to notice the noise. In the blackness they could see nothing, but tried to keep in physical contact so that wherever they went, they'd go together.

Finally they bumped to a stop on a narrow ledge or shelf. It was too dark to see, but probing with his feet, Read could feel nothing ahead or below. He had the uneasy feeling they were on the brink of a sheer precipice, and they decided to stay put until dawn.

It was a sound decision. Daybreak showed they were on the edge of a cliff—only inches from a vertical drop of hundreds of feet to the Aita River. When it grew light enough, they began creeping along the shelf, hoping to find a workable way down.

They had gone about fifty feet when a shower of pebbles indicated that someone else was coming down from above. Flattening themselves against the cliff-face, they drew their guns and waited. Fortunately, at this point they were under an overhang; so whoever it was, they would at least have the drop on him.

Presently they spotted a pair of brown legs feeling their way down from above. Then another pair, and yet another. It looked like a party of natives on their trail. There was no escaping, and both Read and Robinson had always resolved never to be caught alive.

"Wobbie" let go a burst from his tommy gun. There was a yell of pain, and a voice cried out in pidgin English not to shoot. The new arrivals were half-a-dozen of their own scouts trying to escape the same way. Fortunately, the wounded native had only a grazed leg —not enough to put him out of action—and the combined party ultimately reached the river and safety.

Learning that the Japanese raiders had moved on,

Jack Read led his group back up to the camp on June 15. Only charred ruins were left. All stores and gear were gone, the teleradio batteries and charging engine smashed. But the teleradio itself had not been discovered. Read retrieved it and headed for the commando base at Aita, hoping to find new batteries, another charging engine, and some benzine to run it.

The commandos were all gone. Hearing the gunfire at Read's camp only five miles away, they had cleared out and were now somewhere to the west. Offsetting this, Read found Sergeant Falls, Yauwika, and Womaru hiding nearby. His natives were also drifting in, and to his amazement he gradually realized he hadn't lost a single man in the attack. If he could only get the teleradio going again, he'd be back in business.

A charging engine turned up in the gear abandoned by the commandos. Then a 12-volt storage battery was salvaged from the wrecked Catalina. Finally, some benzine was located when Jack Keenan arrived from Lumsis, reporting that he had been attacked again. This time he had to leave the area. His cache of benzine had been abandoned, and a couple of natives were sent to get it.

Meanwhile Read worried about his parties in the west . . . especially Lieutenant Bedkober, who was guarding the injured airmen at Sikoriapaia. When last seen, the Japanese raiders were headed that way. On the 19th he sent Keenan to check the situation and, if possible, use Sergeant McPhee's teleradio to arrange a supply drop.

Jack Read's worries were well-founded. A little after 9:30 on the morning of June 16, as Bedkober's men lazily watched a B-24 duel with several Zeros overhead, a blast of machine gun fire ripped into their camp, catching every one totally by surprise.

Fighting back with submachine guns, five of the party

Sergeant Yauwika, the big, bearded constable who was Jack Read's chief scout on Bougainville. (Courtesy John R. Hubbard)

—three commandos and two flyers—managed to break out of the trap and escape into the bush. Doug Bedkober himself stayed behind. He could have gone with the others, but that would have meant leaving Flying Officer Dunn and Corporal Fenwick, two of the injured airmen.

Cut off from the rest, these three tried to escape into the hills, but it was no use. Early in the afternoon Fenwick was captured and put into a leaf hut guarded by two sentries. Some hours later—just as the moon was rising—Bedkober was brought in too. Finally, at daylight next morning a party of Japanese soldiers appeared, dragging Dunn's body. He was shot through the chest, but it was never clear exactly when or where he was killed.

Along with Bedkober and Fenwick, one other prisoner was taken. The camp cook, a native named Savaan, had gone off on an errand shortly before the attack and walked right into the advancing Japanese.

The three prisoners were lined up during the morning of the 17th, and with troops both to the front and the rear, the force marched to the west coast. On the 20th, as they slowly moved north, Savaan was sent to a stream to wash a saucepan of rice. That was all the opportunity he needed. He plunged into the bush and escaped.

Bedkober and Fenwick were not so lucky. They ended up at Rabaul, where they were eventually executed. Nor did the five who got away survive very long. With few arms and in some cases barefoot, they struggled east across the island, hoping to link up with one of Read's outposts. Near Numa Numa they were seized by local tribesmen and turned over to the Japanese. It was never clear what happened afterwards. Some natives said they were sent to Rabaul and executed; others that they were lined up and shot at Numa Numa.

Two of the injured airmen were still relatively safe. Sergeant Thompson was back on his feet and helping Sergeant McPhee cover the west coast. Corporal Wettenhall, also recovering, had a closer call. Just 45 minutes before the Japanese struck, he had left the camp with three of the commandos to prepare a supply drop site. They heard the firing, guessed what had happened, and went bush.

This party reached Read on June 19, and gave him his first intimation that all might not be well at Sikoriapaia. There was more bad news when Keenan's benzine arrived on the 22nd, and the teleradio worked again. KEN reported that Bedkober's camp had definitely been captured . . . that McPhee was hard-pressed . . . that Mason had gone off the air after reporting that his presence had been betrayed to the enemy.

The game was up. All the parties were either destroyed or on the run. None were producing intelligence, and the Japanese were closing in on all sides. On the night of June 24 Jack Read composed a long message to KEN:

MY DUTY TO NOW REPORT THAT POSITION ALL HERE
VITALLY SERIOUS. AFTER FIFTEEN MONTHS OCCUPA-
TION ALMOST WHOLE ISLAND NOW PRO-JAPANESE. INI-
TIAL ENEMY PATROLS PLUS HORDES PRO-JAPANESE
NATIVES HAVE COMPLETELY DISORGANIZED US. POSITION
WILL NOT EASE. BELIEVE NO HOPE REORGANIZE. OUR
INTELLIGENCE VALUE NIL. IN LAST FORTNIGHT ALL
PARTIES HAVE BEEN EITHER ATTACKED OR FORCED TO
QUIT. RELUCTANTLY URGE IMMEDIATE EVACUATION.

Next morning he showed it to Robinson and asked
what he thought of it. "I like the word 'weluctantly,'"
was Wobbie's only comment. So at 5:13 A.M. on June
25 Jack Read contacted KEN and with heavy heart sent
the message off.

Forty miles to the south Paul Mason and George
Stevenson were still pushing toward Buin with eight
commandos, about 30 native police boys and carriers,
and Usaia Sotutu, the redoubtable Fijian missionary
who had rescued Lieutenant Mackie from Buka in
the early days of the occupation. They had been off
the air since June 22, but this was to foil the enemy's
direction-finding apparatus, not because they were on
the run. True, the Japanese did know the party was in
the general area, but exactly where was another matter.

On June 25 they reached Dubonami, a small village
at the foot of the Crown Prince Range, the dramatic
mountain chain that dominates the southern half of
Bougainville. Mason's goal was to cross the range and
continue south on the eastern side—an area he knew
well from his days of watching the Tokyo Express.

Unfortunately he didn't have enough carriers to get
everything across the range at one time. With the
Japanese riding high, most natives were scared of serving the Coastwatchers these days. The solution was to

divide the party and make two trips. Taking four of
the commandos and half the gear, Mason crossed the
range at 6,000 feet and camped near Moru, at the
head of the Luluai River. Early on the 26th he sent
the carriers back to Dubonami, where Stevenson was
waiting with Usaia Sotutu and the rest of the party.

For Stevenson's group, the wait meant a welcome
opportunity to relax after weeks of hard marching. They
were camped on a ridge that seemed exceptionally safe.
Joined to the mountain by an impassable wall of rock,
it could be reached by only three paths. These could be
easily watched, while a cliff and dense thickets of
bamboo blocked any other access.

The men spent the morning of the 26th bathing in
a nearby stream, then had a leisurely lunch and lay
down for a nap. Stevenson rested in an open shelter
of banana leaves a little way off from the others. He
had sentries posted on two of the paths, but the third
was left unguarded. Known as the "women's path," it
was said to lead nowhere except to a hiding place where
the local tribe kept their women in time of danger.

It was just after 2 P.M. when Sergeant Frank Furner
heard a burst of gunfire. Crying, "What's that?" he
leapt from his cot. Japanese soldiers in green fatigues
were racing down the "women's path" toward the
camp, firing as they came. Stevenson, nearest the path,
was now on his feet too. He reached for his Austin
gun, but too late. Riddled with bullets, he fell on top
of it.

Usaia Sotutu rushed over to help. For the next few
seconds he provided a good covering fire, until his
gun jammed. Then he tried to drag Stevenson to safety.
Finally realizing that the lieutenant was already dead,
he abandoned the effort and joined the rest of the party.
They had now grabbed their guns and were firing back

as they retreated along the path that led down from the ridge.

They spent a miserable night in the bush, then cautiously returned to the camp next morning. The Japanese were gone, but the place was a shambles— the midget radio smashed, Stevenson's body lying where he fell. Sergeant Furner was now acting CO, and he decided to rejoin Mason as soon as possible. He, of course, knew nothing about the area, but once again Usaia Sotutu came to the rescue. He knew the trails, and with a composure that gave them all a new feeling of confidence, he led them swiftly across the range and into Mason's camp.

The disaster had to be reported—even at the risk of breaking radio silence—and on the 27th Mason flashed the bare details to KEN. The news confirmed the wisdom of a decision just reached by Commander I. Pryce-Jones, the somewhat austere officer who had recently relieved Hugh Mackenzie. This was to close down the whole Bougainville operation and evacuate all personnel as soon as possible. After Jack Read's gloomy assessment there seemed nothing else to do, and the top brass in Brisbane agreed.

Pryce-Jones now ordered Mason to retire north to Kereaka, near the west coast. Here he would join Sergeant McPhee's party and wait for a submarine to come.

Early on the morning of June 29 Paul Mason began the long, hard trip back. Once again he would have to travel over half the length of Bougainville, dodging Japanese patrols that knew he was there and were closing in to get him. He had done it in December and January, but this time would be harder. The familiar eastern trail was now blocked by the enemy. The western route was through the roughest imaginable country

—gorges that seemed made for ambush, paths almost lost in lawyervine, chilling ridges and steaming swamps.

The size of his party worked against him too. Like most Islanders, Mason was happiest when working with a minimum of people. Last time he had only Otton and Wigley. Now he had around 50, counting all the police boys and carriers. Finally, his commandos were anything but experienced bushmen; Mason regarded them as an extra responsibility rather than a source of strength.

Trouble came soon enough. As they crossed a gorge on the 30th, shots rang out from a village above them. Mason, at the front of the column with four of the commandos, got his men under cover and began to return fire. Soon four Japanese came charging down the hill toward them. A police boy picked off one, and the others retired. The firing continued.

While Mason's advance guard held off the enemy, the rear was meant to get the teleradio and supplies under cover, but it didn't work out that way. Instead, the carriers dropped everything and fled in panic. When Mason finally pulled his little group back to link up with the others, he discovered the charging engine, three weeks' rations, and all their trading tobacco abandoned on the trail. Farther back he found the rear guard huddled on a path in the gorge, wondering what to do.

Rallying the men, he now led them down the gorge, far below the Japanese outpost, moving generally west. Most of the carriers were gone for good, but it no longer mattered so much, The teleradio receiver and transmitter had been lost in the panic and were never found again. Most of the commandos had lost their packs too, and the group spent a miserable night sleeping in the open under a pelting rain.

July 2, they were still working their way down the

gorge, hoping for an easier place to cross. They could hear native signal drums in the distance, and with all the villages now working for the Japanese, the sound was anything but reassuring. Near the village of Lamparan they caught two natives spying on them. Holding one hostage, they sent the other to warn his people to let them through. As they moved from the gorge into a narrow valley, the hills exploded in gunfire. Another ambush.

In the confusion the hostage escaped, but the Japanese fire soon tapered off—apparently a tactic designed to lure them deeper into the valley. But Mason too could play the waiting game, and his party lay low until night. From time to time they caught a glimpse of Japanese troops searching for them.

After dark they moved on again, slipping and stumbling in the rain. It was pitch black, and to keep the group together, each man fastened to his back a piece of phosphorescent fungus.

Finally clear of the valley, they continued on, always working their way north and west, sometimes through steaming lowlands, sometimes along ridges so high that bitter winds swirled around them at night. Most of the time they had little food—none at all for one 34-hour stretch—but on July 6 they enjoyed a real windfall. Near the village of Mom they shot a stray one-eyed pig, then captured another in somewhat better shape.

The feast that night suffered an interruption that tended to dampen the appetite. One of the missing carriers turned up with a note written on a sheet of paper from one of the lost packs:

My dear Ansacs: We all admire your bravery. You have done your best for Great Britain. You are advised to give yourselves up. The Japanese are not a cruel people, as the lying propaganda of the

United States would tell you. You will die of hunger
in the jungle. You will never reach your friends
in Buka, as all the jungle trails are watched by
the Japanese soldiers and the sharper eyes of the
natives.

(signed) Commander of the Japanese Army

On second thought, Mason found the note encouraging. For the past eight days he had been completely cut
off from the world and had no idea whether Read's
people had been caught or not. Now this note with its
boast that "you will never reach your friends" must
mean that they were still free. With new heart he
trudged on.

By July 12 they were north of Empress Augusta Bay
and up against the jagged limestone ridges of the Emperor Range. It was the toughest climbing of all: again
and again they struggled up to the 5,000-foot level, then
plunged down into a valley, only to face still another
climb. At least the natives were friendlier. Most of
them had never seen either a Japanese or a white man
before, but they cheerfully fed these ragged strangers.

By now the long marches and constant hunger had
taken their toll. Seven of the eight commandos were
in wretched physical shape, and on the 16th Mason decided to give them all a day's rest. As they relaxed,
the local natives told him about some soldiers camped
a day's march to the north. They sounded like Read's
men, but he couldn't be sure. After all, he was dealing
with people who couldn't tell the difference between
an Asiatic and a European.

Playing it safe, Mason sent two police boys ahead to
investigate. They carried nothing in writing—just an
oral message giving his position and numbers, to be
delivered if the soldiers were friendly.

They turned out to be Jack Keenan's party. Under

Read's orders he had taken charge of all operations
in the west and was concentrating every one at Kereaka,
pending evacuation by submarine. Mason's men were
the last to be accounted for, and to spur them on,
Keenan sent guides to meet them with rations of tea
and meat. When they wearily trudged into Kereaka on
the 19th, Paul Mason had pulled off a miracle. He had
led his men 80 miles through enemy territory, over the
most impossible terrain, in the face of constant harass-
ment by hostile natives, and past every trap set by the
pursuing Japanese. It had taken him three weeks.

When Keenan signaled that Mason had linked up,
Jack Read was still some miles to the east, working
his way toward the coast. With him were Eric Robinson and an assortment of police boys and Chinese
refugees. Learning from KEN that a submarine could
be provided on four days' notice, Read gave the go-
ahead signal and radioed Mason to take charge of the
evacuation. His own party, he explained, was blocked
by the Japanese and couldn't get to the beach in four
days, but it was all-important to take off those already
assembled as soon as possible. Then if the submarine
returned for a second pickup in another four days, he
and his people would be on the shore and ready to go.

SOPAC gave its blessing, and Mason began moving
his group to the coast. Collecting at Atsinima Bay,
they were a very mixed bag: 22 commandos . . . the
last two survivors of the Catalina . . . seven Chinese who
had been hiding in the hills . . . 24 native scouts and
police boys . . . four native wives and children . . . a
stray Fijian . . . and, of course, Keenan and Mason.
Conspicuously absent was the tireless Usaia Sotutu,
who went off with five of the best scouts to help Read.

By the morning of July 24 Mason's whole party was
at the beach. A native named Bombay planted two
sticks in the sand, then carefully stretched a white cloth

between them. In the evening there would be signal fires too, but the sub was supposed to make its landfall during the day, and the cloth marked the spot where the party was waiting. It would be easy to miss on this wild, uncharted coast, and Mason could only hope some sharp-eyed sailor would see it. . . .

There it was at last. All day the U.S. submarine *Guardfish* had been cruising submerged along the coast, searching for the white cloth the evacuees were meant to display. The navigator Lieutenant Richard H. Bowers, vainly swept the shore with his periscope. None of the landmarks stood out, and his ancient German charts were hopelessly vague. Where, he wondered bitterly, was that vaunted Teutonic thoroughness?

Then, around 4 P.M., the periscope suddenly picked up a blotch of white against the jungle green. It had to be—could only be—the marker they were looking for. The skipper, Commander Norvell G. Ward, took over. He had been exec on the *Gato* at Teop and was now an old hand at this sort of thing. He eased the *Guardfish* down to the bottom and waited for the night.

After dark Ward surfaced and lay quietly offshore, waiting for the signal fires. As they blazed up, he inched closer to the beach, swinging completely around and backing the last few yards. Now the forward and after torpedo-room hatches opened, and dim figures appeared lugging eight uninflated rubber boats. A series of sharp hisses broke the still night air as the plugs were pulled and the boats inflated. Launched and manned, they moved clumsily toward the shore. They were next to impossible to row, and one sailor muttered, "My shipping-over papers didn't say nothing about this. Next time I'll read the fine print."

On the beach the evacuees watched with mounting excitement as the little flotilla shot the breakers and spun ashore. In half an hour the first boats were loaded and on their way out again. Now they were even harder to row, and one capsized in the surf. Righting it, the men clambered back in, grunting and cursing, but with no loss except an officer's cap that floated away in the night.

On the *Guardfish* "Bub" Ward watched incredulously as the motley collection of Australians, Chinese, natives, men, women and children swarmed aboard. "We gathered a bit more of a crowd than we'd anticipated," Paul Mason explained, adding apologetically, "There are still some more on the beach." When the submarine finally headed out to sea, a total of 62 evacuees were jammed aboard.

Down below, Sergeant Furner could hardly believe his eyes. After those three hungry weeks with Paul Mason, the smell of the coffee—the sight of the hot white bread—was more than he could grasp. Rarely, if ever, has any one regarded Spam with greater awe or keener anticipation.

On Bougainville Jack Read waited until the radio confirmed that Mason's group was safely away, then moved his own party swiftly to the coast. Everything was working out exactly as he planned. There had never been any Japanese blocking his way to the shore—he could easily have made the rendezvous in time—but headquarters had told him there wasn't room in the submarine for all his natives, and he was determined not to leave any behind. The only solution was to cook up a pretext that would require the sub to make two trips.

July 28, Read's party assembled at Kunua, a coastal plantation several miles north of the Mason pickup. This time there were only 22 to go—fourteen loyal natives and Chinese refugees, Usaia Sotutu and his five scouts, Eric Robinson, and Read himself.

That evening he watched the signal fires blaze for the last time. The *Guardfish*—having transferred her first load to a subchaser—reappeared on schedule, and the pickup came off without a hitch. As commanding officer, Read followed the time-honored tradition and made sure he was the last man in the last boat to shove off from the beach.

For Jack Read it was a strange feeling to be leaving Bougainville after these seventeen months of unremitting effort in the face of constant danger. How much had really been accomplished? How did the books balance out? On the debit side, he had been driven off the island. There was no denying that. But there were entries on the credit side too. There were all those plane sightings that gave CACTUS two hours' warning during the desperate fight for Guadalcanal. There was the convoy he reported in November, just before the last great Japanese attack. There were the nuns and refugees he helped save on New Year's Eve. There was the steady flow of intelligence on the enemy airstrip at Buka. There was even the satisfaction of tying up so many Japanese in their final, successful drive to get rid of him.

Nor was the ledger closed. During the past two months, while Read was on the run and generally out of touch with the world, great events were taking place to the south. These developments would dramatically affect the role of the Coastwatchers, and ultimately the fate of Bougainville itself.

11

A VERY PRIVATE WAR

Donald Kennedy knew all about Ferdinand the Bull—
and he fully appreciated why this most docile of animals
was the Coastwatchers' symbol—but his base at Segi on
the southeastern tip of New Georgia was just too valuable to lose, even if it meant fighting back. The location
was superb. Protected by uncharted reefs, it offered
equally good access either to the north and the waters
of the Slot, or to the south and Blanche Channel, busy
with Japanese traffic moving in and out of Munda.
Other Coastwatchers could pick up and move if hard-
pressed—one hill was as good as another—but Segi
was unique.

Yet at the start he had so little to defend the place.
Just a handful of native scouts and a few rifles. Thanks
to the compliant Bogese, the Japanese knew roughly
where he was; if they also knew how weak he was,
Segi would be doomed. They mustn't be allowed to
find out.

His solution was what he called the "forbidden zone."
As long as the Japanese kept a safe distance from Segi,

Segi Point. This seemingly placid shoreline conceals Donald Kennedy's Coastwatching base—a stronghold bristling with well-armed natives. Photographed from a PBY that has come to pick up a downed aviator. (National Archives)

the principles of Ferdinand applied, and he left them strictly alone. But if any patrol or scouting force came within the area he deemed essential to the base's security, then it was in the "forbidden zone" and must be attacked at once. It didn't matter whether the Japanese were actually looking for him at the time—or even whether they knew they were near the base—it was enough that they *might* discover him.

Total annihilation was the rule. Every man in the enemy party must be killed or captured. No one must escape to tell the tale. In this way he would still keep the low profile that was so much a part of the Ferdinand idea. He would just be doing it a different way. Instead of dodging the Japanese, he would swallow them up.

At first some minor successes . . . then a big one. About 10 A.M. one bright morning in November 1942 a native scout burst into camp with the news that two Japanese barges were holed up in Marovo Lagoon only five miles north of camp. They were heading east with supplies—certainly weren't looking for Segi—but they *might* discover the base, and Kennedy wasn't about to risk the chance. They were in the "forbidden zone."

Gathering a force of 23 men, including two American flyers awaiting evacuation, he hurried to the scene . . . first by boat, then on foot. Urging the men on was his second-in-command, a burly, good-humored half-caste who had been somewhat redundantly christened William Billy Bennett. An experienced sailor and competent mechanic, he had also been a medical dresser, cook boy, and school teacher at various times in his 22 years. He was loafing at Munda when Kennedy recruited him in 1941, and he quickly proved an invaluable aide. He was not only versatile, but highly articulate. Before every engagement he would "psyche up" the scouts, like a coach giving a locker room pep talk before the big game.

There's no record what he said this time, but it certainly worked. Kennedy's little force struck at 7 P.M., pouring a devastating fire into the two barges which were moored right against the shore. A Japanese machine gun opened up briefly but was soon knocked out, and all was silent.

Billy Bennett boarded one of the barges, only to be greeted by a Japanese sailor who jumped him with the handle for lowering the landing ramp. Bennett bayoneted him, and there was no more resistance.

He now threw a lighted dry-leaf torch into the second barge and scrambled aboard. In the glow of the flames he saw a Japanese lying on his stomach a few feet away, aiming a rifle at a scout on the shore. Bennett fired at him point-blank, taking off the top of the man's head. Hearing some sounds below, he next tossed a grenade down the engine hatch, slammed the lid, and rashly sat on it. He somehow escaped injury in the blast that

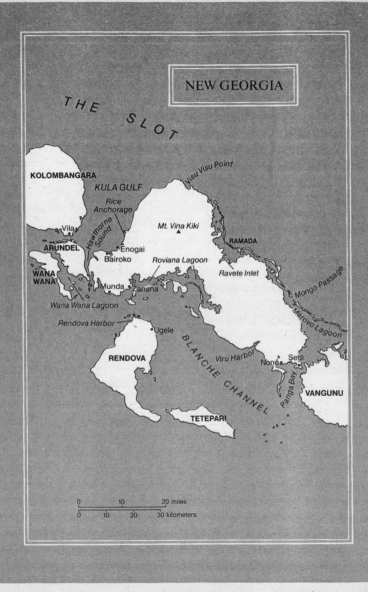

NEW GEORGIA

THE SLOT

KOLOMBANGARA

KULA GULF

Njsu Visu Point

Rice Anchorage

Mt. Vina Kiki

Vila

RAMADA

ARUNDEL

Hawthorne Sound

Enogai

Bairoko

Roviana Lagoon

WANA WANA

Ravete Inlet

Munda

Zanana

Mongo Passage

Wana Wana Lagoon

Rendova Harbor

Marovo Lagoon

Ugele

BLANCHE CHANNEL

RENDOVA

Viru Harbor

Nono

Segi

Panga Bay

VANGUNU

TETEPARI

| 0 | 10 | 20 miles |
| 0 | 10 | 20 | 30 kilometers |

followed, and the battle was over. Every Japanese was killed; their weapons carried off, their barges towed into deep water and sunk. No trace of them remained whatsoever. To the enemy command at Munda it was one more mysterious incident where their personnel simply vanished.

To Kennedy it was a bonanza. He not only built up his arsenal, but he vastly strengthened his standing with the local natives. Ferdinand was too sophisticated a concept to stir much enthusiasm, but a devastating ambush was something else. New recruits began drifting in from the nearby islands and villages. Seni, chief of the Mindi-Mindi Islands just east of Segi, signed on as a scout and received a rifle. He then ambushed a patrol of six Japanese, killed one, and got a second rifle. Recruiting one of his tribesmen, he ambushed five more Japanese— and got five more rifles. He repeated the process until he ended up with 32 armed men, all at Kennedy's service.

Shortly afterwards another local chief, Ngato, asked Kennedy's permission to attack a reconnaissance party of five Japanese on an island 30 miles up the Marovo Lagoon. At the moment Kennedy had only one rifle to spare, but Ngato assured him guns wouldn't be necessary. And so it proved. Taking six of his natives in a canoe, the old chief paddled up to the island and made friends with the Japanese. Then, while they lay sleeping that night, he crawled into their hut and stole all their weapons.

Next morning when the Japanese discovered what had happened, a general scuffle broke out, and at this point Ngato's plan hit an unexpected snag. Two of the enemy happened to be jiu-jitsu experts, and they gave the natives a hard time indeed. Finally the local villagers rushed to the rescue and, with the ratio "about 20 to 1," the patrol was subdued. Trussed up, the Japanese were brought back to Segi in triumph and thrown into Kennedy's POW pen.

More recruits drifted in, until Kennedy ultimately had what amounted to a private army of 70 men—half of them armed—not counting Seni and Ngato's tribesmen. He drilled them relentlessly, even teaching them a certain amount of spit and polish. They could go through the manual of arms like a Guards Regiment, and at Segi the day began with a bugler blowing reveille.

Discipline was always tough. In this kind of warfare the lives of all could depend on one man's performance, and Kennedy demanded unswerving obedience. The disobedient were likely to end up "across the drum"—which meant a good lashing while lying across a 44-gallon drum, feet on one side, hands touching the ground on the other. But Kennedy himself never administered the beating—it was done by other natives—in an effort to avoid racial implications. These harsh punishments did spawn a certain amount of grumbling, but it was not so much resentment as the griping of touch troops who will put up with almost anything for a commander they believe in.

As Kennedy's army grew, so did its arsenal. Each skirmish added more Japanese weapons to the collection. Ultimately the stockpile at Segi included one 20-mm. cannon, 8 machine guns, 2 submachine guns, 12 pistols, and 60 rifles.

Along with his army Kennedy was also accumulating a private navy. On one occasion his men stole a 57-foot diesel barge while the crew was ashore foraging for food. Another time U.S. fighter planes shot up two barges nosed against the shore, causing leaks that flooded their batteries. Unable to start the engines, both crews headed home on foot. Once they were out of sight, Kennedy's scouts plugged the leaks, pumped out the water, and towed the barges back to Segi. Two days later another

Japanese barge appeared with a spare engine for one of the damaged craft. While the crew was off searching for it, the scouts stole the spare engine too.

The Kennedy fleet eventually boasted six barges altogether, one of which he armed with machine guns from a downed B-24.

But the flagship of his navy was no barge. It was the ten-ton schooner *Dundavata,* a marvelously picturesque two-master with wheezing engine that formerly belonged to the Seventh Day Adventist Mission on Choiseul. With Billy Bennett coaxing her along, she could make seven knots in a following sea.

The *Dundavata*'s big chance came in April 1943. Two of Kennedy's scouts arrived one evening to report that a whaleboat loaded with Japanese was coming up the Marovo Lagoon from Wickham Anchorage. It was methodically probing every isle and inlet along the way, obviously trying to locate the Coastwatching base.

There was no time to lose. The information was already late. The scouts had been delayed by a native missionary named Punda, who did not believe in the war and tried to argue them out of reporting back. He failed, but they did listen—and lost some valuable time.

Kennedy hurriedly rounded up a dozen men, and the *Dundavata* shoved off from Segi that night. Turning east down the Marovo Lagoon, the little schooner looked about as warlike as she ever could. Her upper works were camouflaged with leaves and branches, and a .50-calibre Browning machine gun was mounted on the bow. She also carried two lighter machine guns salvaged from a couple of downed Zeros, and nearly all the crew had rifles. Kennedy, Billy Bennett, and most of the men were on the *Dundavata* herself, but a few were towed in canoes trailing behind.

At daybreak one of Kennedy's outlying scouts paddled up to report that the Japanese were ashore on an island just ahead. This was far closer to Segi than Kennedy expected to meet them, and he had to scrap his previous plan for interception. Improvising on the spur of the moment, he anchored behind another island nearby. Assuming the Japanese had sighted him approaching, the *Dundavata* was now screened from their guns. He next posted a lookout in a palm tree with orders to report any enemy move. He was in a good position to intercept, whichever way they went.

Everything taken care of, he settled down with a bottle of whiskey and waited for the Japanese to make the next move. He figured they would stay put until dark—their usual practice—and he decided to take a nap. It was night when one of his chief scouts, John Mamambonima, woke him up, explaining excitedly in pidgin: "Him along. It's time to get up."

Kennedy waited long enough to be sure the Japanese were definitely on their way, then started his engines and slipped out from behind his own island. It was a bright moonlit night, and he soon spotted the whaleboat coming toward him. The Japanese apparently saw him too, for they turned around and began rowing hard for home.

Picking up speed, the *Dundavata* raced in pursuit. Bill Bennett took over the wheel, while Kennedy went forward and personally manned the .50-calibre machine gun. At 500 yards he began firing. A Japanese machine gun opened up in reply, and two bullets clipped Kennedy's thigh. He looked a bloody mess, but he kept blazing away as the distance narrowed between the two vessels.

After three and a half belts, the Browning jammed. Kennedy limped aft, took one of the Zero machine guns, and continued shooting. The Japanese fire fell off, and he sensed he was getting results. Soon the whaleboat lay almost dead in the water, oars smashed or lost, wounded oarsmen slumped in their seats. The *Dunda-vata* was now only a hundred yards away.

Kennedy shouted orders to ram. Billy Bennett was so excited he turned the wheel the wrong way, and there was an instant of total confusion as Kennedy cuffed him on the head and twisted the wheel the other way, shouting, "This way, you bloody fool, port not starboard!"

The bow wavered a second—not long, but enough for some quick-thinking Japanese to hurl a hand grenade onto the *Dundavata*. It exploded with a roar, scattering everyone and knocking Kennedy to the deck.

Next instant the *Dundavata* crashed into the whaleboat, bow rising over the gunwale, capsizing it and dumping the Japanese into the water. The canoes towed by the schooner now cast off and made the rounds, finishing off any swimming Japanese. Kennedy took no prisoners this night.

Some 20 Japanese were wiped out altogether, and as usual the rule was to leave no trace of the engagement. In the morning Kennedy's men buried the ten bodies they found, salvaged some useful gear from the bottom of the lagoon, and sank the hulk of the whaleboat in deep water. His own casualties were miraculously light —thirteen men nicked by grenade fragments, the regular helmsman slightly wounded, and himself with his bleeding thigh. The wound was painful but not serious, and for the present he refused to leave Segi for treatment. He simply "shoved in" some sulfanilamide and carried on.

Such exploits made certain that Donald Kennedy's base at Segi would play an important role as the Allies moved over to the offensive in the South Pacific. The ultimate objective was the great Japanese base at Rabaul. This meant, among other things, clearing the Central Solomons; and this in turn meant seizing the enemy airstrip at Munda near the western end of New

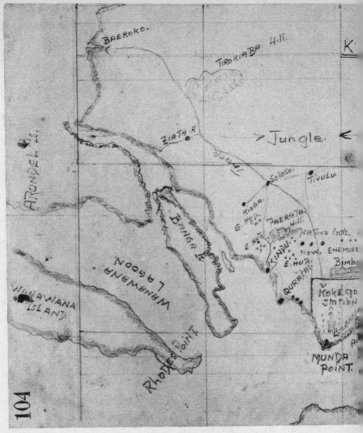

Kennedy's scouts drew meticulous maps of the Japanese installations at Munda. This sketch, probably by Job

Georgia. Admiral Halsey's SOPAC command would be responsible, and the operation was called TOENAILS —a code name that turned out to be uncomfortably prophetic.

Once more the Allies faced landing on shores that were virtually unknown. How to go about it depended on the answers to a number of highly technical ques-

Tamana, was brought back by a Marine patrol visiting Segi.
(Courtesy Mrs. Robert C. Laverty)

tions. Which beaches were long enough for the number of landing craft involved? What were the gradients? Where was the soil of the best consistency for a supporting fighter strip? What size drains would be required? How much Marsden matting would be needed for the airfield?

Not even Kennedy's network could answer questions

like these. But there were men who could, and Segi had
the guides, interpreters, weapons and canoes to help
them.

Lieutenant William P. Coultas was a naval intelligence officer on Halsey's staff who had been to the
Solomons on a scientific expedition before the war,
knew the jungle, understood the natives, and even spoke
pidgin. He was a natural to lead the first of several
tactical reconnaissance teams inserted into Segi to survey the area. With him went Captain Clay Boyd of
the 1st Marine Raiders, who was an officer with long
jungle experience, and three enlisted Raiders carefully
handpicked by Boyd.

"Would you like to go north and fight?" Boyd
asked Sergeant Frank Guidone one day late in February. At the moment Guidone was stuck on New Caledonia, feeling very much at loose ends. He was a boxer,
had been in a good many interservice bouts, and thought
Boyd wanted him to go north for some tournament.

"Sure," he said, and then learned he had just volunteered to go behind enemy lines in New Georgia.
Marine Gunner Jim James and Corporal Robert C.
Laverty presumably understood the question better, but
all three were very, very good at adjusting to even the
most unexpected developments.

On March 3 they flew to Segi by PBY, landing in the
lagoon as fifteen fighters circled protectively above.
Kennedy was waiting at the dock to greet them.

To the new arrivals, the organization of the place was
simply amazing. They were deep in enemy territory and
had expected to find a small hideout manned by a few
furtive jungle fighters. Instead they found a teeming
secret base. The beaches on either side of the dock
were covered by machine guns stolen from the Japanese
or salvaged from wrecked planes. More guns were
planted up the hill around the old Markham plantation

house, which served as Kennedy's quarters. Native look-outs were posted on platforms in the trees, while sentries patrolled the shore in every direction. A chain of signal fires warned of any approaching vessel. The teleradio was in a shack about a half mile into the bush, and even friends were discouraged from learning its exact where-abouts.

Kennedy's organization extended far beyond the base itself. He never expected to hold Segi against a major attack, so "getaway roads" (as he called them) laced the jungle in every direction. He built reserve radio huts as much as ten miles into the bush. Caches of food were stored in secret places. An amazing system of hid-den canoes allowed his people to move in any direction at any time.

The new arrivals found Kennedy himself quiet and rather aloof. Perhaps from months of enforced caution, he did not warm easily to strangers. But professionally they could find no fault. All day he helped them plan schedules and routes. Then as dusk fell, he invited them to join him on his verandah, where they sipped some excellent scotch.

It was dark now, and a houseboy appeared carrying a lighted Coleman lamp. With the Japanese only a few miles away at Viru Harbor to the west and Wickham Anchorage to the east, Clay Boyd was astonished. It struck him as a most reckless thing to do. Kennedy, however, seemed to regard it as a normal amenity, a touch of civilized living he wasn't about to give up sim-ply because he happened to be behind enemy lines.

They dined at 8:00, seated around a table set with silver, china and immaculate linen. Houseboys in jackets served a dinner of chicken and fish with fruit salad. It was all so eye-goggling that it seemed perfectly natural when the party was later joined by a lovely-looking Polynesian girl, who smiled a lot but said little.

Next morning there was more cause for wonder as one of Kennedy's gun crews went through a drill with a .50-calibre machine gun. They simulated firing, then took the gun apart, reassembled it in a speed drill, and continued their simulated firing. It was, Sergeant Guidone felt, a performance that would have put any Marine gun crew to shame. Later in the day he decided to show the natives that he too could do a few fancy stunts with a gun. It was a long time since Quantico, however, and he accidentally fired a shot through the dining room ceiling. Kennedy, Coultas and Boyd were fortunately off somewhere, but the Polynesian girl saw it and dissolved into giggles.

The Marines spent most of the day with Kennedy, poring over a large map of New Georgia. Then at 4:00 P.M. they boarded two large canoes, and with 20 native paddlers and carriers they set out for a first-hand survey of the terrain. All that night they paddled up the Marovo Lagoon. Daybreak, they landed at Ravete Inlet . . . crossed the island on foot . . . then continued up the southern coast by a trail that roughly paralleled the Roviana Lagoon. On the 6th they finally reached a leaf hut known as Horton's No. 2 Camp a few miles short of Munda.

It was hard going all the way, and the natives didn't hide their exasperation. It seemed one more example of the white man's inability to get around. If they had gone by canoe up the Roviana Lagoon, they could have made the trip in twelve hours, as against three days by land. The visitors, of course, weren't interested in speed. They wanted to find out how easily a large body of men could move through the interior . . . how long it would take . . . whether troops could live off the land or must depend on rations. They backed their findings with copious notes and photographs.

Horton's No. 2 Camp proved a disappointment. Even

Amenities at Segi. Donald Kennedy serves tea to U.S. Marine Captain Clay Boyd during one of Boyd's patrols behind enemy lines. (Courtesy Mrs. Eric Feldt)

from the tallest tree they couldn't get a good view of the Munda airstrip (Horton could have told them), and they finally split up for other projects. James, Guidone and Laverty headed back to survey the Japanese camp at Viru Harbor nine miles west of Segi, while Coultas and Boyd visited Horton's station PWD on Rendova, hoping for a better view of Munda.

They were not disappointed. Ferried across by Willie Paia, one of Kennedy's chief scouts in the Roviana area, they found Dick Horton on his ridge, still enjoying his spectacular view. Nothing escaped his scrutiny—whether a staff car tooling down the Munda runway . . . or barge traffic on Blanche Channel . . . or merely some bored Japanese soldier fishing in Rendova Harbor directly below. Natives stationed in the two treetop lookouts shouted down every movement in the local dialect to the camp cook, who translated it for Horton, who whiled away his idle time practicing yoga. If sufficiently important, it was easy enough to switch to the teleradio.

Some fifteen minutes farther up the mountain was another excellent lookout, where it was possible to sit back in an easy chair and watch the Japanese through a mounted telescope. This was Coastwatching at its most comfortable. Horton was, on the whole, very secure in his eyrie, but to be on the safe side, he had a couple of fall-back positions deeper in the interior, where he could always retreat if hard pressed.

Two days of sketching, photographing, gathering data; then on March 13 Coultas and Boyd headed back to Segi, arriving there on the 16th. The others in the party were already waiting after a most successful survey of Viru. They had worked their way to a point only 1200 feet across the harbor from the enemy camp—so close that Frank Guidone amused himself by lining up his carbine sights on a Japanese soldier who was squatting in the water to relieve his bowels.

By March 20 the party was back in Noumea. Their findings, together with data gathered by four Marine teams sent in on the 21st, greatly altered the planning for TOENAILS. Originally the idea was to land in division strength at Segi and push up the coast to Munda. Now this was out. The beach at Segi was too small, and the coastal terrain impassable for any large body of marching troops. But it was also clear that landings could be safely made much closer to Munda . . . that a 200-yard beach at Zanana, five miles east of the airstrip, was a good spot . . . that the reefs around there were tricky but passable . . . that there was a good harbor and few Japanese on nearby Rendova . . . that a separate landing north of Munda would be easier than cutting through the jungle from the east in order to flank the field.

The Japanese outpost at Viru. Photographed through the bushes 400 yards away by U.S. Marine patrol operating out of Segi. (Courtesy Mrs. Robert C. Laverty)

Out of all this grew the final plan for TOENAILS. As hammered out by Admiral Kelly Turner's staff, there would be a two-pronged assault. A Western Group would seize Rendova . . . soften Munda with artillery . . . then cross Blanche Channel and advance on the airstrip; they would be supported by troops landed at Rice Anchorage on the coast north of the field. At the same time, a smaller Eastern Group would take Wickham Anchorage, Viru Harbor, and Segi. As soon as Segi was secure, a fighter strip would be built there to support the advance.

June 13, and Clay Boyd was back at Segi with a team of seven Marine Raiders, including most of the original team in March. With Kennedy providing the guides and carriers as usual, they quickly headed for the interior. By now TOENAILS was set for June 30, and their assignments were very specific—preparing the landing beaches, collecting canoes, cutting paths from Rice Anchorage toward the nearest Japanese stronghold at Enogai.

Operating from a base camp a few miles east of Munda, the group also fanned out on two- and three-man patrols, checking any late changes in enemy dispositions. Toward dusk on one of these patrols Guidone and Sergeant Joe Sciarra were making their way up a mild slope when they suddenly heard a great clatter of pots and pans, along with the sound of Japanese voices. An enemy outpost lay on the other side of the slope, just 50 feet away.

They froze in their tracks. They couldn't go forward, and it was too dark to go back, for fear of the noise they'd make. So for the rest of the night they just sat there, assaulted by a million mosquitoes, listening to Japanese songs, jokes, and laughter. At first light they quietly stole out of range, realizing that only those noisy pots and pans had kept them from walking right into the enemy camp. "If they had been washing the dishes," Guidone later philosophized, "we'd have been caught."

Joe Sciarra did not escape scot-free. He came down with a bad case of malaria and had to be evacuated when Clay Boyd was ordered back to New Caledonia to give Admiral Halsey a personal, last-minute briefing before TOENAILS. The rest of Boyd's party continued hacking trails and preparing the landing beaches on New Georgia's north coast.

The Japanese at Munda were not asleep. The navy

commander, Rear Admiral Minoru Ota, and his army counterpart, Major General Naboru Sasaki, were both very much aware of the U.S. reconnaissance teams prowling about New Georgia. Scraps of American food had been discovered in a nearby hut, and Ota's young intelligence officer, Lieutenant Satoru Yunoki, pieced together a torn letter to a U.S. Marine from his girl, found on a jungle path only half a mile from the Japanese camp. Along with the constant air attacks now hammering the landing strip, the presence of these visitors suggested an early Allied offensive.

Countermeasures must be increased. The Segi area seemed to be the source of the mischief, but exactly what the Allies had there was still a mystery. Every patrol sent to investigate had simply vanished. The answer, the commanders decided, was stronger patrols and better leadership.

On May 13 new outposts were established on Ramada, Mongo, and several other islands in the Marovo Lagoon north of Segi. Kennedy countered on the 16th by annihilating an eight-man scouting party that came within the forbidden zone. Captured papers indicated that the enemy still didn't know the exact position of his camp.

Meanwhile the Japanese also strengthened their garrison at Viru Harbor, on the Blanche Channel side of Segi. The present post commander had shown little energy, and it was hoped that the reinforcements under Major Masao Hara would add some real muscle.

Hara's first attempt was by barge—down Blanche Channel and up toward Segi from the south. As usual, Kennedy's sentries were on the job, and the chain of signal fires blazed their warnings. At Segi Kennedy's army manned their machine guns, ready to give the enemy a lively reception.

But the Japanese still didn't know exactly where the

base was located and piled ashore near Nono, a village some five miles short of Segi. There was, of course, nothing there. The troops—bewildered and with no other instructions—went back to Viru through the bush. Kennedy let them go; he had deployed his men for a last-ditch defense and was unable to invoke the forbidden zone rule.

The next party came by land, chopping a trail through the bush from Viru. Reaching the shore again near Nono, they camped for the night, planning to push on in the morning. Sentries were carefully positioned, covering any approach to their camp by land, but the side facing the sea was left unguarded. The shore was a tangle of mangrove roots, and these seemed protection enough against a surprise attack.

Kennedy and his men came in five canoes. Laying to offshore, the scouts disembarked and began wading in. The mangrove roots were indeed good protection against a sudden charge, but not against the tactics used tonight. On signal from Billy Bennett, the scouts began lobbing grenades into the enemy camp. In the darkness the Japanese had no idea where the missiles were coming from. They huddled together in frightened confusion.

Eventually the grenades were all thrown, and the scouts began using their rifles. But by now the Japanese had taken such fearful casualties, the direction of the attack no longer mattered. The survivors straggled back to Viru along the trail they had carved, dragging their wounded with them. They never fired a shot in return.

Nevertheless, Kennedy was under fire that day. As his men opened up with their rifles, bullets began whining around his ears, and he suddenly realized that somebody in one of his own canoes was shooting at *him*.

He could never prove who did it, but he had his suspicions. Some time earlier he had fired the native in charge of the POW pen at Segi for failing to lock the

The enemy. Japanese snapshots picked up by Corporal Bob Laverty during one of his patrols on New Georgia.
(Courtesy Mrs. Robert C. Laverty)

gate one night. The man denied any blame, but he was relieved of the key and sent to work in the gardens of Chief Ngato—a humiliating demotion. Tonight, without Kennedy's knowledge, the old chief brought him along on the attack because he seemed so handy with guns.

The Japanese at Viru had now been foiled twice in quick succession, but Kennedy sensed the change in command. No doubt about it, the "new bloke" (as he referred to Major Hara) was far more vigorous than his predecessor. It was a development that made Kennedy more receptive than he should have been to a scheme suggested by another shadowy figure at Segi. Belshazzar Gina had been a native missionary at Simba before the war but was now under a cloud, charged with theft and extortion. While locked up at Segi, he volunteered to spy on the Japanese at Viru, presumably in return for his freedom. His latest report indicated that nine barges were moored across the harbor from the Japanese camp, that they were unguarded and there for the taking.

It looked like a golden opportunity to deprive the new bloke of his transportation. Ordering Gina to stay on the scene, Kennedy quickly assembled an armada of 20 canoes and set off for Viru Harbor. They were well on their way when intercepted by a native swimming out from the shore. It was one of Chief Ngato's men, and he urged the party to turn back. He too had been spying at Viru and he warned that Gina was making things up. In fact, Gina wasn't even at Viru—he was enjoying himself at another village—and the "unguarded" barges were really loaded with armed Japanese.

It was a narrow escape. Only a lucky interception by that daring swimmer had saved the day. Gina was recalled, and the natives urged that he be executed on the spot. Not completely sure whether the man was a traitor or simply irresponsible, Kennedy was unwilling to go that far. Instead he ordered 100 lashes over the drum. This was later reduced to 25, but Gina was never again allowed to leave the camp.

As the threat to Segi continued to grow, on June 11 Lieutenant Commander Don Gumz, skipper of the PBY detachment stationed at Tulagi, got some unusual orders direct from Rear Admiral Marc A. Mitscher, who commanded all the planes in the Solomons. COMAIRSOLS ordered Gumz to fly a "Dumbo" mission to Segi the following morning, stopping at Rennell Island on the way back. The squadron had never before flown a mission to Rennell, isolated as it was some 250 miles south of Guadalcanal. Gumz knew nothing about conditions there, or even where he was expected to land.

A mildly worded plea to COMAIRSOLS for more dope brought only a laconic reply that there wasn't any more. Nor was any explanation offered on the purpose of the mission. Gumz assumed that some hot-shot fighter pilot had gotten himself lost and was on Rennell waiting for a ride home.

Early next morning he took off, and one hour and 48 minutes later set the PBY down in the lagoon off Segi Point. So far the trip had been just another milk run. Now he supposed Kennedy would be bringing out some downed flyers and maybe give him a little info on the Rennell part of the mission.

But there were no downed flyers this morning. Instead, Kennedy had in his canoe the Polynesian girl others had noticed at Segi. In her lap she held a baby, while an older amah-type woman hovered close by. Two young Polynesian men completed the party.

Coming alongside, Kennedy sang out to stand by for passengers. The PBY crew gaped in silent astonishment. It had been far too long since they had seen any girl, much less one as pretty as this. But no one had any comment. Among the grateful American airmen in the Solomons it was well understood that what Kennedy wanted Kennedy got, and Gumz saw no reason to quote him Navy regulations about civilian female passengers on a man-of-war.

The two women were helped aboard and settled on bunks in the cabin, while Kennedy went forward to the cockpit. He asked if Gumz knew Rennell Island, and the Commander said no, but he could probably find it if it was anywhere near the position shown on his chart. Kennedy glanced at it, said it was "good enough," and explained the location of Lake Tungano, where the PBY was to land. Once on the water the two Polynesian boys would guide him to the spot where the passengers would disembark—it was their home. A few more navigating tips; then he scrambled back into his canoe and cast off.

Kennedy now lay to, watching, as Gumz taxied into position for takeoff. He was still watching as the PBY circled back overhead before turning south. Gumz had made other trips to Segi, but he had never seen Kennedy watch a departing plane so long and hard before.

The flight to safety was just in time. Four days later, on June 16, Kennedy's scouts ambushed an enemy patrol of 25 men advancing overland from Viru Harbor. The Japanese got away in the darkness, but left behind an assortment of diaries and sketches. From these it was clear that Major Hara now knew exactly where Kennedy's headquarters lay.

On the 17th Hara launched his biggest drive yet. Half a battalion moved out from Viru and headed cautiously for Segi Point. Kennedy didn't know the details, but he knew he was threatened from three directions, and that he couldn't possibly hold Segi against the attack that was taking shape. On June 20 he radioed

KEN that he'd have to take to the hills unless he got help.

Admiral Kelly Turner, the Amphibious Force commander for TOENAILS, reacted immediately. Segi must not be allowed to fall. It was needed for the fighter strip that would support the attack on Munda. He had planned to land there June 30; now that would obviously be too late. Instead, they must go at once— tonight!

At 8:30 P.M. the old four-pipers *Dena* and *Waters* left Guadalcanal with two companies of Colonel Michael Currin's 4th Marine Raiders. Racing west, they veered into Panga Bay and headed for Segi Point. They reduced speed now—these waters were still uncharted and no one knew whether the channel was deep enough for ships of this size. Twice they scraped bottom, wriggled free, and ploughed on. Soon Kennedy's signal fires began blazing—but this time as beacons rather than warnings.

At 5:50 A.M. they were there. The 400 Marines piled into Higgins boats and chugged toward the beach. As Colonel Currin splashed ashore, he was greeted by a big man in singlet and khaki shorts, with weapon slung casually over his shoulder. He seemed quiet and cultivated, and Currin wondered what such a man was doing in a place like this. It was Donald Kennedy.

Two Japanese parties were approaching too, but the nearest was still at a village called Regi, busily burning the place down. In the race for Segi, Mickey Currin had beaten Major Hara by a good three miles.

Next morning, the 22nd, two companies of U.S. infantry arrived to bolster the position. With them came a Navy survey party led by Commander Wilfred L. Painter. He was in charge of building the fighter strip that would turn Segi into an "unsinkable aircraft carrier."

Commander Bill Painter, who promised to build a fighter strip at Segi within ten days from the time the Marines landed.
(Naval Construction Battalion Center)

Bill Painter was a brash, boastful officer, tolerated at headquarters only because he had a knack of living up to his boasts. This time it looked as though he had bitten off more than he could chew. He would be starting completely from scratch, yet he promised he'd have his strip ready ten days after the main landings on June 30. To many people 30 days seemed more likely.

Painter tore into the job as soon as he was off the ship. He had been to Segi twice before—once in February, again in May—to examine the lay of the land. Now he knew exactly what he wanted. Under his crisp directions, the surveyors got out their instruments, began taking sights, driving stakes and unwinding reels of line. His basic idea was to lay out the strip completely in pegs and cord. Then, when the bulldozers and graders arrived on the 30th, he would start building immediately. In this crisscross of string, he could already see taxi loops, drains, gasoline tanks, ammunition dumps, repair shops.

Rendova had visitors too. Around June 20 Kennedy forwarded a team of nine U.S. infantry and artillery officers by canoe. Led by Navy Lieutenant "Red" Redden, they made their way to Dick Horton's camp overlooking Munda. Their job was to explore the shore around Rendova Harbor, where the troops would land on the 30th, and also to find positions for the big 155-mm. guns that would be used to soften up the Japanese. After several days of poking around, most of the party left with the data they needed. Redden and two other officers remained to help guide in the landing craft on D-Day.

About this time RAAF Flight Lieutenant R. A. Robinson led still another party to Horton's camp. "Robbie" Robinson—never to be confused with "Wobbie" on Bougainville—was a free-spirited, beer-drinking old-timer who had been a Burns Philp plantation manager on New Britain before the war. Stationed at KEN, he was sent up via Kennedy with two radio operators and a coder to give Horton some extra strength.

At Rendova Harbor and Ugele village the Japanese garrisons warily watched all this activity. Lieutenant (j.g.) Naoto Niyake, a young naval doctor, noted that U.S. planes were constantly overhead, with no Japanese fighters to oppose them. In his diary he compared himself to "a lonely candle standing in the midst of a fierce wind."

And well he might. There were only about 200 Japanese on Rendova altogether. Lieutenant Suzuki, normally in charge of the infantry unit on the island, was down with malaria at Munda, and there was a feeling of futility about the whole defense effort.

Lieutenant Niyake thought about his mother and his girl a good deal, and for solace dipped into his "comfort bag." All he seemed to find was an article entitled "Worry Comes with Birth." Small comfort. By June 25 he was resigned to the end: "I know I shall really feel helpless when the enemy lands. Our reactions now are slow, just like that."

On the night of the 29th Dick Horton put Robinson in charge of the camp and went down to the west coast with Redden and the other two officers. Canoes were waiting, and they paddled to Bau, a tiny islet just north of Rendova Harbor. Landing, Horton led Redden to a tree he had picked out on the northeastern tip of the island. From here Redden was to flash a light between 5:00 and 5:15 A.M., guiding in the first troops, a specially trained group of jungle fighters styled "Barracudas." Their leader, on his first mission since the dark days of Guadalcanal, was that tough old Islander Snowy Rhoades.

A fierce rain squall and gusts of wind buffeted Horton and Redden as they waited by the tree. Peering into the night, they could see nothing, but at 5 o'clock Redden began flashing his light as directed. Five, ten, fifteen minutes passed. No answering flash . . . no indication that their signal had been seen . . . no sign that any one was coming. . . .

Steaming up Blanche Channel, Snowy Rhoades peered into the mist and could see nothing. He had been chosen to guide in the Barracudas because he had once been manager of the Lever Brothers plantation at Rendova Harbor and knew every inch of the place. But that didn't help tonight. He couldn't pick out the barrier islands that screened the harbor, nor was there any sign of the white light that was meant to mark Renard Entrance, where the landing craft would go in.

The *Dent* and *Waters,* the pair of destroyer-transports bringing the Barracudas, groped along the coast, finally stopping several miles west of where they were meant to be. The Barracudas piled into the Higgins boats, started for the shore, then were recalled at daybreak, when it became clear they were in the wrong place. The other ships in the invasion armada could now be seen gathering off the harbor entrance. Belatedly the *Dent* and *Waters* hurried into position, and once again the Barracudas embarked in the Higgins boats.

They were an odd spearhead. Instead of landing first and wiping out any resistance, they arrived ten minutes behind the troops they were meant to be leading. Making the best of it, Snowy Rhoades led his group through the men already on the beach and advanced into the plantation. Almost at once he walked right into two Japanese soldiers with raised rifles. They seemed undecided whether to fire or run, and before they could make up their minds, he shot them both.

Despite all their forebodings, the Japanese were unprepared when the blow finally fell. At Rabaul, Admiral Kusaka had noted the increase in Allied radio traffic and concentrated his planes for a counterblow, but when the traffic fell off after June 26, he dispersed them again. At Munda, General Sasaki positioned his guns to cover a frontal assault, apparently discounting a landing anywhere else. On Rendova the garrison had gone on the alert during the night, but when nothing happened immediately, they relaxed and were literally caught napping. One outpost managed to fire off four blue flares, trying to warn Munda as the transports arrived.

The garrison at Rendova Harbor opened up briefly with a machine gun, but seeing the size of the U.S. force, the men soon scattered into the bush. Lieutenant Niyake, the pessimistic young doctor, found himself with an isolated group of 22 men. Driven from the plantation, they headed up a trail that led into the mountains.

Holding down Horton's camp PWD at the 2000-foot level, Robbie Robinson had his first hint of trouble early on July 1, the morning after the landings, when a stray Japanese soldier was sighted wandering nearby. Robbie got his Owens submachine gun, sprayed the bush without results.

Around 11:30 scout Pelope Lomae was sitting by a fire cooking tara with several other natives, when they sighted troops advancing up the trail toward the camp. It must be the Americans, they agreed, and delegated Lomae to meet them as the only one of the group who spoke English. He was greeted by a burst of gunfire. Lieutenant Niyake's contingent, retreating up the mountain, had stumbled across the Coastwatchers' hideout.

Robinson and his men began firing back, but the Japanese opened up with a light machine gun, and that proved decisive. No time to do more than grab the codes and maps, remove the crystals from the teleradio, and scramble into the bush. The Japanese chased them for nearly a mile, then retired to pillage the camp. They smashed the teleradio, burned the rifles, took the rice supply, and shot the camp dog "Spring." One enemy soldier also had the time and curiosity to disassemble Robinson's Rolls razor, then couldn't get it back together again.

On the run and buffered by a torrential rain, Robbie's party slipped and slid down the trail that led to the east coast. They were almost at the beach when they met another party coming up. A group of natives was bringing Lieutenant (j.g.) Arthur B. Wells, a downed Navy fighter pilot, to what they thought was the safety of PWD.

Robinson had no time to find this out. Taking one look at Wells, he simply blurted, "I don't know who you are, but fall in line—they're right behind me!"

The combined group now headed downhill, stopping just short of the beach. There were several enemy outposts nearby, and they didn't dare take to the water in daylight. Dusk, and two big canoes appeared. They all got in and started north up the coast. Then a close call with a Japanese barge . . . a wet night on a barrier island . . . and finally on the morning of the 2nd they reached the American perimeter and comparative safety.

Safety—and chaos. The landing craft piled cargo on the beaches far faster than things could be sorted and stored. Soon rations, medical supplies, fuel and ammunition were mixed in a hopeless jumble. To make matters worse, the rain continued. The few plantation roads turned into ribbons of muck—one bulldozer almost sank out of sight.

It looked like a golden opportunity for the Japanese, but at Rabaul Admiral Kusaka was still trying to reassemble his planes. He mounted small strikes on June 30 and July 1, and did manage to torpedo Kelly Turner's flagship *McCawley*. But the *coup de grâce* was supplied by a PT-boat which inadvertently sank the "Whacky Mac," thinking she was Japanese.

On the 2nd Kusaka finally put together a full-scale attack, and it was devastating. Sneaking in from behind the mountains, 68 bombers and fighters caught the Americans by surprise. Fuel dumps exploded in flames, and over 200 men were killed and wounded.

Dick Horton was lucky. He missed the full brunt of the strike. Escaping the confusion on the beaches, he had established himself on a small offshore islet, and it was here that Robinson's party caught up with him. Learning the details of the attack on PWD, Horton now sent a reconnaissance team up the mountain to learn what was left of the camp. Luckily the Japanese missed the hiding place of the spare teleradio. It was brought down to the beachhead, and PWD was soon on the air again.

Beyond the perimeter, Snowy Rhoades took charge of mopping up the scattered Japanese. Learning that a small party was hiding up a river near the southeast coast, he loaded a barge with eighteen U.S. infantry and ten armed natives and went after them. They sneaked to the spot undetected and found the Japanese cooking rice in a small depression near the river bank.

Rhoades asked the lieutenant commanding the infantry to plaster them with a few rifle grenades. The lieutenant pointed out that half his men had taken a wrong turn, and he didn't want to attack until he was at full strength. He then went off to look for the strays, while Rhoades and one of the natives crept closer to watch the Japanese.

Suddenly an officer, wearing a Samurai sword, left the group, strolled to a bush ten yards from Rhoades, and began taking a leak. Snowy froze, hoping the Japanese wouldn't see him and spoil the element of surprise. The officer finished, glanced casually around, and his eyes fell on Rhoades, standing right there in his jungle fatigues.

He let out a startled yell, and Rhoades fired a burst, killing him instantly. As the rest of the Japanese grabbed their guns, Snowy ran for better cover by the river bank. Here he and the native crouched down, listening to the enemy search the bush a few yards away. The native rose up, hoping to get off a shot, but was almost cut in two by a Japanese machine gun. Fighting on alone, Rhoades kept firing at every sound he heard, hoping to give the impression that there was more of him than one.

Finally the U.S. infantry unit moved up and began firing rocket grenades at the roots of a banyan tree where the Japanese machine gun seemed to be located. They silenced the gun, killed a warrant officer manning it, and routed the rest of the enemy party.

By the time Rhoades checked the body of the officer he shot, some American souvenir hunter had already beaten him to the Samurai sword. But he learned the officer's name from his diary. It was Naoto Niyake, the moody young naval doctor. Despite the sword, Niyake met something less than a Samurai's end. He was not filled with martial zeal; he was filled with gloom and self-doubt. He did not die gloriously; he died taking a leak.

Meanwhile the drive on Munda was moving ahead. Early June 30—even before the Rendova landings began—two companies of the 169th Infantry seized the barrier islands guarding the entrance to Zanana beach. They were guided by Clay Boyd, back for another patrol behind enemy lines. July 1, the big 155-mm. guns were landed on Rendova and commenced bombarding the airstrip. On the 2nd Major General John H. Hester began ferrying his troops across Blanche Channel to the Zanana beachhead. Early on the 5th Marine Lieutenant Colonel Harry Liversedge's mixed force of Raiders and infantry began landing at Rice Anchorage to block off Munda from the north.

Frank Guidone was offshore in a native canoe, marking one flank of the landing beach with a flashlight. A few miles to the west Rear Admiral W. L. Ainsworth's cruisers and destroyers were pounding the Japanese posts at Bairoko and Enogai to cover the landings. As the salvos thundered louder and nearer, Guidone's two native paddlers decided they had had enough. They dived overboard, leaving him teetering alone in the canoe, trying to keep his balance and the light steady at the same time.

Both here and at Zanana the Americans found the going far tougher than expected. Initially taken back, General Sasaki quickly beefed up his defenses with 3000 men brought over from the island of Kolombangara. At Rabaul on July 4, General Imamura promised another 4000 from the northern Solomons, as Admiral Kusaka reactivated the Tokyo Express.

The terrain too proved worse than anticipated, and General Hester's troops were less than prepared to cope with it. Mired down in the swamps and jungle, beset by spirited defenders, the men's morale began to suffer. The advance fell behind schedule. The situation called for a number of remedies—one of them closer fighter support.

At Segi Commander Bill Painter watched the bull-dozers clear the coconut palms from the area where he planned his runway. The Eastern Force of TOENAILS had arrived on schedule, bringing the heavy equipment Painter needed to translate his layout of pegs and string into a real fighter strip.

Work began while the ships were still unloading on June 30, and it didn't stop even at night. Correctly gambling that the Japanese were too busy at Munda to bother with Segi, Painter rigged floodlights, and his Seabees worked all night, clearing trees and grading the site. July 1, his trucks began hauling coral from a nearby pit and spreading it on the runway. By noon on the 2nd his rollers were busy smoothing it out.

Then the deluge. On the night of July 3 a blinding tropical storm swept in, stopping work, drenching everything, dissolving the freshly laid coral paving. In a few rain-soaked hours Bill Painter was almost back where he started. He had guessed wrong in using "dead" coral from the pit. Now his only hope was "live" coral from the reef offshore. That wouldn't dissolve, but it was hell to dig.

Dynamite did the trick, cracking the reef, producing great chunks that the Seabees crushed and spread on the runway. Painter urged them on, trying to make up for lost time. He seemed everywhere at once, rarely stopping to eat or sleep. By July 7 he figured he was back on schedule.

Then "Washing Machine Charlie." On the night of the 7th a lone Japanese float plane—probably from Rekata Bay—droned over Segi, disturbing the peace with occasional bombs. They did little damage but stopped all work, as the lights were doused and the men took to their foxholes. It was the same story on the 8th and 9th.

Once again Painter desperately tried to make up for lost time. During the daylight hours practically everyone in the outfit was put to work spreading coral. Clerks and carpenters found themselves wielding shovels.

As night fell on the 10th, Bill Painter's ten days were up, but he needed another twelve hours. The rollers were still working one end of the runway. But they could finish during the night—and complete the job on schedule—if Washing Machine Charlie didn't turn up.

Finished on time. The Segi airstrip built by Bill Painter. Photographed July 1943 by a U.S. bomber returning from a raid on Munda. (U.S. Marines)

Painter and Captain C. S. Alexander, who would be in charge of the strip, examined the evening sky. Clouds were rolling in, and it looked like no night for Charlie. They radioed that the field would be ready for 30 fighters at daylight.

But Charlie came. The clouds drifted away, and the familiar sound of his engine droned over Segi. When dawn broke, the rollers were still at work. Painter wondered whether to call off the fighters, but Alexander, an old flyer himself, was sure the planes could get in anyhow. The tower would simply warn them to land long. An hour later they began coming in—every landing perfect—and Bill Painter had made good his boast.

Donald Kennedy watched it all a little ruefully. It was his organization and leadership that had held Segi for the day when the Americans needed it. Yet now that they were here, he was almost a misfit. He really didn't belong in this teeming world of bulldozers, supply dumps and repair shops, supported by the hordes of GIs now swarming in. He belonged to a far smaller world built around personal loyalty, personal authority, personal initiative, personal contact.

Now no one even knew who his scouts were. And after some trigger-happy sentry almost shot Kennedy himself one night, he finally moved his headquarters across the channel to Vangunu Island. Here he still serviced KEN with intelligence, but the private war of Donald Kennedy was over.

12

165 UNINVITED GUESTS

Later, after it was all over, Lieutenant Commander John L. Chew decided that his big mistake was shaving that day. Chew was Assistant Gunnery Officer on the light cruiser *Helena* and a typically superstitious sailor. He always wore the same pair of old brown shoes and flashproof jumper. (The jumper, in fact, was so important he wouldn't let it be washed.) He always carried his lucky hunting knife on his belt, his lucky four-leaf clover in his wallet, his lucky silver dollar in his pocket. And he never, never shaved before going into battle.

This time it had seemed perfectly safe to spruce up a little. After a hard night's work supporting the landings at Rice Anchorage, the *Helena* was steaming south of New Georgia, away from the action, presumably for a few days of rest.

Then late in the afternoon of July 5 came word that the Tokyo Express was on the move again. Ten destroyers were heading down the Slot, bringing reinforcements for General Sasaki's hard-pressed defenders at Munda. The *Helena,* along with the rest of Admiral

Ainsworth's force of cruisers and destroyers, was ordered to turn around immediately and intercept. For Jack Chew the word came too late—he had already shaved.

By 1:30 A.M. on the 6th the force was off the mouth of Kula Gulf, racing up the Slot at 25 knots. Clouds hid the moon, but the towering volcanic cone of Kolombangara Island loomed to port. At 1:36 the radarman made contact—seven to nine ships coming out of Kula Gulf, hugging the Kolombangara shore.

Japanese lookouts soon sighted the Americans too, and when Ainsworth's force opened fire at 1:57, the enemy destroyers had a nice aiming point for their "long lance" torpedoes.

At 2:04 a roar split the night, and the *Helena* gave a sickening lurch. One of the torpedoes had found its mark, completely tearing off the ship's bow. Thirty seconds later a second torpedo hit . . . then a third. The *Helena* sagged, back broken amidships. All power was gone; guns were silent; communications cut; lights out, except for a few dim emergency bulbs.

Jack Chew, in charge of the combat information center, checked the bridge for instructions. Captain Charles P. Cecil's orders were no surprise—abandon ship.

The word spread, and men poured onto the slanting decks. Chew and Lieutenant Commander Warren Boles, the *Helena*'s gunnery officer, struggled to get the life rafts off the forecastle into the water. Further aft, Major Bernard T. Kelly, commanding the ship's 42-man Marine Detachment, checked the main deck forward to make sure no one was left behind, then climbed down a cargo net into the sea. Near the stern, Ensign George Bausewine, a young assistant damage control officer, carefully removed his shoes and slipped into the water.

Swimming clear, they all turned for a last look at

the *Helena.* The bow and stern rose high in the air to form a V. Then with a rumble she slid straight down, disappearing at about 2:30. Watching her go, Major Kelly felt as if his home had burned to the ground.

For the next hour hundreds of men milled around in the water, hoping that some ship might pick them up. The lucky ones found rafts; the rest gathered in clusters where they might be more easily seen. Chew and Boles collected a group of about 75 around a Jacob's ladder that came floating by.

Some time before dawn they heard ships approaching, and soon Major Kelly made out the number "449" on the bow of a destroyer. That meant the *Nicholas,* one of Ainsworth's force. The Admiral had detached her with destroyer *Radford* to look for survivors, once he realized the *Helena* was missing. The rest of the task force was now high-tailing it back to Tulagi, convinced

The U.S. light cruiser Helena, *sunk in Kula Gulf July 6, 1943. She went down in 25 minutes, leaving most of her crew swimming in the Slot.* (National Archives)

they had wiped out most of the Japanese fleet. Actually, they had sunk only one destroyer, with another driven on a reef through bad navigation.

The *Nicholas* and *Radford* lowered nets and boats, began taking survivors aboard. For Chew's group, it would be a long, hard swim to safety, but for others like Ensign Bausewine rescue seemed only seconds off. He was floating on his back right next to one of the destroyers, awaiting his turn to climb aboard. Then, without warning, she suddenly got under way at high speed and began firing her guns. Another Japanese destroyer had been sighted coming out of Kula Gulf. The fight was on again.

Dawn was now breaking, and with Japanese planes controlling these skies, there was no chance for the destroyers to come back again. Amazingly, in the short time they were at the scene, they managed to pick up 745 survivors; their boats—left behind as they steamed off—took another 100 to a safe spot on the New Georgia coast.

The rest of the *Helena* survivors, including Jack Chew's group, remained treading water in the Slot. With daylight they found a curious rallying point. The *Helena*'s bow, severed from the ship by the first torpedo, was still afloat. Standing vertically about 20 feet above water, it soon became a popular refuge. Chew and many of the others paddled over, feeling it should be the first thing spotted by any friendly planes that came looking for them.

And so it proved. About 10 A.M. a B-24 appeared, circled, and dropped three rubber rafts. One sank but Chew's group managed to inflate the other two. Unfortunately each could hold only four men. Chew put in his most seriously injured, and the group continued waiting.

Soon more planes arrived—but this time they were Zeros. Watching them approach, Major Kelly recalled the recent Bismarck Sea affair, where Allied aircraft strafed the Japanese life rafts after sinking their transports. This was no gentleman's war, and he steeled himself for the worst.

But the Zeros didn't shoot. The nearest pilot simply pulled back his canopy and looked at them closely. Circling, the planes made a second run, and again held their fire. As they circled for a third run, they got off a few short bursts, and Kelly felt sure that this time would be "it." As they roared by, practically touching the water, the lead pilot grinned, waved, waggled his wings . . . and then they were gone. The relieved but puzzled survivors figured they were so coated with fuel oil, the flyers couldn't tell whether they were American or Japanese.

But it was a close call. It drove home to Chew that these were indeed enemy waters, and the bow was far more likely to attract Japanese than American planes. He decided his group, now down to about 50, should clear out as soon as possible. Kolombangara lay only eight or nine miles to the south. If they used the rafts to get there, maybe they could then work their way to the U.S. lines on New Georgia.

They shoved off around 11 A.M., with the two rafts tied loosely together and the men divided evenly between them. The injured continued to ride as passengers, while two or three hands straddled the rims and paddled; everyone else remained in the water, clinging to the sides, kicking and pushing the craft along.

All that day they inched toward Kolombangara, gradually losing touch with the other rafts and oil-soaked swimmers that dotted the Slot. For Chew's party it was hard, exhausting work, and he tried to ease the strain by developing a system of rotation. Every so often one of his swimmers would take a turn in the raft itself, along with the injured. But there was room for only one or two at a time, and as things worked out, a man could expect only ten minutes rest every two hours.

Nightfall, and Kolombangara seemed as far away as ever. One of the injured men died, and all were badly off. They had now been in the water for eight hours, were bone-tired, hungry, and utterly discouraged. Under a tropical sky studded with stars that seemed far nearer than the island they were trying to reach, Chew led them all in the Lord's Prayer.

As the night wore on, the yearning for sleep grew overwhelming. No matter how hard they fought it, some succumbed . . . loosened their grip . . . and were gone for good. Major Kelly knew the danger, and tried desperately to stay awake. Once he nodded, found himself floating away from the group, barely made it back. Next time, he stayed asleep, and when a mouthful of salt water woke him up, it was almost dawn and he was alone in the sea.

He started swimming north, and if he needed any stimulant, it was provided by two fish, about three or four feet long, that showed great interest in his bare feet. He splashed, shouted, kicked, and they departed.

He continued swimming and finally lucked into one of Chew's two rafts. They had become separated, and this was not Kelly's original one, but no sight was ever more welcome.

All day, the 7th, the flotsam of the *Helena*—rafts, bits of wreckage, individual swimmers—drifted up the Slot. On Chew's raft the men gradually realized that they would never get to Kolombangara. The wind and current were sweeping them by. Their best hope lay in the next island to the northwest, Vella Lavella.

Someone suggested rigging their shirts as a sail. Two paddles were lashed together to form a crosstree, and the shirts were then stretched between them. Warren Boles was the guiding light. He was from Marblehead, Massachusetts, and knew how to sail before he could ride a bike.

The men's spirits rose, and they perked up even more when a crate of potatoes floated near. For most it was their first food since leaving the *Helena*. But at sundown they were still a long way from Vella Lavella, and it was clear they would be spending another night in the water. Their hearts again sank.

It was as bad as they feared. Kelly's raft lost ten during the night—mostly men who quietly slipped off while the rest were blindly kicking away. By now the men were so exhausted, hallucinations were common. George Bausewine, dozing on the edge of one of the *Helena*'s doughnut rafts, awoke going under water to get to a bunk he felt sure was there. A groggy, water-logged Ensign David Chennault kept asking Bausewine for a cigarette.

Daylight on the 8th, discipline collapsed completely on Chew's raft. The men wouldn't rotate any longer. Those resting simply refused to get back in the water, and Chew was too weak to make them do it. Seeing he had lost control, he decided to swim for it. Vella Lavella looked pretty close now; once ashore, maybe he could get some native help.

Warren Boles and two other men joined him, and around 7 A.M. the four pushed off. Two hours . . . three hours . . . six hours passed. Clearly Vella Lavella was much farther off than it looked. Exhausted, they drifted apart and lost sight of each other. By mid-afternoon Chew was only half-awake. Sometimes he found himself swimming in the wrong direction; other times, deep under water for no logical reason. He kept thinking he

was going to meet a man who would take him to a cock-
tail party at "the Residency"—whatever that was.

Boles, the best swimmer, seemed more aware of
things. Spotting a stretch of beach he liked, he methodically made for it. Stumbling ashore, he found a coconut in the sand, cracked it open for a drink. Then he
crawled under a bush a few yards inland and went to
sleep.

By 4 P.M. Chew was just about all-in, when he sighted
two natives paddling a canoe toward him. They eased
alongside and asked, "You American?"

"You betcha!" he replied, and they rolled him into the
canoe. One of the natives looked so venerable, Chew
thought of him as Moses. Reaching shore, they explained they would hide him and asked if he could walk.
Certainly, Chew replied . . . and collapsed in his tracks.

For ten miles along the beach a remarkable scene began to unfold. Native canoes darted out, plucking men
from the water. At other points, rafts and individual
swimmers rolled in with the surf. Here and there dazed
men wandered about, trying to get their bearings.
Coxswain Chesleigh Grunstad felt overwhelmingly content. He had no idea where he was, but even if he had
been told the truth—that Vella Lavella was a Japanese-
held island 60 miles from the nearest American outpost
—at this moment he wouldn't have cared. He was on
dry land at last.

Looking down the beach, he could see others coming
ashore. Then one man was washed up almost at his
feet. He was wearing a red money belt, and it reminded
Grunstad of his own money, a roll of two-dollar bills
fastened to his dog tags. He loosened the roll and began
drying the bills. The other man began doing the same—
only his bills were all twenties.

Major Kelly stuck to his raft all the way in. Finally
ashore, he had his party hide it under some trees. They

were just in time. Minutes later a flight of Japanese dive bombers roared by, only 500 feet overhead. Kelly next sent a man along the beach in each direction to scout out the situation. The man who went southward returned in a few minutes with a 25-pound can of coffee—at last they were beginning to get some breaks. The other man returned with a *Helena* sailor and a dignified, middle-aged native who introduced himself as Aaron, "a good Christian and a good Methodist." He quickly produced some coconuts, then disappeared to get help.

It was a quiet day at Toupalando, the little village high in the interior of Vella Lavella where the Coast-watcher Henry Josselyn had recently moved his camp. Josselyn had now been on the island more than eight months, reporting Japanese ship and plane movements, rescuing downed airmen, keeping an eye on Iringila, the main Japanese strong point in the area.

So far he had easily dodged the enemy patrols, but they were increasing in number, and when one party landed only 300 yards from his supply depot at Kila Kila, he had shifted his station NRY deeper into the interior. This eased the pressure a little, and today he had gone off on some errand, leaving the station in charge of Sub-Lieutenant Robert Firth, who had replaced Jack Keenan as his assistant. A former Burns Philp accountant and ship's purser, Firth was a small, cheerful Australian who quickly adapted himself to Coastwatching life.

At the moment, it was not an especially taxing assignment—just a lazy, tropical afternoon. From time to time Firth raised his binoculars and checked the Japanese post at Iringila, but nothing unusual was going on.

Suddenly the torpor was broken by a native scout hurrying up the path to the camp. Rushing up to Firth, he breathlessly reported "plenty Americans" coming ashore along the east coast. To prove it, he produced a set of U.S. Navy dog tags.

Bobby Firth needed better proof than that. Like most Allied fighting men, he attributed almost limitless guile to the Japanese. He feared this might be just one more of their tricks: a clever charade staged to make the Coastwatchers reveal themselves. He quickly called KEN on the teleradio, supplied the name and serial number on the tags, and asked them to check it out.

In an hour KEN was back. The dog tags belonged to a machinist's mate, 3rd class, assigned to the *Helena,* sunk in Kula Gulf on the 6th.

Now convinced, Firth sent for Josselyn, who agreed that it looked like "something big." As yet there was no hint as to how many *Helena* survivors were involved, but they seemed to be concentrating in two main groups along the coast—one in the Paraso Bay area, the other twelve miles east near Lambu Lambu village. The Japanese had outposts near both places, and fast work was needed to clear the castaways from the beaches before enemy patrols began picking them up.

A runner dashed off to alert Bamboo, the native chief in the area where the survivors were landing: Send out canoes to pick up any men still in the water . . . plant a string of sentries to watch for Japanese patrols . . . stand by to help on food and housing.

Another messenger hurried to the Reverend Silvester, the Coastwatching missionary, who was currently at Maravari on the southeast coast. He should take charge of the eastern group of survivors landing near Lambu Lambu. Josselyn himself would take on the western group, at Paraso Bay and Java. Firth would stay at Toupalando—later at a camp still deeper in the interior —handling the teleradio traffic with KEN. They would all keep in touch through two walkie-talkies and a somewhat larger set used by Josselyn, and to help Firth

VELLA LAVELLA

Iringila
Toupalando
Deneo
Paraso
Java
Mundi Mundi
Lambu Lambu
SAM CHUNG'S HOUSE ■
Paramata
Kundurumbangara Point
Orete Cove
BAGGA
Supato
Maravari
Barakoma
WILSON STRAIT
Bilua
Liapari
VELLA GULF
RANONGGA
0   2   4   6   miles
0 2 4 6 8 kilometers
GIZO

out they had the fortuitous services of a "guest"—Lieutenant Eli Ciunguin, a P-38 pilot awaiting evacuation.

Everything set, Josselyn headed for the village of Java, where the first survivors had been sighted. Time was so important that he traveled all night to get there.

Ensign Bausewine's group—rescued from their doughnut raft by native canoes—spent the night in leaf huts on the beach near Java. Supper was a hodgepodge of papaya, coconuts, taro, and fish stew. Normally indigestible, perhaps, but after three days of nothing to eat, nobody complained. It was food.

Shortly after dawn next morning, July 9, they were awakened by their hosts. Using a mixture of pidgin English and sign language, the natives explained that everyone must leave the beach area. Then, as the group sleepily formed up in the early daylight, out of the jungle appeared a slim white man, hair almost down to his shoulders. It was Henry Josselyn.

Asking for the senior officer present, Josselyn took Bauswine aside and explained how urgent it was to move inland at once. The coast was alive with Japanese patrols and barge traffic. The men were still weak from their three days on the raft, but there was no time for rest. They hobbled inland, camping later in the day, deep in the jungle, where giant trees hid them even from snooping planes.

Twelve miles down the coast a native named Mickey organized the rescue of the other group of survivors at Lambu Lambu Cove. When Ensign Don Bechtel came ashore on the evening of the 8th, one native undressed him, another fed him, a third led him to a clearing where he could rest. More survivors were collected; then, with Mickey leading, the group started inland. Those who couldn't walk, like Commander Chew, were carried on litters of poles and copra bags.

Mickey led them first through a jungle swamp, where the men sank up to their knees; then along a hard, rocky trail that climbed into the hills. Finally, after two and a half miles, they came to a clearing with a wooden shanty. To Jack Chew it looked like a typical summer vacation shack on the Chesapeake Bay. It was the house of a Chinese trade named Sam Chung, who was hiding out in the hills with his family. Sam tactfully moved out, and the place became an impromptu camp for the *Helena* survivors brought up by Mickey. When Chew arrived, MM1/c Lloyd George Miller and several others were already there.

Inside, Chew found a few pieces of crude furniture, a shot gun with one shell, a pair of white shorts and a pair of sneakers. With his own dungarees split and chafing his skin, he tried on the shorts. Miraculously, they fit. Then he tried on the sneakers. Even more miraculously, they fit too.

During the evening more survivors turned up, and then the Reverend Silvester arrived, looking anything but clerical in a short-sleeved shirt and old khaki shorts. A native walked beside him with the walkie-talkie. Searching out Chew, the senior officer, Silvester explained he had "access to a radio" and would have the American headquarters notified.

Next day, the 9th, a few more survivors trickled in. Last to arrive was Warren Boles, who had spent the night on the deserted beach where he landed. Looking around in the morning, he encountered a giant native ("he looked about ten feet tall") armed with a huge machete. Boles had only a six-inch knife; so he did the diplomatic thing. He threw his own knife to the ground and gestured friendship. The native understood no English, but he knew exactly what to do. He led Boles to Sam Chung's house, and with his arrival the group reached a grand total of 104 men.

The Reverend A. W. E. Silvester, Methodist missionary on Vella Lavella. He helped hide 165 Helena survivors for eight days, while arrangements were made for their rescue. (Courtesy Warren C. Boles)

This was no longer a small band of castaways; this was a whole village—a village deep in enemy territory. To survive, Commander Chew realized they must have rules, assignments, lines of authority, and all the trappings of an organized community.

As senior officer, Chew automatically became the "mayor," and it's hard to imagine a better one. A thoroughly professional career officer, he nevertheless had an informal touch that came in handy in these weird surroundings that no naval manual ever anticipated. In the Annapolis world dominated by conservative "black shoe" officers, he belonged not only figuratively but literally to the more relaxed "brown shoe" minority. In fact, on the *Helena* his lucky brown shoes had been a trademark.

His "chief of police" was, of course, Major Kelly. He would be in charge of defense, sanitation, and maintaining law and order. As a force, Kelly had five of his own Marines plus a number of petty officers and natives.

Weapons were a more difficult problem. At the start

the survivors had only a .38 revolver and a .45 automatic. Then Chew discovered the shotgun in Sam Chung's house, and Josselyn sent over seven very assorted rifles, including a Japanese model with exactly three bullets. Two men were assigned to each weapon— if one were hit, the other was to save the gun. The force inevitably became known as "Kelly Irregulars."

With the Irregulars in the field, Kelly turned his attention to sanitation. Knowing that digging a latrine is not a sailor's idea of fun, he set an example by helping dig it himself. This was no easy task, for their only implement was a steel helmet, unaccountably worn by the ship's barber during the entire three days he was in the water.

They also needed better sleeping quarters. So far, the men were packed in Sam's shack and a curious outbuilding that rather resembled a hen house. The Reverend Silvester said he thought he could remedy this problem, and a team of his mission boys appeared the next morning. Cutting poles and vines from the jungle, they quickly lashed together a framework, then covered the sides with palm leaves, and thatched a roof with grass. By the evening of the 10th they had finished a shed some 40 or 50 feet long. To dedicate it, the Reverend Silvester held a service, with survivors and natives joining together in "Onward, Christian Soldiers."

Food posed another problem. The natives were short themselves, and the addition of scores of *Helena* survivors proved a serious drain. Once again the Reverend Silvester came to the rescue. He organized native foraging parties that systematically combed the area. Soon the camp was getting a steady flow of potatoes, tapioca, yams, pau pau, taro root and bananas. When ripe, the fruit was given to the injured. Everything else was dumped into a huge copper pot, also provided by Silvester's natives. It reminded Jack Chew, a little uncomfortably, of the pots he had seen in cartoons of cannibals cooking missionaries.

The pot was kept boiling by two experienced cooks— Seaman 1/c J. L. Johnson and Marine Bert Adam, a massive bartender from Bourbon Street in New Orleans. Twice a day they ladled out a watery stew, laced with a few chunks of Spam scavenged from the beach. The men never ceased to marvel at the results. Sometimes it was rich purple, next time pink, then almost white, and again almost black. There were no complaints, although Coxswain Ted Blahnik later confessed that he tried to dodge the fish eyes.

On medicine too the Reverend Silvester proved invaluable. Pharmacist's Mate Red Layton did a superb job with the injured, now bedded down in Sam's shack, but his task was made easier by the sulfa drugs and pain killers that came from the mission stores.

Every evening Silvester dropped by to chat with Jack Chew—not just about the problems of the day, but about life in general. Gradually a close bond developed between them. Bern Kelly and the others felt it too, and they all agreed that this devoted man who did so much for them deserved far more than to be a mere "Reverend." He should at least be a bishop, and so they made him one, unofficially. From this time on, they always called him "Bish."

By July 12 life in "Mayor" Chew's community almost bordered on the routine. In the morning the men got up with the sun—about 6:00. Washing up without soap was somewhat futile, but they learned that a lime peel was excellent for cleaning teeth.

Breakfast (stew, of course) came around 10:00, when Chief Cook Johnson would ceremoniously announce, "Chow is ready." Finishing, the men washed the coconut shells that served as plates . . . then two laps around the camp for exercise . . . then clean-up. Nearly every one had some specific assignment; most sought-after duty was the canteen detail because it meant an opportunity to bathe in the crystal-clear stream at the bottom of the hill.

Lunch (more stew) came at two o'clock, and that was the last meal of the day. The rest of the afternoon most of the men relaxed, gradually regaining their strength, until evening prayers around 5:30. Not quite knowing how this mixed and involuntary congregation would react, Chew passed the word that no matter how they felt, he expected the men to show proper respect during the Reverend Silvester's service.

He need not have worried. Perilous hardship had brought most of the men closer to God than they had ever been before. Survivors and natives joined together in singing the hymns, especially "Rock of Ages." The natives sang in their language, the *Helena*'s crew in theirs, but the effect was strangely unifying. The common melody seemed to mean a common bond that many of the men found enormously reassuring. It was not unusual to see them in tears as the service ended.

And so the days passed, one pretty much like another —except for the big feast. This took place after a party of natives butchered one of the stray cattle that roamed the island. Lugging the beef back to the camp, the natives were held up by Japanese patrols, and by the time they reached Sam's place, the meat was ripe indeed. Chew consulted Chief Cook Johnson; they reluctantly agreed that it was hopelessly spoiled, and they had it buried.

This was more than MM2/c R. G. Atkinson could stand. He was the oldest member of the *Helena*'s crew, and among other things in life, had been in the Klondike gold rush. He told Chew that in the Yukon no one would throw away beef like that. He knew how to salvage it and would like to try his skill.

The meat was hastily disinterred, and Atkinson went to work. No one ever knew what he really did. Obtaining an iron pot from the natives, he boiled the beef for three days, occasionally tossing in bits of fruit and herbs he found growing in the jungle. Finally he announced that his treat was ready, and to the astonishment of the other 103 men, it turned out to be delicious.

Despite Atkinson's genius—and the continuing efforts of the more orthodox cooks—food was always short, and always on everyone's mind. The men no longer talked about the girls in Sydney—it was the steaks back home. So it was not too surprising when Major Kelly stormed up to Chew one day, reporting that some one had stolen one of the few cans of Spam salvaged from the rafts. "If I find out who it is, will you sentence him to death?"

Chew said he thought this was a little drastic. The thief was probably some poor devil so hungry he really didn't know what he was doing. Kelly was adamant, and the "Mayor" was caught between approving what he felt was a Draconian measure and undermining his "Chief of Police." To his enormous relief, the culprit was never caught.

A graver crisis arose the day a four-man Japanese patrol came too close to the camp. The native scouts intercepted, and in the skirmish that followed, three of the enemy were killed. The fourth was taken alive, posing a serious dilemma. With his men hiding-out deep in Japanese territory, and the enemy now on their heels, Chew felt it was too dangerous to have a prisoner on their hands, yet they certainly couldn't turn him loose. In the end he reluctantly ordered the Japanese executed. Technically, perhaps, against the rules of the Geneva Convention, but surely that body never contemplated a situation like this. Nevertheless, it was a hard decision, and it was comforting to Chew that the Reverend Silvester understood and agreed.

The next Japanese thrust was no four-man affair. Twenty well-armed troops landed from a barge in Lambu Lambu Cove and started up the trail toward Sam's house. Warned by their native scouts, the Irregulars deployed to meet the threat, while the rest of Chew's group prepared to move deeper into the interior.

Major Kelly hoped to ambush the Japanese as they climbed single file up the trail. He selected a spot that gave him both good observation and cover for his own men. The Irregulars moved into position with their grab bag of weapons and waited.

Soon they heard the Japanese coming, hobnailed boots clanging against the rocks, their voices casual and quite audible in the distance. Kelly wondered how they got their reputation as stealthy jungle fighters.

Still, they were plenty dangerous, and the outnumbered, outgunned Irregulars steeled themselves for a last-ditch fight. Then, just as the head of the enemy column came into view, several blue Corsair fighters streaked by overhead and began firing at the Japanese barge on the coast. Black smoke boiled up, and the patrol, voices babbling in excitement, hurried back to the beach.

Kelly never knew what triggered the attack—probably the fighters just happened by and saw the barge—but he did know that Corsairs were generally land-based. This must mean that the U.S. now had a field within fighter range of Vella Lavella. He was right: Bill Painter's strip at Segi had begun paying off.

Twelve miles up the coast at Paraso Bay—but in touch by radio—Henry Josselyn wasn't thinking about these small triumphs; he was thinking about all the other Japanese on Vella Lavella. Some 300–400 enemy troops were now on the island, and the number was growing. There were new outposts at Kundurumbangara Point and Baka Baka, both near Chew's camp, and another at Marisi, about three miles west of Ensign Bausewine's group at Paraso.

There was no time to lose, if the men were to be saved. COMSOPAC said they could provide a couple of destroyer-transports, so the problem boiled down to the mechanics of evacuation. A total of 165 *Helena* survivors were involved—104 with Chew, 50 with Bausewine, and another 11 a few miles to the northwest with CWO William Dupay. Even after adding Dupay's men to Bausewine's group, it was impossible to concentrate everybody in one place, so Josselyn planned two separate evacuations. He was already at Paraso Bay with Bausewine; so he would send this group off first. Then he would go down to Lambu Lambu and do the same for Chew's group.

July 12, and Bausewine's party received a surprise addition—a captured Zero pilot, brought in by native scouts. Here, too, arose the agonizing question of what to do with the prisoner. The general consensus was to kill him, but as Bausewine later recalled, "Nobody would go through with it; so he lived." Happily, he seemed cowed and thoroughly docile, but to be on the safe side his hands were bound and he was kept blindfolded whenever the group moved. A final and far more welcome newcomer was Lieutenant Ciunguin, the downed P-38 pilot who had been helping Firth with the radio traffic.

By nightfall on the 12th all were assembled on the beach, waiting for the pickup at 2 A.M., but the Japanese Navy didn't cooperate. The Tokyo Express came barreling down the Slot that night with 1200 more reinforcements for Kolombangara. Admiral Ainsworth rushed to intercept them, and the rescue operation was postponed first to the 13th, then to the 14th. But now it fell too close to the 15th, when Josselyn planned to get Chew's group off. In the end he proposed to do the whole job on the night of the 15th: the ships would first pick up Bausewine's party at Paraso Bay, then steam down the coast and get Chew's group at Lambu Lambu.

COMSOPAC approved, and two tense days of waiting followed. Josselyn knew the Japanese were getting close to Chew, and his own group seemed to be living on borrowed time. He moved the camp every night. He shifted the teleradio after every message. He grew nervous, irritable, smoked incessantly. Bausewine's men gladly smoked his butts, for they had the jitters too. Some jungle bird had a call just like the *Helena* general quarters alarm, and the men jumped every time it sounded off.

On the evening of the 15th the party once again went to the beach. Most of them still had on the shreds of oil-soaked dungarees they wore when they landed, but Bill Dupay was resplendent in the Japanese pilot's uniform. The pilot, blindfolded and hands still tied behind his back, was guided along in his underdrawers —the fortunes of war.

Twelve miles down the coast Jack Chew's group was on the move too. With the strongest serving as stretcher-bearers for the sick and wounded, they left the camp at 3 P.M.—a time nicely calculated to get them to Lambu Lambu Cove just before dark. They were in no shape to travel at night, and the coastal plain was too exposed to wait there in broad daylight. Now added to the party were sixteen of the local Chinese—mostly Sam Chung and his relatives.

Kelly's Irregulars screened the movement, taking position between the line of march and the nearest Japanese outpost. Behind them the evacuees plodded along, reaching the coast at dusk, just as planned.

The spot selected for the rendezvous was not on the open sea, but at a former trading-post dock a mile or so up the Lambu Lambu River. This was a broad estuary with several tricky turns, and Chew assigned Warren Boles, the old Marblehead sailor, to go out in a native canoe and pilot the rescuers in.

It was a far cry from cruising the New England coast. The canoe was paddled by a single native who couldn't speak English and didn't understand any instructions. There was a moon, but the shadows of the jungle hid the shoreline. The only channel markers were natives literally planted in the water by "Bish" Silvester to mark each bend in the river. Boles longed for the days of neatly numbered red-nun buoys as he tried to meet the challenge of picking out a black man in a black river on a black night.

Now they were off the mouth of the river, bobbing in the waters of the Slot. Here they waited for some sign of the rescue ships. Once they heard the whine of destroyer blowers and vessels going by at high speed . . . then a few flares and explosions. Japanese ships were apparently on the prowl, sniffing trouble. Then it was dark again, and the wait continued.

On shore Major Kelly also felt the strain of the long wait. Finally he slipped away from his defense line and consulted with Chew. If the ships didn't come soon, it would be dawn, and they couldn't risk staying here during the day. They began discussing the possibility of returning to camp.

Twelve miles up the coast at Paraso Bay it was a long night for Bausewine's group too. The rescue was set for 2 A.M. on the 16th, and at midnight Josselyn pushed off in a large canoe to guide in the rescuers. With him went three natives and Gunner Bill Dupay, to help make contact. For the next two hours they bobbed up and down in the empty night a mile or so offshore.

Then, toward 2 A.M. they spotted the shadowy forms of several blacked-out ships approaching through the dark. There was no clue whether they were friend or foe, but Josselyn hopefully flashed a series of Rs—the recognition signal.

On shore George Bausewine and the others restlessly waited as the hours ticked by. He hoped for the best, but he had always been fatalistic about the group's chances. That Admiral Kelly Turner would send 3000 men in ten destroyers to rescue them was a thought that never occurred to him.

From the start Kelly Turner was determined to rescue the *Helena* survivors on Vella Lavella. It was more than a matter of saving 165 good men; it was important to the whole Navy's morale. As he explained, "It means a lot to know that if the worst happens and you get blown off your ship and washed ashore somewhere, the Navy isn't going to forget you."

But how to do the job? PBYs, submarines, PT-boats —all the usual ways were out. They just couldn't hold enough men. Ships were clearly the answer, and the destroyer-transports *Dent* and *Waters* seemed the best bet. Painted a mottled jungle green, these APDs (as they were called) had the right size and speed, with crews specially trained in amphibious operations—and looking at it one way, this was just an amphibious operation in reverse.

Protecting the two APDs was the problem. They were lightly armed, and this would be the Navy's deepest penetration yet into enemy-controlled waters. The Japanese not only held Vella Lavella, but had airstrips at Kahili and on Ballale plus their anchorage in the Shortlands only 60 miles away.

Kelly Turner took no chances. As the *Dent* and *Waters* steamed toward Vella Lavella on the afternoon of July 15, they were escorted by four destroyers under Captain Thomas J. Ryan. Out of sight but very much in the picture were four more destroyers under Captain Francis X. McInerney. They would hover in the Slot during the pickup, ready to intercept any Japanese ships coming down from the Shortlands. McInerney was in overall charge of the operation.

Midnight, and Ryan's six ships, coming up from the south, entered Vella Gulf. The moon was full, and it was hard to believe they hadn't been sighted. At 1:12 a white flare went up from Vella off to port, and the crews braced for an attack. Nothing happened. Five minutes later, a red parachute flare shot up from Kolombangara on the starboard side. Again the men steeled themselves; again nothing happened.

At 1:30 they were off Paraso Bay. Now the destroyer *Taylor* turned inshore and, using both lead lines and

The USS Dent, *one of the two destroyer-transports assigned to rescue the* Helena *survivors hidden on* Vella Lavella. (National Archives)

sophisticated depth-finding equipment, guided the *Dent* and *Waters* into the bay toward the mouth of the Paraso River. The other three destroyers formed the inner screen, patrolling the bay's entrance. Ten miles out, Captain McInerney's four destroyers took their station as the outer screen. A Japanese patrol plane spotted them, dropped a bomb or two, but apparently did not call in support. Their luck was holding.

On the bridge of the *Dent* Commander John D. Sweeney peered into the darkness, trying to follow the movements of the *Taylor* just ahead. He was commodore of the two APDs and gloried in the code name PLUTO. The *Taylor,* with deeper draft, finally reached a point where she couldn't go any farther. She backed away, signaling over the TBS radio, "PLUTO, you're on your own. Good luck."

The *Dent* and *Waters* crept on a few yards, now so close to land that the shadows of the trees hid the shoreline. Suddenly a signalman called, "Captain, there's a light."

Sweeney rushed to the wing of the bridge, looked down, saw a canoe coming out of the dark. A voice in the canoe called, "I am the Gunner of the *Helena!*"

When he called the words out, Bill Dupay still wasn't sure whether these darkened ships creeping into the bay were American or Japanese; he simply decided to take a chance. It worked out, and a minute later the canoe was alongside the *Dent*. He and Josselyn clambered aboard.

The *Dent* and *Waters* now hove to and lowered their Higgins boats. Each ship contributed three, and with Josselyn acting as pilot, the little armada chugged through the reefs to the river mouth, where Bausewine's party was waiting.

In a remarkably short time the boats were all back, and Henry Josselyn was escorted to the bridge of the

Dent. Commander Sweeney needed no introduction: He had landed Josselyn a year earlier at Tulagi as a guide with the Marines. To his surprise, the commander now learned that these were less than half the men to be evacuated. No one had briefed him about the second group at Lambu Lambu. He didn't know the coast, and in a few hours it would be daylight.

Don't worry, said Josselyn, he'd guide the ships there. Sweeney advised the screen, and the rescue fleet got under way. Toward 4 A.M. the *Dent* poked into Lambu Lambu Cove, and the bridge quickly spotted a light off the starboard bow flashing the *Helena*'s number, "50." The *Dent* flashed a long red light back and cut her engines.

Warren Boles never did see the answering red flash. He only knew that these ships were coming from the wrong direction. Nobody had told him that the rescue fleet was going to Paraso first, and he was expecting ships from the southeast, up from Tulagi.

He flashed his signal anyhow, but when he failed to catch the answer, he really began to worry. He wondered whether to turn tail and run for shore, but finally decided the die was cast—rescue was now or never—so he kept flashing his light.

Pretty soon he heard the sound of small-craft engines . . . then in the darkness a British voice sang out, "Hello there." It was Henry Josselyn in the first of the *Dent*'s Higgins boats. Skippered by Ensign Rollo H. Nuckles, the boat drew alongside the canoe, and Boles climbed aboard. It wasn't easy: The ten-day ordeal had taken its toll. He had a gimpy leg, and a gash on his left arm was so badly infected it hung useless by his side.

With Boles acting as pilot, the landing craft continued on, traveling in a column of six. Somehow he found the mouth of the river, and then began the difficult business of navigating the various bends and turns. The live channel markers were still in place, but it was debatable whether they were more a help than a hazard.

At last the boats reached the rickety dock where Chew's group was waiting. The pier could handle only one boat at a time; so they took turns going in. As each was loaded, Jack Chew stood at the edge of the water, counting the men as they scrambled aboard. Nearly every one paused to shake hands with some native, and many of the men handed out all the cash they had. Far more useful on Vella Lavella was the sheath knife that Chesleigh Grunstad gave a native he had grown to know and like.

Through it all the men kept as quiet as possible. They were always half-convinced that the Japanese lay just out of sight, waiting to pounce. A Chinese baby started to cry, and to Ted Blahnik, "It was the loudest noise I ever heard."

Soon the crowd on the dock thinned down to a few dozen, and Major Kelly began to pull in his Irregulars. As they prepared to board the last boat, one by one they handed their assorted rifles and pistols to the native scouts. Kelly watched the transfer of the last weapon; then he too stepped aboard.

As senior officer, Chew was the last to go. He conveyed his thanks to Josselyn, whom he had just met, and turned to Silvester. It was hard to find the right words, and maybe a small gesture conveyed his gratitude better than anything he could say. Jack Chew, the most superstitious of old sailors, handed Bish his most prized talisman of all, his lucky silver dollar.

The Higgins boats got under way; Silvester and Josselyn gave a final wave and faded into the bush.

On the *Dent* and *Waters* the rescued men swarmed below to rediscover a host of basic pleasures—good chow, cigarettes, hot water, soap, clean underwear. In

Helena *survivors, rescued from Vella Lavella, line up for new clothes and gear at Tulagi.* (National Archives)

the wardroom of the *Waters* Jack Chew downed five bowls of pea soup, then enjoyed the luxury of a real shower. He was too excited to sleep; so he wandered into the wardroom again and talked the rest of the night away. He had been cut off from the world for ten days, and like the other survivors, he wanted to know how the war was going.

The Munda campaign, it seemed, had bogged down. The Japanese still held the airstrip; the U.S. infantry at Zanana were stalled in the jungle. The Tokyo Express was putting reinforcements ashore on Kolombangara but took a pounding on the 12th. Ainsworth had losses too—destroyer *Gwin* sunk, cruisers *Honolulu, St. Louis,* and *Leander* damaged. Biggest news involved the top command: General Hester was out, General Griswold had taken over on New Georgia. Kelly Turner had been relieved by Rear Admiral "Ping" Wilkinson.

The wardroom of the *Waters* wasn't privy to the information, but Army morale was near collapse on New Georgia, requiring the shake-up there. Turner, on the other hand, was going on to greater things—command of all amphibious operations in the Central Pacific.

Daylight, July 16, and American fighters from Segi appeared overhead. The rescue fleet pounded on toward Tulagi, out of danger at last. On the bridge of the *Dent* Commander Sweeney wondered what sort of men did the things Henry Josselyn did. Their parting gave him little clue. Sweeney had offered to take Josselyn to Tulagi, but he said no, there was still work to be done. Then Sweeney offered him some cases of canned food, but Josselyn again said no: The natives might leave the empty cans around, giving away his position.

"Can't we do anything for you?" Sweeney asked.

"Yes," said Josselyn, "I could use a couple of pairs of black socks, some Worcestershire sauce, and a few bars of candy."

13

THE OTHER KENNEDY

Jack Kissane, a young code clerk with the Coastwatching organization, felt utterly heartsick. On temporary duty at Ken, August 2, he overheard some American pilots talking about a search mission they were scheduled to fly. To his stunned dismay, they said that "Kennedy" was missing.

Kennedy! The legendary Coastwatcher of Segi. Donald Kennedy had been living on borrowed time for over a year, waging his private war against the Japanese; so it was probably inevitable that fate would catch up with him in the end. Still, it was hard to swallow. Jack Kissane's immediate impulse was to drop everything and volunteer for any rescue effort being planned.

Then to his immense relief, he learned it wasn't Donald Kennedy at all. It was some other Kennedy they were talking about—a U.S. PT-boat skipper, missing with his crew in Blackett Strait.

The other Kennedy had a prominence of his own. As the son of a conspicuous millionaire and former U.S. Ambassador to Britain, Lieutenant (j.g.) John F. Kennedy was automatically a minor celebrity. He had also parlayed a lively intellect with a knack for making the most of his contacts to write a well-received book. *Why England Slept*—developed from his senior thesis at Harvard—was a most unusual achievement for a young man just out of college.

Athletic enough to have been on the Harvard freshman swimming team and practically raised on small boats at his family's summer place on Cape Cod, Kennedy had been drawn—like many of his background— to the Navy's glamorous PT-boat program. He was predictably good at it; but beyond his skill and his easy Ivy League charm, he had an earthiness—born of a rough-and-tumble Irish heritage—that made him both tough and warm at the same time. He was highly regarded by officers and enlisted men alike in the small world of the PTs.

The 26-year-old Kennedy arrived in the Solomons early in April 1943 and on the 25th was given command of *PT 109,* one of a number of boats based at Tulagi. As the fighting moved westward, the squadron was shifted first to the Russells, and then in mid-July to Rendova Harbor. Here its job was to seal off Blackett Strait as an avenue for bringing Japanese reinforcements to Vila and Munda. Almost every night the PTs slipped through Ferguson Passage and poked around the strait. There were occasional encounters with barges but, for the first two weeks, no heavy stuff.

Then on August 1 an urgent message arrived from Guadalcanal. Based on radio intercepts, it predicted that the Tokyo Express might be running that night. It ordered Rendova to put a maximum number of PTs in Blackett Strait and warned that the Japanese air command was out to get the squadron.

The warning proved true all too soon. Early in the afternoon 18 bombers barreled in, sinking two of the

Lieutenant (j.g.) John F. Kennedy at the wheel of PT 109.
(John F. Kennedy Library)

boats and damaging another. If the radio intelligence
was as accurate about everything else, it should be a
busy night.

At 6:30 P.M. fifteen PTs—all that were still in shape
—churned out of Rendova Harbor and headed west for
Ferguson Passage and Blackett Strait. Under the plan
worked out by the squadron CO, Lieutenant Commander Thomas G. Warfield, they were deployed in
four divisions to block the southern and western approaches to the strait. Kennedy's *PT 109* was one of
four boats in Lieutenant Henry Brantingham's Division
B, operating all the way to the west.

By 9:30 Division B was on station, and the long wait
began. Lieutenant Brantingham's *PT 159* had radar, but

the other boats had to depend on eyes and ears, and these were no help tonight. The sky was cloudy, and the men could see no distance at all. Nor could they hear anything; there was strict radio silence.

On *PT 109* Kennedy stood at the wheel, occasionally chatting with Radioman 2/c John E. Maguire in the cockpit beside him. Machinist's Mate Patrick McMahon was in the engine room, but the engines were just idling and there was little to do. The rest of the twelve-man crew were standing by on deck, watching and waiting.

On the bow was a thirteenth man—an extra hand. Ensign George Ross was temporarily without a boat and had asked Kennedy if he could come along for the ride. Kennedy said sure: He could take charge of a 37-mm. antitank gun mounted as an experiment on the foredeck. Now Ross was standing by his weapon—one more pair of eyes peering into the black, empty night.

Shortly after midnight Lieutenant Brantingham's radar showed four blips approaching from the west, hugging the Kolombangara shore. They looked small, and Brantingham guessed they were probably barges. He turned to attack but apparently didn't break radio silence to report either the contact or his own movements. He closed to 1800 yards, planning to strafe, but the Japanese shot first. A withering blast of gunfire dispelled any notion that he was dealing with mere barges.

The four Japanese destroyers didn't budge from their course. Their mission was far too important to go off chasing some pesky torpedo boat. They were on their way from Rabaul to Vila with 900 troops and 120 tons of supplies for the hard-pressed defenders of Munda.

Three of the destroyers carried the troops and supplies. The fourth—Commander Kohai Hanami's *Amagiri*—herded them along, sniffing for trouble like an industrious sheep dog.

Entering Blackett Strait around midnight, they were now on the most dangerous leg of the trip. To port was the towering cone of Kolombangara Island; to starboard, Gizo and a string of small, outlying islets. At its narrowest the strait was no more than five miles wide, and there were plenty of reefs on both sides. Twelve knots would have been a safe speed; the destroyers were doing 30. It was all-important to reach Vila, unload, and get out again before daylight and the American bombers came.

Fending off Brantingham with a well-placed salvo, the destroyers hurried on. Then they brushed aside a few other PTs, also in the way. By 12:30 A.M. they were at Vila, surrounded by a swarm of barges and lighters. While the other ships unloaded, the *Amagiri* cruised restlessly back and forth, guarding the anchorage from attack.

To the west, all was confusion. After discovering his mistake in identification, Lieutenant Brantingham fired two torpedoes and cleared out. So did *PT 157,* operating with him. In the other divisions down the line, several other PTs also sighted the Express, fired their torpedoes, and ran. None of them got a hit. None of them radioed a contact report, or if they did, the unengaged boats never heard it.

On *PT 109* Jack Kennedy didn't know that Brantingham had attacked and pulled out . . . didn't know that some of the other PTs were also in action . . . didn't even know there were Japanese destroyers around. From the flashes, he did know there was gunfire to the east, but it seemed to be inshore, and he figured some enemy coastal battery had found the PTs.

Hard by was the other boat in his section, *PT 162,* but her skipper Lieutenant (j.g.) John R. Lowrey was equally in the dark. As the two boats idled uncertainly in the strait, they were joined by Lieutenant (j.g.) Philip

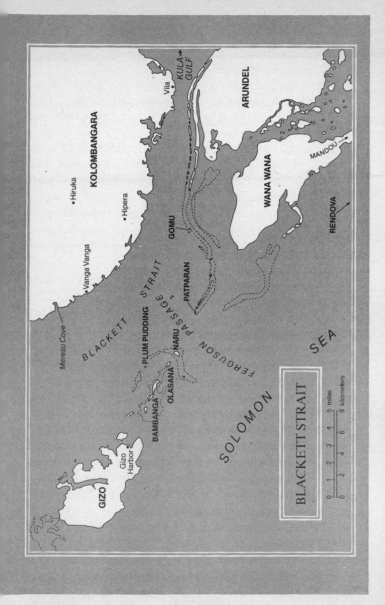

A. Potter's *PT 169* from Division A. He had lost touch
with his group too, and didn't know any more than
Kennedy or Lowrey did.

The three boats tried to get instructions from Rendova but were simply told to resume patrolling; so they
continued on station, hoping they'd run across someone
they knew.

Sixteen miles to the east the three Japanese destroyers
finished unloading their troops and supplies at Vila. The
flagship flashed "Let's go home," and about 1:30 A.M.
they all started back. The signal was relayed to *Amagiri,*
still covering the anchorage, and Commander Hanami
swung his ship around too. Putting on an extra burst of
speed to catch up with the others, he headed northwest
up the strait.

The three PTs continued blindly patrolling—no sign
of either friend or foe. As they moved slowly west, Kennedy suggested that they reverse course: They'd have
more chance of finding the other boats if they went back
to where they started from. This seemed sensible; so
about 2 A.M. the PTs swung around. With Kennedy now
in the lead, they headed southeast down the strait.

"Ship at two o'clock," Motor Machinist's Mate 2/c
Harold Marney sang out from the forward gun turret.
At the 37-mm. gun Ensign Ross saw it too and pointed
off the starboard bow. Kennedy looked and made out a
shape even blacker than the night. For an instant he
thought he had at last found one of the other PTs, but
quickly changed his mind. No PT-boat ever looked like
this—a big curved prow, growing every second, kicking
up tremendous phosphorescent bow wave as it hurtled
toward him.

On the *Amagiri* Commander Hanami decided to ram.
When sighted, the PT was already too close for his
guns. He ordered his coxswain to turn the wheel hard

to starboard, and the destroyer veered toward the target.

Kennedy had no such maneuverability. He was running on only one engine, holding down his wake to avoid detection from the air. Now, as he desperately spun his wheel, *PT 109* responded only sluggishly. On the bow George Ross slammed a shell at the 37-mm. gun, but the breech was closed.

Then the crash. *Amagiri* piled into the starboard side, slicing *PT 109* in two just behind the cockpit. Hurled to the deck by the impact, Kennedy looked up at the steel hull of the destroyer sweeping by. A roar of flame from one of his fuel tanks gave him a brief but unforgettable glimpse of a sleek, raked funnel.

On the *Amagiri* some gunner got off two parting shots —both misses—at the blazing debris as the destroyer raced on into the night. Watching in horror from one of the nearby PTs, the skipper buried his face in his hands, sobbing, "My God, my God!"

The men on the ships in Blackett Strait were not the only ones to see the flames roar up as the *Amagiri* sliced through *PT 109*. On Kolombangara, about three miles away, two Coastwatchers—Sub-Lieutenant Arthur Reginald Evans of the Royal Australian Navy and his assistant, Corporal Benjamin Franklin Nash, U.S. Army —were sitting on a hillside about 1400 feet up, trying to pick out Japanese shipping. Suddenly their attention was caught by the burst of fire spreading over the water.

Evans focused his glasses to see what he could make of it. Some vessel seemed to be burning, but whose or what kind remained a mystery. Nor could Nash figure it out. The night had been a strange one—occasional gun flashes, but never the sustained fire of a real sea fight. Possibly some stray Japanese barge had been caught and was burning.

Coastwatcher Reg Evans, who saw a strange burst of flame on the water from his post on Kolombangara. (Courtesy Reg Evans)

Reg Evans had been Coastwatching on Kolombangara for more than four months now, and not a day of it was easy. A thin, pleasant man in his late thirties, he came from Sydney and had been a Burns Philp accountant and purser on an interisland steamer in peacetime. He knew the Solomons well, but his experience lay on the water and in the office rather than in the bush.

Serving in the Australian Army during the early years of the war, he managed to transfer to his first love, the Navy, in October 1942 and was soon snapped up by Eric Feldt. He was working as a general assistant at KEN in February 1943, when evidence piled up that the Japanese were building an airstrip at Vila Plantation on the south shore of Kolombangara in support of their larger base at Munda. Neither Donald Kennedy nor Dick Horton was near enough to cover the new strip adequately; so Hugh Mackenzie decided to set up a separate station under Evans.

On March 21 he landed alone at Kuji on the southern coast of Kolombangara after a long and dangerous trip from Segi. His canoe passed so close to Munda that he could hear Japanese trucks working on the airfield.

His arrival was no surprise to the local natives—Dick Horton had come over from Rendova and prepared the way. Now a leaf house was waiting for him at Hiruka, a hilltop overlooking the Japanese position, and a team of native scouts was recruited and ready to work.

Just as well. It was hard enough to be an office worker in the bush, but to be one on Kolombangara was especially trying. There were less than 500 natives on the island, and they all lived on a corner of the southwest coast. They had never ventured into the interior—it was as strange to them as to Evans. Nor had any of them ever worked on the plantations—they didn't even know what a truck looked like. They had seen steamers but were very vague about warships and certainly couldn't identify any types.

A single exception to all this was Rovu, the hereditary chief of the settlement at Vanga Vanga village. He was sixty years old and couldn't speak even pidgin English, but he did know every rock on Kolombangara. Though now a venerable elder by island standards, he had to lead every patrol, just to get the others back home again.

Evans cheerfully dived into his assignment anyhow. Reaching Hiruka about noon on March 22, he unpacked the teleradio, strung the aerial, and contacted KEN. For his own call letters he chose GSE—his wife's initials.

He had no trouble recruiting natives to serve as sentries and lookouts, and he soon had a good network of scouts on the islands that fringed the strait. Scouting on Kolombangara itself remained a problem; the natives knew nothing about firearms, and he never dared trust them with anything more sophisticated than knives and axes.

Evans also found his tree-top lookout less than perfect, and on April 15 he moved his camp to a nearby hill he called "Square Top." This gave him a wider view of the Vila area, and was slightly nearer Blackett Strait.

He scored his first triumph on the morning of May 8. At 3 A.M. four Japanese destroyers, racing down Blackett Strait with supplies for Vila, piled into a minefield just laid by an American task group. One sank almost at once; two others lay damaged and burning. The fourth was still picking up survivors when Evans spotted them at daybreak. He fired off a message to KEN, and nineteen SBDs soon appeared. They polished off the two cripples, while three fighters worked over the only destroyer to escape.

On this same day, KEN sent Evans an assistant. Actually, Evans himself felt perfectly happy as matters stood, but there were considerations he didn't know about. The buildup for TOENAILS—the operation to seize Munda—was in full swing, and Kolombangara would clearly be in the center of things. Enemy barge traffic would increase as the Japanese pumped reinforcements into Vila, and every target must be reported. Given the difficulties of operating on Kolombangara, a second man should allow more flexibility, more opportunity for patrol work. There was, in short, nothing unusual about the idea of sending Evans an assistant; what was unusual was the choice.

Corporal Frank Nash grew up on the family cattle ranch near Canon City, Colorado. It was life in the wide open spaces, a throwback to an earlier frontier America. Physically, he was big and rangy—perfect for a Hollywood western. By temperament, he was quiet, conservative, independent, and intensely idealistic.

When war came, he didn't wait to be drafted; he volunteered. When it looked as though his signal outfit would be stuck in California, he told his commanding officer he wanted to go overseas, and if necessary he'd get transferred to the infantry. Since it was unheard of for anyone to *request* infantry duty, the CO decided he must mean it, and by the end of 1942 Nash was in the New Hebrides.

In January 1943 his outfit, the 410th Aviation Signal Company, was ordered to Guadalcanal to help install and operate a new control tower going up at Henderson Field. While stationed there, Nash began hearing the pilots talk about the Coastwatchers. It sounded like interesting duty.

Then in April he heard the 410th was going back to the New Hebrides for rear area work. "This was not my idea of the war," as he later put it, and one day he dropped by KEN to ask whether they could use him.

Hugh Mackenzie could always use another hand—especially a good radio operator. The 410th didn't seem to care; so the papers were filed for a formal transfer. It would, of course, take months to clear a U.S. Army corporal for duty in the Australian Navy. Meanwhile, Nash "sort of deserted."

He soon proved far more than a good radio operator. An enterprising non-com is a godsend in any military organization, and this was particularly true at KEN. Supplies were short on Guadalcanal, and as the only non-U.S. outfit at Henderson, the Coastwatchers were always at the end of the line for everything. They wallowed in praise from the admirals, but getting a roll of toilet paper was hell.

Frank Nash changed all that. Borrowing here and there, authorizing his own requisition slips, moving deftly both in and out of channels, he opened the pipelines. KEN soon enjoyed a steady flow of light bulbs, stationery, office equipment, everything.

When it was decided to send Evans an assistant, Nash immediately volunteered. Mackenzie thought this an absurd idea—what did a U.S. corporal know about the bush? Lieutenant Forbes Robertson, Mackenzie's chief assistant, thought differently. A resourceful man was what counted, and Nash was certainly that. He could learn about the bush when he got there. In the end, Mackenzie gave in—one of his last decisions before being relieved by Commander Pryce-Jones.

May 8, and Nash was on his way. First, a pause at Segi for one of Donald Kennedy's patented briefings . . . then by canoe to Kolombangara. He arrived on the 17th —essentially still a Colorado cattleman loose in the tropical jungle, but ready and eager to learn everything he could from Reg Evans. As it worked out, neither was really at home in the bush, and in the end they lived mostly off rations and Spam. But Forbes Robertson was right: Resourcefulness was what counted, and both men had plenty of that.

Blackett Strait was "heating up" now—Japanese barges down every night . . . planes coming and going . . . an occasional destroyer, as reinforcements poured into Vila and Munda. GSE radioed a steady flow of sightings, but Evans worried that they weren't catching everything. On June 14 he again moved the camp— this time down to Hipera, only a mile from the coast and well below the cloud line.

With the launching of TOENAILS on June 30, Kolombangara became hotter than ever. The Japanese began using Vila as their main staging point for ferrying troops to New Georgia. Again Evans worried that they weren't seeing enough, and on August 1 he asked KEN for permission to shift GSE to Gomu, a small island between Kolombangara and Wana Wana. This would be more central, and local communications would be better too. Canoes could come and go, day or night.

Nash would remain on Kolombangara, in touch by walkie-talkie.

Evans was still waiting for an answer that night, when he and Nash spotted the blaze that marked the pyre of *PT 109*. At daybreak they could see something floating in the water where the fire had been, but even with their 15-power telescope they couldn't make out what it was. In reporting to KEN, Evans suggested it was "possibly" the remains of a barge. Certainly it didn't occur to him that it might be the shattered wreckage of a PT-boat.

Nor did it occur to KEN, or to the advanced Coast-watcher base PWD on Rendova. Apparently overlooking any possible connection, at 9:30 A.M. PWD radioed Evans:

PT BOAT ONE OWE NINE LOST IN ACTION IN BLACKETT STRAIT TWO MILES SW MERESU COVE. CREW OF TWELVE. REQUEST ANY INFORMATION.

Evans immediately moved into action: All natives were to watch for survivors; the scouts would start searching the coast. Nobody found anything, except an extraordinary number of spent American torpedoes washed up on the shore. As for the mysterious object floating in the strait, it was too far off to be investigated by canoe in daylight. At 11:15 he radioed PWD no luck so far. He added that the "object" was still in sight.

At 1:12 P.M. KEN confirmed the loss and position of *PT 109*, and at 4:45 Evans reported he was still searching, and that the "object" was now drifting south-east. Optimistically, he predicted that his Gizo scouts would pick up any survivors who landed on the other side of the strait.

A reasonable assumption until now, but during the night of August 2 some 200–300 Japanese troops landed on the north coast of Gizo. This was a major threat to the network and must be reported immediately. On the morning of the 3rd scouts Biuku Gasa and Eroni Kumana took a canoe and hurried down Blackett Strait to alert Evans, still on Kolombangara awaiting permission to move.

During the morning Evans was again in touch with PWD and KEN about the missing *PT 109*. All searches were "negative"; no sign of survivors anywhere. Nor did he have any better news on the 4th after seeing Biuku and Eroni. At 10:25 A.M. he regretfully radioed PWD:

NO SURVIVORS FOUND AT GIZO.

By now KEN was very interested in the "object" that Evans had earlier reported floating in Blackett Strait. It had finally occurred to somebody that there must be a connection with *PT 109*. At 11:30 KEN radioed:

WHERE WAS HULK OF BURNING PT BOAT LAST SEEN? IF STILL FLOATING, REQUEST COMPLETE DESTRUCTION. ALSO REQUEST INFORMATION IF ANY JAPS WERE ON OR NEAR FLOATING HULK.

Reg Evans had the precise mind of a good accountant, and wasn't that sure the "object" was part of *PT 109*. He radioed back:

CANNOT CONFIRM OBJECT SEEN WAS FLOATING HULK OF PT. OBJECT LAST SEEN APPROX TWO MILES NE BAMBANGA DRIFTING SOUTH. NOT SEEN SINCE PM SECOND.

But August 5, the "object" was sighted again, now in Ferguson Passage drifting south. It ended up on a reef, where scouts later identified it as the "forepart of a small vessel."

Meanwhile Biuku and Eroni had left Evans and were paddling back to Gizo. Breaking their trip at Wana Wana, they headed across Ferguson Passage on the morning of August 5. As they approached Naru, first island on the other side of the passage, they spotted the wreckage of a Japanese boat, stranded a few hundred yards offshore. They anchored their canoe and waded over to investigate.

The pickings were slim. Nothing worth scavenging except a couple of rifles. Then, as they climbed out of the boat, they were horrified to see two men staring at them from the beach. Had the Japanese caught them looting? Biuku and Eroni didn't wait to find out. Scrambling into their canoe, they paddled off as fast as possible.

Were these two native scouts for the Japanese? Lieutenant Kennedy and Ensign Ross weren't taking any chances. They bolted into the bush. Four harrowing days had passed since the Japanese destroyer had sliced through *PT 109,* and it looked like one more narrow escape.

"This is how it feels to be killed," had been Kennedy's first thought as the crash hurled him against the side of his boat. But the severed bow miraculously stayed afloat, and he gradually collected the survivors onto the hulk. There were eleven altogether—only two lost—another miracle.

All morning, August 2, the men perched on the listing bow, waiting for some PBY or PT-boat to pick them up. Nobody came. Around 10:00 the bow turned turtle, and Kennedy realized they couldn't stay with it much longer. If it didn't sink, the current could easily deliver them to the Japanese. Scanning the horizon, he decided they should swim to one of the tiny islets that stretched southeast from Gizo. He chose one called

Plum Pudding, which lay about three and a half miles away. It seemed just the right size—big enough to hide on, yet too small for a Japanese outpost.

They set out about 1:00 P.M., with most of the men hanging onto an eight-foot plank from the wreck. Pat McMahon, however, was so badly burned he couldn't swim. Seeing this, Kennedy took the strap of McMahon's life jacket in his teeth, and using the breast stroke, he towed the injured man all the way to the island—a four-hour swim.

Nor was he through for the day. Taking a battle lantern salvaged from the boat, he swam out into Ferguson Passage that evening, hoping to flag down one of the PTs as they entered Blackett Strait on their regular patrol. It was a wasted night. Abandoning their usual practice, the boats took a different route to the north.

Next night, the 3rd, Ensign Ross pinch-hit for the skipper. Taking the lantern, he too swam into Ferguson Passage, but with no better luck. Again, the PTs used the northern route.

On the 4th Kennedy shifted every one from Plum Pudding to Olasana Island, about a mile and three-quarters to the southeast. It was a little larger, had more coconuts, and lay closer to Ferguson Passage. As before, he towed the badly burned McMahon with his teeth.

The swim was exhausting, and this night nobody went out with the lantern. Inevitably the PTs switched back to Ferguson Passage.

On the morning of the 5th Kennedy decided to explore Naru Island, a half mile to the east and the last bit of land before the passage. He recruited Ross, and they swam over together, about the same time that Biuku and Eroni were approaching by canoe from the opposite direction. Starting down the beach, Kennedy and Ross noticed the same Japanese wreck that attracted

Plum Pudding (center), the tiny islet where the survivors of PT 109 first landed. Photographed from Gizo Harbor, in Japanese hands at the time. (Author's collection)

the two natives, and they came upon a crate that must have been part of its cargo. To their delight, it was full of crackers and hard candy.

Continuing on, they made an even more exciting discovery: a dugout canoe with a can of water hidden in the bushes. Unknowingly, they had stumbled across a secret cache planted for emergencies by one of Evans's scouts.

They paused for a moment of rest, then went back to the beach. To their consternation, they now spotted Biuku and Eroni scavenging the wreck. The two Americans leapt into the bushes without noticing that the natives—equally alarmed—were scrambling back to their canoe.

After a while Kennedy and Ross cautiously returned to the beach. No one was in sight. The place seemed safe; so that evening Kennedy took the dugout and again ventured into Ferguson Passage. Again, no PTs appeared, and at 9:00 P.M. he returned to Naru, picked up the candy, crackers, and water and paddled back to the rest of the group on Olasana. For lack of room in the canoe, Ross remained on Naru the whole night.

Reaching Olasana, Kennedy was surprised to find two new additions to his party. Biuku and Eroni had landed there after fleeing Naru and encountered the other *PT 109* survivors. The two natives had at first been suspicious, but their fears were allayed when Kennedy's executive officer, Ensign Leonard J. Thom, pointed to the sky and shouted, "White star! White star!"

That they both understood. The white star marking on U.S. planes was something every Coastwatcher drilled his scouts to know and recognize. It meant American . . . friend . . . some one to be helped.

Reassured, they joined the castaways and warned them of the two "Japanese" they had spotted on Naru. Nobody connected this sighting with Kennedy and Ross; so the relief was enormous when the skipper himself casually reappeared with his crate of sweets.

On the morning of the 6th Biuku and Eroni paddled Kennedy back to Naru for another look around. On the way over they gathered in Ross, who was now swimming "home" to Olasana. Once on Naru, the natives showed the two Americans another secret cache, complete with a two-man canoe. It would come in handy later, but Kennedy's immediate attention was focused far to the southeast. There he could see Rendova Peak, pin-pointing the location of the PT base. It was 38 miles away, but unlike Ferguson Passage, it meant certain help.

Pointing to it, he somehow conveyed the idea that he wanted Biuku and Eroni to paddle there for assistance. With the same thought in mind, Ensign Thom had already scribbled a message on an old Burns Philp invoice found lying on Olasana. It briefly described the group's location and condition, spelling out recognition signals for any rescue effort. Now Kennedy added a message of his own, showing a bit of the flair that seemed to touch everything he did. Taking a piece of coconut shell, he used his sheath knife to scratch out these words:

> NAURO ISL
> NATIVE KNOWS POSIT
> HE CAN PILOT   11 ALIVE NEED
> SMALL BOAT
>
> KENNEDY

Carrying both messages, Biuku and Eroni set out in their canoe. Kennedy and Ross remained on Naru until evening, when they took the new two-man canoe out for one more try in Ferguson Passage. Again no luck; worse, a squall upset the canoe. Tossed against the reef, battered by sea and coral, they barely made it back to Naru.

Meanwhile Biuku and Eroni once again crossed Ferguson Passage and broke their trip at Wana Wana. This time they contacted Ben Kevu, Reg Evans's principal scout in the area. Formerly the district officer's clerk at Gizo, Kevu spoke excellent English and served as a perfect bridge between Evans on Kolombangara and about a dozen scouts operating in Wana Wana Lagoon. Constantly on the go, he moved back and forth among the Japanese barges with no apparent difficulty.

How he managed to appear so inconspicuous—or so innocent—was his own trade secret.

Kevu plunged into action. Knowing that Evans had at last received permission to move and would be arriving on Gomu this very evening, he rushed a scout there with the news. Biuku and Eroni meanwhile continued on toward Rendova.

It was nearly 11 P.M. when Evans reached Gomu and found Ben Kevu's scout waiting for him. Too late to do anything tonight, but first thing on the morning of the 7th he ordered Kevu to collect a good crew, take a load of provisions to the castaways, and bring back the senior officer to help plan the evacuation. Then at 9:20 A.M. he radioed KEN:

ELEVEN SURVIVORS PT BOAT ON GROSS IS* HAVE SENT FOOD AND LETTER ADVISING SENIOR COME HERE WITHOUT DELAY. WARN AVIATION OF CANOES CROSSING FERGUSON.

KEN passed the good news to Rendova, where it was almost immediately confirmed by the arrival of Biuku and Eroni with Thom's message and Kennedy's coconut shell. They had paddled all night, reaching the first American outpost on Roviana Island shortly after daybreak. From here they were rushed by whaleboat and PT to the base in Rendova Harbor.

Headquarters immediately decided to send PTs to pick up the men that night. But where? Kennedy's message mentioned Naru, but on the radio Reg Evans indicated that the survivors might be coming by canoe to Gomu. Evans cleared the air a little by explaining he had been able to man only one canoe. It wasn't back yet, but it certainly couldn't hold everybody. Rendova

---

* Another name for Naru Island.

now decided to send the boats direct to Naru. Evans
would return separately any men brought out by Ben
Kevu.

Meanwhile, with six good paddlers at work, Kevu
made fast time across Ferguson Passage. Finding Kennedy and Ross still on Naru, Kevu walked up and announced with clipped English accent, "I have a letter
for you, Sir." Kennedy stepped forward and opened it
up:

On His Majesty's Service

To Senior Officer, Naru Is.
Friday, 11 p.m. Have just learned of your presence
on Naru Is. and also that two natives have taken
news to Rendova. I strongly advise you return
immediately to here in this canoe and by the time
you arrive here I will be in radio communication
with authorities at Rendova and we can finalize
plans to collect balance of your party.

A R Evans Lt.
RANVR

Will warn aviation of your crossing Ferguson Passage.

Ben Kevu now took Kennedy and Ross back to
Olasana, where they rejoined the rest of the group.
As Kennedy announced the good news, the natives unloaded the canoe and began cooking a feast that seemed
scarcely believable to the famished men of *PT 109*—
yams, C-rations, roast beef hash, potatoes . . . even
cigarettes to top it off. While some of the scouts cooked
the food over Sterno stoves, others built a lean-to for
the badly burned McMahon.

Mid-afternoon, and it was time to go. With Kennedy
now lying in the middle of the canoe covered with palm

Ben Kevu, Reg Evans's scout, who hid Lieutenant Kennedy in his canoe and brought him to Evans on Gomu Island. Photographed at Gizo thirty years later. (Author's collection)

fronds, Ben Kevu steered east, again across Ferguson Passage, heading for Gomu. Once three Japanese planes buzzed them. Kevu gave a friendly wave. Reassured, the planes flew off.

Toward 6 P.M. Reg Evans spotted the canoe and went down to the beach to meet it. At first he saw no passenger; then a smiling young American popped out of the palm fronds and greeted him: "Hello, I'm Kennedy."

"Come to my tent and have a cup of tea," was Evans's polite rejoinder as he introduced himself.

Over their teacups he explained the rescue arrangements as they now stood. The PTs would be at Naru at 10 P.M. for the other survivors; Kennedy himself would go direct from Gomu to Rendova in Ben Kevu's canoe.

Kennedy would have none of it. As a practical matter, he pointed out, he was the only one who knew exactly where the men were. Besides, he wasn't about to leave the rest of his crew and go home by himself. Instead, he should join up with the PTs and guide them in.

Convinced, Evans radioed a new plan at 6:50 P.M. Kennedy would now meet the PTs at 10 P.M. near a tiny islet called Patparan on the eastern side of Ferguson Passage. Recognition signal: four shots from the boats, which he would answer with another four. He'd then come aboard and pilot the PTs the rest of the way.

Around 8 P.M. Kennedy said good-bye, climbed back into Ben Kevu's canoe, and headed for the rendezvous at Patparan. There, another of those long waits began. The boats were meant to show at 10:00, but at 11:20 Kennedy watched the moon go down, and there still was no sign of anybody.

At last he heard it—the welcome rumble of PT engines. Then four shots in the night, which he an-

swered with another four. A familiar shape loomed out
of the dark, and Ben Kevu eased his canoe alongside
Lieutenant (j.g.) William F. Liebenow Jr.'s *PT 157*.

"Hey, Jack," hailed a voice from the deck.

"Where the hell you been?" Kennedy asked, memories
of all those hours of treading water in Ferguson Passage
briefly blotting out everything else.

"We've got some food for you," the voice said cheerfully.

"Thanks," said Kennedy, not quite ready to forgive,
"I just had a coconut."

But next moment he was aboard, and all was forgotten in the glow of seeing old friends again. Biuku
and Eroni were on board too, and with their help Kennedy guided the boat through the reef to Olasana. Joy-
ful shouts rang out in the night, and the tattered survivors of *PT 109* were safe at last.

For Reg Evans it was all in the day's work. The
Americans had finally taken Munda on August 5, and
these were exceptionally hectic times in Blackett Strait.
He thought no more about the pleasant young officer
with whom he had spent just two hours. As for Kennedy, it was another of those brief encounters typical
of the war in the South Pacific—so crucial, life itself
hung in the balance; yet so casual that in this case Kennedy never even remembered Evans's name.

14

THE FINAL TRIUMPH

Frank Nash joined the Coastwatchers because rear area duty with the Signal Corps "was not my idea of the war." If a real challenge was what he wanted, he must have been satisfied on August 6, 1943. That day, when Reg Evans moved to Gomu, Nash became the only Allied fighting man on Kolombangara—one U.S. Army corporal against 5000 Japanese.

Fortunately the Japanese were soon too preoccupied with other things to notice him. On August 15, 4600 American troops landed on the southeast corner of Vella Lavella, inaugurating the Allied strategy of leap-frogging over important enemy bases and leaving them to die on the vine. Admiral Kusaka and General Ima-mura hastily began withdrawing their men from the Central Solomons before they could be cut off, and for the next six weeks a steady flow of Japanese barges plied the Slot, evacuating one strongpoint after another —Rekata Bay, Bairoko, Arundel, Gizo, and finally Kolombangara itself.

From his post behind Vila, Nash sent a steady flow

of barge sightings by walkie-talkie to Evans on Gomo, who relayed them to KEN and PWD for use by the air strike command. The fighters and bombers then swept in strafing anything that moved, all too often including friendly villages and sometimes Evans's own scouts and canoes. Evans fired off a stream of angry protests, which did little good. In the end he asked to be recalled and was replaced by Forbes Robertson, an easy-going old-timer. The only abstainer in the entire Coastwatching operation, he was known as "Dry Robbie" to distinguish him from his colleagues "Robbie" and "Wobbie" Robinson.

As the Japanese barge traffic tapered off, Frank Nash came down from the hills of Kolombangara and joined "Dry Robbie" on Gomu. Life turned out to be far different from the old days when he and Evans were a couple of neophytes in the bush, surviving on Spam and C-rations. Forbes Robertson knew everything about Island life—which fruits and fish were the best, how to cook them, and so on. For a few brief weeks Corporal Nash lived the idyllic life of a South Seas island king: superb food, not much work, and very little danger.

Early October, their idyll was over. As the last Japanese pulled out of Kolombangara, Robertson and Nash closed down Gomu and headed for Munda, where the captured Japanese airstrip was already operating "under new management." The Coastwatchers' advance base PWD had shifted here from Rendova, with Lieutenant "Robbie" Robinson in charge.

All attention was now focused on CHERRYBLOSSOM, the next move north. It called for large-scale landings on Bougainville itself, and as a preliminary the Treasury Islands—Mono and Stirling—were to be seized. They lay just south of Bougainville, only seventeen miles from the big Japanese base in the Shortlands, and nobody knew what to expect. In August a Marine

U.S. Army Corporal Frank Nash, the only American Coastwatcher behind enemy lines in the Solomons. (Courtesy Jack Kissane)

reconnaissance team had uncovered only an enemy observation post on Mono, but that was two months ago. What was there now? And what about recent reports that a small party of downed American flyers was hiding out on the island? It was said they'd been there so long they'd gone native.

SOPAC command wanted a new reconnaissance and naturally turned to Lieutenant Robinson. Just as naturally, "Robbie" turned to Frank Nash, back from Gomu and restless for a new assignment.

October 21, a PT-boat roared north carrying Nash and his party. It was one of those highly diverse groups that seemed to work so well together in the South Pacific. Sergeant Bert Cowan was an old New Zealand bushman; Frank Wickham, another member of the enterprising family that dominated the Central Solomons; Sergeant Ilala, a Fijian stalwart in the Islands defense force. Lashed to the deck of the boat was a native canoe.

They arrived in the dead of night off Lua Point on Mono's east coast. Launching the canoe, the four men paddled ashore to an empty beach—no sign of the Japanese or anyone else. They had no idea where they were, but it was no time to start exploring. They hid the canoe under some trees and spent the rest of the night on the beach.

At dawn they discovered to their surprise that they were only a couple of hundred yards from a native village. Friendly or hostile? It was impossible to tell; so Ilala, a man who could blend into any surroundings, slipped into the settlement to find out. He returned to report that the people were friendly.

Nash and the rest now moved into the village; and Frank Wickham, who knew the area best, took over. It turned out that indeed there were Allied flyers on the island—three of them—and a couple of natives went off to bring them down from their hideout.

An hour later the natives were back, explaining that the flyers feared a Japanese trick and wouldn't come without seeing a white man first. Bert Cowan was selected and went off with the natives for a new try.

This time, success. When Cowan reappeared another hour later, he was accompanied by three of the most unmilitary-looking military men ever to represent an armed service. Their uniforms were in shreds, and one man in particular could have passed for Robinson Crusoe. Barefoot, he wore a pair of ragged blue dungarees held together by string, and the remnants of an old civilian shirt.

For Radioman Jesse Scott, Jr., it was the bizarre climax to an unbelievable 148 days. On June 16 he had been shot down into the Slot while flying as radioman on a TBF piloted by Lieutenant (j.g.) Edward M. Peck. Together with the third crewman, Machinist's Mate Stanley W. Tefft, they launched their raft and started paddling for Vella Lavella, where they knew a Coast-watcher was operating.

Wind and current were against them. They were carried north and three days later washed ashore on Stirling Island—small, inhospitable, with high bluffs battered by a pounding surf.

The three men had no idea where they were, but they sensed they must be deep in enemy territory. Scott imagined Japanese marksmen lurking behind every tree and could only wonder, "Why don't they shoot us?" Yet nothing happened, and they soon found a cave that offered a good hiding place for both themselves and the raft.

Next morning, June 20, they cautiously began to explore. It gradually became clear that their little island was uninhabited, but just to the north, only a hundred yards across a channel, lay a much larger island. This was Mono (although they didn't know that yet), and they could see a couple of natives down by the shore. Taking a chance, the Americans hailed them.

On Mono, Roy Riutana and his wife had no idea who these strangers were, but they didn't expect to see any one on Stirling. They had always been taught to report anything unusual to the authorities, and these days the authorities were Japanese. They turned and ran for the nearest command post.

The three flyers ran too, back to their cave to hide again. They stayed there the rest of the day, and the next as well, while a Japanese search party roamed the island looking for them. On the 22nd all seemed quiet again, and Scott ventured out on another reconnaissance. He hadn't gone far, when to his horror he spotted three Japanese soldiers trailing him, about 200 yards behind.

He dived into a large hole in the coral, trying to make himself as small as possible. For the next eight hours he huddled there, his gun at the ready for a last-ditch fight. The Japanese searched all around but never found him.

Late afternoon, they were gone. Scott now emerged from the hole and resumed his reconnaissance, including a swim across the channel for a brief look at Mono. There was no sign of the Japanese on the beach where he landed.

When he reported back to the cave that evening, all agreed that Stirling was now too hot, and the bigger island would be a safer bet. Late that night they launched their raft and began working their way clockwise around Mono, looking for a good place to land. They finally picked Maloaini Bay, a secluded spot on the north coast.

All the next day and night they hid near the shore, listening in terror to the ordinary sounds of the jungle. To a lively imagination the smallest branch, shaken loose by the breeze, sounded like the whole Japanese army. On the 24th they finally decided to try their luck once again with the natives.

Following a jungle trail, they soon came to a group of 30–40 natives gathered together on a beach. The three Americans advanced toward them, hands held out in what they hoped looked like a gesture of peace and friendship. This time the natives didn't run away. On the contrary, several said "Good morning," and one of them, John Havea, had been to the Methodist mission school and spoke passable English.

John immediately grasped the situation. He led them to a cave, gave them some Japanese soap and a razor. Then, to their surprise he offered them "mates." When they looked somewhat nonplussed, he elaborated, "I mean would you like mates for sleeping?"

They thought of all those indoctrination lectures— "never get mixed up with the native girls"—and virtuously declined. It was only after a restless night on the stone floor of the cave that they learned John Havea's English had its limitations. He meant "mats," not "mates."

But they could not have fallen into better hands. The local chief Ninamo organized the village to hide and shelter the stranded Americans. This was no easy task: The Japanese were now sure the castaways were somewhere on Mono, and a search party of 24 men combed the area for them. Lieutenant Peck and his crew were moved five times the first week.

June 30, and life took a turn for the better. This was the day the Americans landed on Rendova, and the Japanese immediately began consolidating their forces in the Central Solomons. All troops were withdrawn from Mono, except a seven-man observation post.

The result was an informal truce, presided over by Ninamo. It was tacitly understood that the natives would leave the observation post alone, while for their part, the Japanese wouldn't look too hard for the flyers.

Both sides thrived on the arrangement. The Japanese proved remarkably amiable, even alerting the natives when their radio indicated air strikes might be expected. Free from immediate danger, the three Americans began to relax.

They were now hidden in the interior of the island, living first at "Peter's house" under a huge rain tree; and later at "Ula's house," where Ula herself presided over their fortunes. Anything but pretty, she was articulate, witty, and immensely shrewd. She spoke no English, but by now Jesse Scott was beginning to catch on to the local dialect. The three castaways relied on her advice.

Gradually they became a sort of tourist attraction, and a steady stream of native visitors turned up with yams, fruit, fish, plus an assortment of old Methodist magazines. When the native women came to call, they invariably wore their best things.

As the days drifted by, Jesse Scott found himself more and more fascinated by island life. He began learning the various native skills, and was immensely pleased when he finally could start a fire by rubbing two sticks together—something he never accomplished as a Boy Scout.

July 22, and the calm of Mono was broken by a commotion offshore. Two Zero float planes were circling low, strafing something in the water. Eventually they flew off, and a lone American aviator appeared, none the worse for his ordeal, paddling a small aluminum raft. He was Second Lieutenant Benjamin King, an Army fighter pilot whose P-38 had been shot down in the Slot six long days ago.

The natives rushed into the water, hauled King ashore, and took him to Ula's house, where he joined the other three flyers. The very next day three more boarders arrived. This time it was another downed TBF pilot, Ensign Joe Mitchell, who paddled ashore with his crewmen Dale Dahl and Chauncey Junior Estep.

The castaways now numbered seven, and for the first time there were enough men to do something about their situation. After a long discussion they decided to ambush the seven Japanese, kill them, and take their launch. With luck, it could carry the seven Americans to safety.

Jesse Scott and one or two of the others were against the plan. They felt it was one thing to capture the Japanese—or kill them in self-defense—but not quite right to go out and "get" them.

The issue was finally settled by the old chief Ninamo. He decreed that there would be no ambush. The war, he said, was no concern of his, but peace *was,* and the present arrangement of seven Japanese and seven

Americans seemed fair. Everyone must keep to his place. Since native cooperation was essential to any decision taken, Ninamo's delicate balance of power prevailed.

But several of the men were determined to do something. Not all of them took to this isolated life as cheerfully as Jesse Scott, who could by this time identify all the plants and build a leaf house as well as the natives. The group now had two TBF rafts, and perhaps by lashing them together they could make the 53-mile paddle to Vella Lavella. Recalling the wind and the current, Scott thought it was hopeless, but on August 20 Peck set out with Mitchell, Estep and Tefft.

Next day they were back. Scott was right. No raft—even two lashed together—could buck the Slot. But the disagreement left its mark. The others couldn't understand how Scott could resign himself so philosophically to this isolated existence. He couldn't understand why they fretted so endlessly, when there were fascinating things to watch, like land-crabs that glowed in the night.

The luxury of such bickering didn't last long. On August 25 fourteen more Japanese arrived from the Shortlands, and on September 10 another 135 landed from Rekata Bay—the first of the forces being driven back by the Allied advance. The days of live-and-let-live were over. The new Japanese were tough customers, in the ugly mood that often goes with a troop withdrawal. They didn't hesitate to steal the natives' property, kill their pigs, and plunder their gardens.

Ninamo turned against them, and when Lieutenant Peck organized a new attempt to escape on September 12, the old chief provided a large war canoe. This time Mitchell, King and Tefft went along. As before, the two TBF rafts were lashed together, but the canoe ferried the party well out to sea, giving them a shorter and presumably easier paddle. Transferring to the raft, they still had a rough time with the wind and the current but were luckily sighted by a passing PBY. It gave them a lift the rest of the way to Vella.

Here they reported that Scott, Estep and Dahl were still on Mono, and a search plane flew over the following night, signal light blinking| No answering flashes were seen, and headquarters decided the remaining three men had probably been captured.

Actually, they were as free as ever. They had seen the search plane signaling and tried to blink back, but as so often happened in these night-time contacts, their answering light was missed.

How long they could stay free was another matter. Mono was now swarming with Japanese, and unlike the old days, the new troops were roaming and pillaging all over the island. On September 22 the three flyers regretfully left Ula and moved to "Reuben's house," much deeper in the jungle.

Reuben was an expert native bushman—just the person to be in immediate charge—and he had plenty of help. By now, protecting the Americans had become a way of life on Mono. The whole population was in on the secret. Young boys like 15-year-old John Lotikena ran in a steady flow of fruit and vegetables. A team of elderly "Marys" did the cooking and laundry. Older men took turns scouting the trails and guarding the hideaway.

The Americans nearly did themselves in on October 4. That night they heard a launch and decided for some reason that it was an Allied reconnaissance party. They blinked their signal light—and discovered too late that the launch was Japanese. The signals were seen, and next morning enemy search parties converged on the area. Again the natives saved the day. They solemnly swore that they were the ones who had been flashing the light. Just hunting crabs, they said.

Yet the net was drawing tighter, and when 100 more Japanese landed at Falamai village on October 21, it seemed impossible that the flyers could last much longer. But this day Frank Nash and his party landed too, and on the following morning the three castaways found their long wait was over. By now Jesse Scott could pick up things with his toes and scamper up trees like a native.

That evening there were heartfelt good-byes, and the three flyers shoved off with Frank Nash for a rendezvous with the PT-boat. Life on Mono returned to normal, but the natives would long remember the days when the whole island turned "Coastwatcher" and hid the American airmen. As one of the natives observed with pride, "It was the only time in history that the thousand people on Mono ever managed to keep a secret."

The whole face of the war had changed during the 148 days of Jesse Scott's enforced but not unpleasant confinement. When his TBF splashed on June 16, the Japanese still controlled all the Solomons north and west of the Russells. That very day, in fact, the Imperial "sea eagles" staged a 120-plane raid on Henderson Field; an enemy patrol trapped Lieutenant Bedkober on Bougainville; and Major Hara was about to start after Donald Kennedy on Segi.

Now, four months later, Guadalcanal was a quiet rear area; New Georgia, Isabel, Kolombangara, Gizo, and Vella Lavella had all been taken by the Allies; the Tokyo Express was no more. Most of the Coastwatchers had turned into welcoming committees or liaison officers, or joined the ranks of the military unemployed.

But not Nick Waddell and Carden Seton. Choiseul lay on the road back from Kolombangara, and the west coast was crawling with Japanese. Station DEL, at 1200 feet on Mount Alikana, offered an excellent view of the shore, and day after day the Coastwatchers radioed their barge sightings, then enjoyed a grandstand seat as the fighters and bombers swept in for the kill.

Sometimes the Japanese ran out of barges, and then the troops themselves could be seen painfully plodding northwest toward the Shortlands or Bougainville. They offered an easy target, and at one point Seton begged KEN to let him organize some guerrillas and finish them off. He was sternly reminded that Ferdinand's mission was to watch, not fight. "You will not repeat not be rendering the best service if you undertake offensive action at present except in your own defense."

In September, American reconnaissance teams began arriving to examine the coast, and Seton spent most of the month guiding them around. Typical of the jaunty way he and Waddell ran DEL was a banquet for the Americans, who had brought only K-rations and expected the most Spartan conditions. Seton served them a magnificent repast featuring chicken cooked in coconut milk and served with sweet potatoes.

October, and life took a more serious turn. CHERRYBLOSSOM—the big Allied landing on Bougainville —was scheduled for November 1, and as a preliminary, Marine Lieutenant Colonel Victor H. Krulak's 2nd Parachute Battalion was to be landed on Choiseul on October 27. It was purely a diversion, but an important one. SOPAC hoped that Krulak's 725 leathernecks could raise enough hell to make the Japanese think that Choiseul, not Bougainville, was the main Allied objective.

Around the middle of the month Seton was whisked off the island by PT-boat to brief the Marines and later guide them in. With him he brought two of his best native scouts, Lance Corporals Pitakere and Pitaniu.

Carden Seton, who served as a Coastwatcher on Choiseul for over a year. Photographed in 1943 while playing host to a U.S. reconnaissance team mapping the coast. (Courtesy Harold Hulesberg)

All went as scheduled. Around midnight on October 27 four destroyer-transports hove to off Voza, halfway up the Slot side of Choiseul, and a flotilla of rubber boats ferried Krulak's men ashore. Lance Corporal Pitakere led the way, but it turned out to be an easy job. No Japanese were near, and Nick Waddell had collected a large number of native canoes, scouts, and carriers to help.

It took two days to get squared away; then on October 30, Krulak moved against the enemy barge station at Sangigai. The Marines attacked from both front and rear, with Krulak and Seton leading the interior party that advanced from behind the village. The plan was to catch the Japanese in a cross fire, but they wouldn't cooperate. Spotting the Marines approaching along the coast, they retired inland and ran smack into Krulak's force. Seton was in his element, blazing away with his carbine. At last there was no one to tell him to act like Ferdinand the bull.

The Japanese scattered; Sangigai was taken, and the enemy barge station destroyed. In the midst of it all, Krulak was knocked down by a Japanese bullet. Coming to, one of the colonel's first recollections was of Seton's great red beard a few inches away as he apprehensively leaned over his injured friend.

As it turned out, Krulak was not badly hurt, and the operation rolled on. The Japanese force at Sangigai was largely wiped out, and on November 1 another Marine force attacked an enemy concentration at Choiseul Bay. This was less successful, partly because Seton wasn't along, and none of the Marines could understand the pidgin English spoken by the native scouts.

There were now signs that the Japanese were on to the diversion and were bringing up large forces from southern Choiseul to wipe out Krulak's battalion. Orders came to evacuate, and as the Marine reembarked on the night of November 4, the colonel urged Seton to come along. He politely declined, explaining that Choiseul was his post and that the natives needed him.

Actually, neither Seton nor Waddell thought there was much danger of a Japanese counterattack. To them the risk was more than offset by the blow to native morale that would result from the Marines' departure. The local tribes were far too unsophisticated to appreciate the tactical niceties of a diversion in support of a landing on Bougainville. They were bound to regard the

withdrawal as a sign of Allied weakness, a retreat somehow forced by enemy activity.

So it proved. Hopes raised high were unexpectedly
dashed, and it took all Seton's and Waddell's persuasive-
ness—plus their annihilation of another Japanese patrol
—before the native villagers dared give any further help
to the Allies.

Meanwhile the big show was building up in the
north. The planners at SOPAC picked Cape Torokina
at the northern end of Empress Augusta Bay as the best
place to land on Bougainville. Halfway up the west
coast, it was reasonably removed from the main Japanese
bases on the island, yet only 210 miles from Rabaul—
perfect for a fighter strip. Rear Admiral Theodore S.
Wilkinson was in overall charge; General Vandegrift of
Guadalcanal fame returned to command the ground
forces. L-Day would be November 1. Troops, supplies,
transports began assembling at Espiritu Santo, Efate,
and Koli Point on Guadalcanal.

On October 27—the same day that Krulak landed on
Choiseul—the New Zealand 8th Regiment stormed
ashore on tiny Mono as the first step. The natives
showed the same resourcefulness they had displayed in
hiding the seven American flyers. One of them, Andrew
Kimisi, helped cut the wires between the Japanese observation post at the entrance to Blanche Harbor and
their main base at Falamai.

Seventy-five miles to the north, also on this eventful
27th, the U.S. submarine *Guardfish* surfaced at 6:15
P.M. and crept cautiously toward Cape Torokina. On
board were six Coastwatchers, two Marine officers, and
40 Bougainville natives. All were to be put ashore
to help pave the way for the coming landings. For three
of the Coastwatchers—Jack Keenan, Eric Robinson and
Jack McPhee—it was an exceptionally satisfying moment. Just three months ago they had been driven off

the island by the Japanese. Now they were going back —and on the same submarine that took them out.

Commander Norvell Ward maneuvered the *Guard-fish* to a spot off the mouth of the Laruma River and hove to. Four rubber boats were launched; Keenan, McPhee, Lieutenant J. H. Mackie, and 20 natives slipped into them and shoved off. These men composed what was known as the Southern Party, and would take position in the hills below Empress Augusta Bay. For Lieutenant Mackie too this was something of a home-coming; he had been in charge of the original commando detachment evacuated by the *Gato* last March.

Bub Ward waited for thirty minutes—long enough to make sure Keenan's party had landed safely—then, still on the surface, headed up the coast. He hoped to drop Robinson and the Northern Party off Kuraio Mission but could see Japanese campfires burning there. He continued on until he came to a very familiar place indeed—the beach where he had picked up Read and Robinson in July.

At 12:30 A.M. he stopped his engines about five miles out and let the sub drift in. At three miles two more campfires suddenly blazed on the shore. For Ward it was a ticklish moment. He didn't dare land his passengers until he knew more about those fires, yet he didn't dare hang around here indefinitely.

The situation was finally checked out by Sergeant Yauwika, the old Bougainville scout who was also coming back. Taking one of the rubber boats and four native paddlers, he examined the shore. While the fires were uncomfortably close to the beach, he reported they were far enough apart to land between them.

No more time to lose. A few quick good-byes; and at 3 A.M. the four rubber boats carrying Robinson and the Northern Party vanished into the night. Heading between the fires as Yauwika recommended, they soon reached the shore, which at this point turned out to be no romantic tropical beach, but a thick, nearly impenetrable mangrove swamp.

They plunged in, hoping to squeeze their rafts through the tangle of roots and trees far enough inland to be well clear of those Japanese campfires. Sixty yards and they could go no farther—the growth was just too much. Making the best of it, they sat in the boats the rest of the night waiting for daylight. For the time being they were safe from the enemy but fair game for clouds of mosquitoes.

Dawn on the 28th, they slashed their boats, hid the remnants as best they could, and began cutting their way through the mangroves, wading inland toward hard ground. Finally they cleared the swamp and made camp. They were still only a mile from the beach, but they were too tired to go any farther.

The next three days "Wobbie" Robinson led his party into the mountains along the northwest coast, renewing old contacts in the native villages as he went. At Kiakara he barely missed colliding with a Japanese patrol —60 to 80 strong, judging from their empty cigarette packs.

October 31, the party camped at Toki, another friendly village, but nobody slept much that night. At 12:30 A.M. on the 1st of November they heard the continuous roar of heavy guns to the southeast. The great moment was at hand: CHERRYBLOSSOM had begun.

By H-Hour, 7:30 A.M., the first units were already ashore. A steady stream of landing craft churned in from the fourteen transports anchored in Empress Augusta Bay. They caught the Japanese completely by surprise: There were 2000 enemy troops along this part of the coast, but only 270 men and one 75-mm. gun at Cape Torokina where the troops swarmed in.

Some 7000–8000 Marines and GIs landed in the first wave. With them came Captain R. A. Robinson, moving up from Rendova and Munda with another party of Coastwatchers. In the group was Corporal Frank Nash, who had latched on to one more interesting assignment.

Just behind the beach lay a large swamp running parallel to the shore, but Robbie Robinson quickly spotted a breadfruit tree—meaning firm ground—and led his men to it. Here he found a hut, evacuated by the Japanese so hastily their washing was still on the line. Perfect for headquarters, and he soon had the teleradio assembled and working.

During the afternoon he made contact with Eric Robinson at Toki but had no luck in reaching Keenan and the Southern Party. Their set had been knocked out by torrential rains, and it would be three weeks before they came on the air. Fortunately, "Wobbie's" location was far more important. On November 2 he found an excellent lookout that covered the whole northwest coast all the way to Buka Passage. It was like old times: Anything that moved was promptly reported.

With the Torokina beachhead secure, the battle for the Solomons was really won. Much fighting lay ahead —on Bougainville Paul Mason would become a master of guerrilla tactics—but the leapfrog strategy was working, and soon Rabaul itself would be left to die on the vine.

The war had been turned around, and it all began in the Solomons. If Midway ended forever any chance of a Japanese victory, it was the Allied seizure of Guadalcanal and the recapture of the Solomons that started Tokyo down the road to final defeat. In November 1943, while the staff at KEN enjoyed their evening

The American landings on Bougainville, November 1, 1943. Two Coastwatching teams are already ashore, put in by submarine five days earlier. (National Archives)

games of deck tennis, it was hard to believe that only fifteen months ago Japanese soldiers had been relaxing under these same coconut palms, with eyes already on New Caledonia.

Many contributed to this remarkable reversal: the unsupported Marines who clung to Henderson Field after the naval disaster of Savo . . . Colonel Edson's 700 weary men who hurled back Kawaguchi's 2100 from Bloody Ridge . . . the overworked destroyers and cruisers that took on Admiral Yamamoto's battle-wagons . . . the little band of fighter pilots who crushed the great air armadas sent down from the north . . . the coordinated sea and air effort that ultimately derailed Admiral Tanaka's Tokyo Express.

They all did their bit, but none played a larger part than Commander Feldt's handful of Coastwatchers, together with the intriguing assortment of missionaries, local people, and natives who helped them. Their numbers were small—six teleradios behind enemy lines in June 1942; still only fourteen a year later—but their contribution was enormous.

Jack Read's dry "40 bombers heading yours" became a sort of South Pacific legend, but it little suggests the cumulative value of his and Mason's radioed warnings. From August 20, when Henderson Field opened up, to November 15, when the strip was finally secure, the CACTUS Air Force—outnumbered 2:1—knocked down 263 Japanese planes while losing only 101 of their own.

This wasn't due to the overwhelming weight of arms that Americans would later come to expect. For weeks there were only a few dozen patched-up planes. Nor did it stem from any inherent superiority of U.S. aviators, as the home front liked to believe.

The real secret was the two hours' warning that Read and Mason gave. This allowed time to collect the exhausted fighter pilots for one more mission . . . time to warm up and take off . . . time to coax the slow-climbing Grummans up to 30,000 feet, where they hovered, waiting to pounce. Admiral Halsey summed it up well when he later observed, "The Coastwatchers saved Guadalcanal, and Guadalcanal saved the Pacific."

As Japanese air power shriveled away and the Tokyo Express came into its own, the Coastwatchers again proved invaluable. Radio intercepts played a priceless part in tipping off these destroyer runs, but it was usually the Coastwatchers who first picked up the actual targets. At its best the process ran like clockwork: The Express would be sighted by Paul Mason as it left the Short-

lands . . . then by Seton and Waddell as it passed Choiseul . . . then by Josselyn on Vella, and sometimes by
Kennedy's network on New Georgia. This flow of bul-
letins usually gave the Americans time to organize a
lively reception committee.

The toll of lost destroyers proved too heavy. The
Japanese were forced to shift largely to barges in the
fight for the Central Solomons. But the routes and lay-
overs were well-defined, and the Coastwatchers knew
them all. Once again a steady stream of sightings flowed
into KEN, which promptly fed them to the PTs and the
air strike command.

As the U.S. planes ranged ever farther north and
west, slashing at Japanese shipping, staging points, and
air strips, some flyers were inevitably shot down, and
the rescue of these airmen became another great Coastwatcher contribution. The best estimate, island by
island, adds up to an impressive figure:

Guadalcanal	6
Isabel	28
New Georgia	22
Rendova	8
Vella Lavella	31
Choiseul	23
	118

There was less opportunity to help the crews of
sunken ships, but when the occasion did arise, the
Coastwatchers were there. The survivors of the *Helena*
and *PT 109* could attest to that.

The value of all this rescue work went far beyond the
numbers actually saved. The effect on overall morale
was enormous. It helped every flyer operating out of
Henderson Field to know that if the worst came to the

worst, and he was washed ashore on some unknown island, there was likely to be someone there who might appear out of the bush and give him a helping hand.

When the Allied drive up the Solomons finally began, the Coastwatchers made still another great contribution. Through their intimate knowledge of the islands—and their excellent relations with the natives—they proved perfect advance men. They helped chart the coasts. They pinpointed Japanese strongholds. They cleared and marked the landing beaches. They supplied carriers, guides, and canoes. They pointed out the best trails and streams for moving through the jungle.

All this was accomplished by volunteers who were anything but professional military men. They included government officials, plantation managers, gold miners, a department store buyer, a pub keeper, an accountant, a rancher—the variety was staggering. They seemed to have nothing in common.

But they did. In recruiting them, Eric Feldt applied an important criterion: They should all know the South Pacific. How to tell the difference between a cruiser and a destroyer could be learned in minutes, but not an awareness of the intricate relationships and loyalties that governed life in the Islands. Sending a native to a Chinese with a message for a missionary involved the sensitivities of three totally different groups of people, and an effective man had to know all the nuances.

The only important exception to Eric Feldt's standard was Frank Nash, the Colorado rancher, but the commander was inactivated by his stroke by the time Nash came aboard. (Besides, Feldt later explained somewhat cryptically, Colorado wasn't all that different from the South Pacific.)

If an Island background explains why these particular men were recruited, it still doesn't explain why they said yes. "But why did he, of all men out here, volunteer?" asks the iconoclastic Tony Fry, puzzling over the Remittance Men, the fictional Coastwatcher in James Michener's *Tales of the South Pacific*. "A single man goes out against an island of Japs? Why?"

"I've asked myself a 'housand times," said the very real Coastwatcher Snowy Rhoades to a curious visitor, "and I still don't know."

Certainly it wasn't rank or material reward. Rhoades had no rank at all until June 1942, when Feldt managed to get him commissioned as a naval lieutenant in the illusory hope that this might help if he were captured by the Japanese. Other Coastwatchers didn't even do that well. Paul Mason was only a naval petty officer much of the time; Geoffrey Kuper, only a private in that haziest of all military organizations, the British Solomon Islands Protectorate Defense Force.

Nor was there the satisfaction of being a hero and basking in the limelight. For understandable security reasons, the Coastwatchers were never mentioned in the press. The great air victories were attributed to skill, tactics and equipment, with a faint hint of Anglo-Saxon superiority. The downed pilots magically "walked home." The *Helena* castaways on Vella Lavella simply "let the Navy know" they were there.

Little matter, the Coastwatchers weren't publicity hounds anyhow. For seventeen years no one knew who the Coastwatcher was who rescued John F. Kennedy. In a 1944 article published first in the *New Yorker* and later in the *Reader's Digest,* John Hersey called him "Lieutenant Wincote" of the New Zealand Army. As Kennedy grew more prominent, enterprising editors tried in vain to find the mysterious Wincote. Finally, after *Pacific Islands Monthly* launched an all-out search during the 1960 presidential campaign, Eric Feldt said that actually the Coastwatcher must have been Reg

Evans. Later Evans himself phoned the magazine that indeed it was he. Would he tell the full story, the excited editors asked. Yes, he said, he'd drop by in three or four weeks. He ultimately appeared.

Yet these men did have their reasons. After considering the question for the 1001st time, Snowy Rhoades observed in the last analysis, "Here I was at this place, responsible for it, and nobody to look after it or the people if I left. So I stayed."

Don Macfarlan, the department store buyer, decided that "It was something different." Bobby Firth, stuck in an army cargo handling unit, felt it was far more interesting than loading ships. Geoffrey Kuper wanted to be on Donald Kennedy's team, wherever that might lead. Martin Clemens, the aspiring young Colonial Office career man, "just couldn't see Europeans walking out on the natives." Frank Nash pursued his eternal quest for "my idea of the war."

There were, in short, as many reasons as there were Coastwatchers. Nor was this surprising, for they were above all individualists. A yearning to escape the standard mold was one reason they came to the Islands, and they weren't about to exchange their independence for conformity simply because there was a war.

They showed their freedom every day. Carden Seton in his bush shirt, usually open to the fourth button . . . Kennedy in his digger hat . . . Josselyn in pressed shorts with officer's cap cocked at a jaunty angle—no two of them even dressed alike.

They also had a casual approach to the command structure that was the exasperation of their superiors and the envy of their peers. It was against General Vandegrift's explicit orders to take the *Ramada* and pick up Snowy Rhoades, but Dick Horton did it anyway. Brisbane told Jack Read that he couldn't bring

Eric Feldt (middle row, fourth from left) poses with a group of his Coastwatchers. Snowy Rhoades is on his right, Hugh Mackenzie on his left. Frank Nash, only American in the picture, is seated in the bottom row on the right. (Courtesy Frank Nash)

out his natives when he left Bougainville—but in the end they were on board the submarine. Whatever else the Coastwatchers did, they enjoyed to the hilt the rare luxury of ruling their own destinies in battle.

Along with their individualism ran a deep sense of personal loyalty—another characteristic of Island life—and this in turn became another reason for what they did. The South Pacific area covered over a million square miles, but it was also a small world where everyone seemed to know everyone else. The personal ties were exceptionally strong. Eric Feldt—an Islander himself—recognized this and built upon it.

It was this streak of loyalty that led Eric Robinson and J. A. Corrigan into the rugged hills of central

Bougainville one February Sunday in 1944. This time they weren't looking for Japanese—the war was winding down and the jungle lay quiet—they were searching for the wreckage of an airplane.

Ten months had passed since Flight Lieutenant Clark's Catalina had crashed on the ridge near Aita while delivering supplies to Jack Read. Six of the crew had gotten out alive, but Clark, Flying Officer J. N. E. Potts, and Sergeant D. J. Ward had been killed by the impact and left pinned in the tangle of twisted metal. Before anything could be done about this, the Coast-watchers were driven off the island.

But now they were back, and that shattered plane in the jungle, with its three imprisoned victims, preyed on the mind of Robinson, who had been with Read at the time. These flyers had given their lives to help him; he just couldn't leave them this way. He had no trouble persuading Corrigan to come along.

Up the winding, slippery trail they climbed, past the ravines and fallen logs that were familiar landmarks to Robinson, yet so different from those harrowing days last June. Then every shadow looked like a Japanese sniper. Now all was calm—only the occasional call of a bird, or the rush of some mountain stream.

At last they came to a stretch where the trees were scarred, and in some cases snapped in two. The jungle was fast healing these wounds, but there was no doubt they had reached the scene. Continuing a few yards, they came to the wreckage itself, now half-hidden by new ferns and vines.

They hacked their way into the cockpit, and found two complete skeletons—the dog-tags identified them as Clark and Potts. A few yards away they found the remains of Sergeant Ward.

Clearing a small plot of ground, they dug three graves

and carefully buried the fallen airmen. The crumpled plane itself became the "headstone." What prayers were said—what thoughts ran through their minds—was a private matter. Their mission complete, their loyalty reaffirmed, the two Coastwatchers turned and headed back down the trail.

Acknowledgments

"I note that you are doing a book on the Coastwatchers," writes Lieutenant General R. C. Mangrum, who commanded the first dive bomber squadron to operate from Guadalcanal. "We owe a great debt of gratitude to those heroes who, literally, made it possible for us to hang on through the grim early days of the Solomons operations. I don't know that any American has heretofore told their story, and it is high time."

High time indeed, but piecing the picture together is, to say the least, a complicated problem. The people involved are today scattered over five continents. The written records are sparse and buried in half a dozen different repositories. To dig out the facts has required the patient and continued help of over two hundred individuals, and I'm immensely indebted to them all.

First, the Coastwatchers themselves. In the course of my research I managed to locate Martin Clemens, Reg Evans, Bob Firth, Dick Horton, Henry Josselyn, Geoffrey Kuper, Don Macfarlan, Bill McCasker, Frank Nash, Doug Otton, Jack Read, Snowy Rhoades, and

Nick Waddell. As with the cause they so gallantly served, they never failed me.

In several instances where the Coastwatchers have now passed on, their families have been wonderfully helpful with pictures, letters, and other material. I'm especially grateful to Mrs. Eric Feldt, Mrs. Paul Mason, Mrs. Carden Seton, Miss Borghild Marie Schroeder, and Mr. John Dalrymple-Hay.

Then there are those who were part of the Coastwatchers organization, although not actually behind Japanese lines in the Solomons. Walter Brooksbank—formerly Civil Assistant to the Director of Naval Intelligence, RAN—gave me whole days of his time. Keith McCarthy did his Coastwatching on New Britain, but he knew many of the men in the Solomons and generously shared his knowledge with me. Peter Figgis, Jack Paterson, and Mrs. Frank Jones (Ruby Olive Boye) also served in other areas, but helped fill in missing chinks.

Parenthetically, it's important to remember that there were Coastwatchers on many islands besides the Solomons, and that there were other clandestine organizations in the South Pacific besides the Coastwatchers. Some, like the Lugger Maintenance Section, based in Australia, bore intriguing if deliberately misleading names. All did valuable work, but in the end it was the little group in the Solomons who stood in the strategic spotlight and who therefore deserve a measure of special attention.

Yet the full story is far more than a record of the Solomons Islands Coastwatchers per se. They are the "stars," but there is an immense supporting cast: the natives who helped them; the missionaries, commandos, and occasional Chinese who worked with them; the downed flyers, castaways, and refugees they rescued; the Marine patrols they guided; the airmen and submariners who serviced them; the Japanese who chased them. The variety is enormous—surely this must be the only subject in the world on which I could be doing research in a home for Catholic Sisters one week, and in Las Vegas the next.

All have been wonderfully generous with their time—one perhaps too much so. Douglas Otton, an AIF commando who served with Paul Mason on Bougainville, gave me a whole Sunday in the final week of his campaign for a seat in the Australian Parliament. He lost by only a few hundred votes, and I've often wondered whether that lost day made the difference.

Tracking down these participants was not always easy, and I'm especially indebted to a number of people who paved the way. In this country Anna C. Urband of the Navy's Public Information Division was a tower of strength. Other helpful emissaries include Al Bonney, Vice President, Association of Guadalcanal Campaign Veterans; Lowell V. Bulger, Executive Secretary, United States Marine Raiders Association; William S. Bunker, USS *Helena* Organization; Professor John T. Mason, Jr., Director of Oral History, United States Naval Institute; J. M. "Boats" Newberry, PT Boats, Inc.

In Australia, many contacts were made through Don Latimer, Secretary of the NSW Commando Association; and in New Zealand, key addresses were supplied by the Reverend G. G. Carter, General Secretary, Overseas Division of the Methodist Church. At the War History Office in Tokyo, Lieutenant Colonel Yutaka Fugita was invariably helpful in identifying Japanese participants and their units. Takami Takeshita, the office's Solomons expert, was equally generous with his time.

This was a project that involved research in strange and faraway places, but plenty of knowledgeable people helped the neophyte along. In Australia, for instance, I owe a lot to Lieutenant Colonel Stanley S. Caporn,

Harry Hansen, Stuart Inder, John H. McGowan, Jeff O'Neill, Professor Robert J. O'Neill, Professor B. M. Primrose, and Professor L. C. F. Turner.

At Rabaul, Fred Archer was both a good host and a good source. Elaine Bruce also provided excellent leads, and thanks go to Ed Farley for putting me in touch with her. In the Solomons, Mr. D. C. C. Luddington, then British High Commissioner for the Western Pacific, gave me access to government facilities and communications without which the job could not have been done. Jim Tedder, formerly the Protectorate's chief information officer, took me under his wing, and I could not have had better luck. So many people rallied to the cause: Francis Aqorau, Paul Brown, David Garisi, Roy Kelosi, Graeme Kent, and Isaac Quoloni—to name just a few.

Of course, interviews and personal observation have their limits, and I also relied heavily on the written record. The official material is haphazardly filed in a variety of places. Finding it taxed the ingenuity of archivists in Washington, Melbourne, and Canberra, but they always came through.

At the U.S. Naval History Division, Vice Admiral Edwin B. Hooper never turned down a request. Within the Division, Dr. Dean C. Allard performed his usual magic at Operational Archives, ably abetted by Kathleen M. Lloyd. At the Naval Construction Battalion Center, Mary Hinojosa came up with just the right information on Wilfred Painter. At the USMC Historical Division I leaned mercilessly on Lieutenant Colonel Herbert M. Hart, Major John C. Short, and Benis Frank; while at National Archives I could always count on Roland Wilson. I'm especially grateful to Jim Trimble of the Audiovisual Division of the Archives for his fine help on pictures, and to Alan Goodrich of the Kennedy Library, who also came through when needed.

In Australia Vice Admiral Sir Richard Peek, Chief of Naval Staff, RAN, gave the project his blessing; and John Ware, then head of the Royal Australian Navy's Historical Section, guided me through a labyrinth of files. When Mr. Ware retired before the completion of my research, his shoes were ably filled by John M. Mackenzie. I'm indebted to them both.

For digging out additional records in Australia, I'm also grateful to Mr. Alan P. Skerman and his fine staff at the Commonwealth Archives Office in Melbourne, and to Mr. W. R. Lancaster, then director of the Australian War Memorial in Canberra.

Besides the official records, a great deal of unofficial material has been provided by helpful people on both sides of the Pacific. Martin Clemens made available his radio message log and his correspondence file covering the period he operated on Guadalcanal. Both are invaluable in fixing dates and the movement of personnel, as is the copy of his diary at the War Memorial in Canberra. Father Emery de Klerk carefully reconstructed his lost diary from reams of contemporary notes. Merle Farland, Patricia Penrose, and Sister M. Irene Alton all lent me their diaries, and Sister Irene also provided a copy of the diary kept by Sister M. Hedda Jaeger on Bougainville.

John Dalrymple-Hay lent me a copy of the journal written by his uncle, the fabulous Ken Hay, on Guadalcanal; Charles Colt contributed fascinating material on the early days at Lunga beachhead; Douglass Hubbard at the Admiral Nimitz Center provided a copy of Snowy Rhoades's unpublished memoirs; Mrs. Robert Laverty made available the papers of her late husband, who operated behind enemy lines on New Georgia and Rendova. A special word of thanks goes to Sherman Lee Pompey, who gave me access to the diary and letter book kept by the Reverend A. W. E. Silvester on Vella Lavella.

The transcripts of two important recordings have also been made available. Dr. James Boutilier has generously provided a taped interview with Donald Kennedy in 1969; and Mrs. Eric Feldt has lent me an LP record, full of reminiscences, made during the dedication of the Coastwatcher Light at Madang, Papua New Guinea, in 1959.

All this material—official and unofficial—is especially important because so little has been published on the Coastwatchers. I know of only four books devoted entirely to the subject: Eric Feldt, *The Coast Watchers,* Melbourne, Oxford, 1946 (Oxford also published an abbreviated American edition the same year); D. C. Horton, *Fire Over the Islands,* Sydney, Reed, 1970; M. Murray, *Hunted: A Coastwatcher's Story,* Adelaide, Rigby 1967; and Malcolm Wright, *If I Die,* Melbourne, Lansdowne, 1965. Only Feldt has ever been published in the United States.

There is also a long chapter on the Solomon Island Coastwatchers in Allison Ind, *Allied Intelligence Bureau—Our Secret Weapon in the War Against Japan,* New York, McKay, 1958, and parts of the story can be found in other books. I found the following especially useful: Robert J. Donovan, *PT-109,* New York, McGraw-Hill, 1961; G. Hermon Gill, *Royal Australian Navy in World War II,* Canberra, Australian War Memorial, 1957–58; Samuel B. Griffith, *The Battle for Guadalcanal,* Philadelphia, Lippincott, 1963; Hugh Laracy, *Marists and Melanesians,* Honolulu, University of Hawaii, 1976; Thomas G. Miller, Jr., *The Cactus Air Force,* New York, Harper & Row, 1969; and A. A. Vandegrift, *Once a Marine,* New York, Norton, 1964.

In this connection I owe particular thanks to Bob

Donovan and Reg Evans for their permission to quote from Evans's message file, which is featured in *PT 109*.

From time to time informative articles have also appeared in various magazines and newspapers. *The Pacific Islands Monthly*—indispensable for any one interested in the South Pacific—has carried the recollections of Andy Andresen (January 1944) and Ken Hay (July–August 1971), as well as an interesting piece on Reg Evans (January 1961). The *United States Naval Institute Proceedings* has also touched on the subject at various times; see especially "Bougainville Rendezvous," by Commander Richard H. Bowers (July 1952); "The Segi Man," by Rear Admiral George Van Deurs (October 1958); and "Bush Navigation in the Solomons," by Captain Charles F. McGivern (February 1974).

Other pertinent articles: "Survival," by John Hersey, *New Yorker,* June 17, 1944; "Rescue in the Pacific," by Gilbert Cant, *Saturday Evening Post,* January 29, 1944; "Nights to Remember," by Leonard J. Baird, Benjamin Katz, John D. Sweeney, and John L. Chew, *Shipmate,* July–August 1975; an unsigned feature story on John Mackie's AIF commando unit in the Australian paper *Daily Mirror,* October 28, 1963; and a six-part series by Colin Simpson in the Sydney *Sunday Mail Magazine,* November 1–December 6, 1953. For locating and copying various Australian articles, extra thanks are due the staff at the University of Queensland Library in Brisbane.

Many others, too, took a special interest in the project and came to my rescue at crucial moments. These include Rear Admiral H. J. Dyson, Brigadier General Samuel B. Griffith II, A. N. Garbarino, Commander Clarence C. Hawk, Colonel R. D. Heinl, Ben Horn, Lieutenant General R. C. Mangrum, Rear Admiral A. H. McCollum, Captain Roger Pineau, Stuart Revill,

Larry Reineke, Major Edna Loftus Smith, Donald B. Thompson, John and Toshiko Toland, and Jac Weller.

Finally, there are those who virtually lived with the project over the years. In Japan nothing was ever too much trouble for Yuzuru Sanematsu or Y. Horie. In Australia Barbara Land performed miracles in locating various participants, and on several occasions handled interviews when I was "out of position." Her tact and good humor I am sure won the help of many people who might otherwise have been reluctant to come forward.

In New York Dorothy Hefferline handled most of the voluminous correspondence, while Florence Gallagher notched her thirtieth year of deciphering my scribbled foolscap.

But all these people—helpful as they were—would not have been enough without the cooperation of the 141 participants listed on the following pages. In the last analysis it is *their* story. They get none of the blame for my mistakes but all the credit in the world for whatever new light is thrown on the remarkable role played by the Solomon Islands Coastwatchers in winning back the Pacific.

List of Contributors

All contributors are listed together—regardless of nationality and of civilian or military status. Each name is followed by the participant's vantage point. Where supplied, present rank is also included.

Sister M. Irene Alton—missionary, Buka and Bougainville

Lt. Paul O. Anderson, USNR (Ret.)—*Helena*

Col. Henry Aplington, II, USMC (Ret.)—Torokina landings, Bougainville

Fred Archer—civilian planter, Bougainville

J. P. Ayres—rescued U.S. flyer, Vella Lavella

George Bausewine—*Helena*

William Bennett—Coastwatcher network, New Georgia

Alesasa Bisili—mission student, Munda

Theodore Blahnik—*Helena*

Jefferson J. de Blanc—rescued U.S. flyer, Vella Lavella

Capt. Warren C. Boles, USN (Ret.)—*Helena*

Capt. Richard H. Bowers, USN (Ret.)—*Guardfish*

Col. Clay A. Boyd, USMC (Ret.)—Marine Raider patrols, New Georgia

Capt. H. C. Bridges, Jr., USN (Ret.)—PBYs, Solomon Islands

Rear Adm. William H. Brockman, USN (Ret.)—*Nautilus*

G. J. Brooksbank—Naval Intelligence Division, RAN

Walter H. Brooksbank—Naval Intelligence Division, RAN

Lowell V. Bulger—Marine Raider patrols, Guadalcanal

H. W. Bullen—Coastwatcher staff, Guadalcanal, Segi

William S. Bunker—*Helena*

Ed Burckhard—*Helena*

Col. R. C. Burns, USMC (Ret.)—Seventh Fleet Intelligence

Jack Campbell—Coastwatcher network, Guadalcanal

Norman L. Carlson—*Helena*

Vice Adm. John L. Chew, USN (Ret.)—*Helena*

Cdr. Archie J. Church, USN (Ret.)—*Patapsco*

W. F. Martin Clemens—Coastwatcher, Guadalcanal

Charles C. Colt—Air Combat Intelligence, Guadalcanal

Cdr. Robert C. Corlett, USN (Ret.)—PBYs, Solomon Islands

R. J. Cream—AIF detachment, Bougainville

Col. Michael S. Currin, USMC (Ret.)—Marine Raider patrols, New Georgia

Solomon Dakai—Coastwatcher network, Guadalcanal

Cdr. George S. Davis, USN (Ret.)—*Nautilus*

Terrence T. Dempsey—*Helena*

Eugene R. Dilts—*Helena*

R. W. Dolby—AIF detachment, Bougainville

C. W. Duke-Yonge—Coastwatcher staff, Townsville, Brisbane

William Dupay—*Helena*

Cdr. Philip F. Eckert, USN (Ret.)—*Nautilus*

Major Halstead Ellison, USMCR (Ret.)—Lunga beachhead, Guadalcanal.

Cdr. L. D. Emerson-Elliott, RN (Ret.)—Naval Intelligence Division, RAN

A. R. Evans—Coastwatcher, Kolombangara

Capt. Leonard E. Ewoldt, USN (Ret.)—rescued U.S. flyer, Guadalcanal

Merle S. Farland—mission nurse, Vella Lavella

Adm. James Fife, Jr., USN (Ret.)—SOWESPAC, Brisbane

Peter E. Figgis—Coastwatcher, New Guinea, New Britain

Capt. Gordon Eugene Firebaugh, USN (Ret.)—rescued U.S. flyer, Santa Isabel

R. L. Firth—Coastwatcher, Vella Lavella

Rear Adm. Robert J. Foley, USN (Ret.)—*Gato*

Gonshiro Funada—Kure 6th Naval Landing Force, Rendova

Frank Furner—AIF detachment, Bougainville

Cdr. Joe L. Gammon, USN (Ret.)—*Guardfish*

Lt. Col. Ritchie Garrison, USA (Ret.)—U.S. Army, Efate

J. C. H. Gill—Coastwatcher staff, Townsville, Brisbane

Walter B. Gillette—LCTs, Segi landings

Harold Grieff—Lunga beachhead, Guadalcanal

Chesleigh S. Grunstad—*Helena*

Capt. Frank J. Guidone, USMC (Ret.)—Marine Raider patrols, New Georgia

Capt. Donald G. Gumz, USN (Ret.)—PBY supply and rescue missions

Clive M. Hamer—RAAF Catalina base, Tulagi

Solomon Hitu—mission student, Munda

D. C. Horton—Coastwatcher, Rendova

John R. Hubbard—U.S. Navy Photo Reconnaissance Group, Guadalcanal

Harold Hulseberg—U.S. Army mapping reconnaissance, Choiseul

Robert M. Hurst—RAAF Catalina supply missions

Akijiro Imai—8th Combined Naval Landing Force, Rabaul, Munda

Jaku—Coastwatcher network, Guadalcanal

W. T. Jolly—Marine Raider patrols, New Georgia

Mrs. Frank Jones (Ruby Olive Boye)—Coastwatcher, Vanikoro

Henry Josselyn—Coastwatcher, Vella Lavella

Col. Bernard T. Kelly, USMC (Ret.)—*Helena*

Capt. Robert B. Kelly, USN (Ret.)—PT-boats, Rendova

Frank A. Kemp—Marine Raiders, New Georgia landings

Lt. Roger Kent, USNR (Ret.)—Air Combat Intelligence, Guadalcanal

Ben Kevu—Coastwatcher network, Wana Wana Lagoon

LCDR Richard L. Kile, USN (Ret.)—radar unit, New Georgia

J. A. Kissane—Coastwatcher staff, Guadalcanal

Father Emery de Klerk—missionary and Coastwatcher network, Guadalcanal

Gordon Knightley-Smith—Burns Philp, Tulagi

Lt. Gen. Victor H. Krulak, USMC (Ret.)—Paratroop Battalion, Choiseul

Geoffrey Kuper—Coastwatcher, Santa Isabel

Father Albert Lebel—missionary, Bougainville

Dale M. Leslie—rescued U.S. flyer, Guadalcanal

Pelopi Lomae—Coastwatcher network, Rendova

John Lotikena—native civilian, Mono

J. Keith McCarthy—Coastwatcher, New Britain

A. W. McCasker—Coastwatcher, Ontong-Java

Capt. Charles F. McGivern, USN (Ret.)—*Gato*

D. S. Macfarlan—Coastwatcher, Guadalcanal

Capt. Roderick K. MacLean, USN (Ret.)—*Gato*

David R. Maltby—PT-boats, off Bougainville, Choiseul

Cdr. W. Robert Maxwell, USN (Ret.)—rescued U.S. flyer, Rendova

Lloyd George Miller—*Helena*

Major Paul R. Montrose, USAFR (Ret.)—fighter pilot, Segi

John V. Murray—Armed Guard, USN, Guadalcanal

B. Franklin Nash—Coastwatcher, Kolombangara

Rear Adm. William T. Nelson, USN (Ret.)—*Peto*

Gen Nishino—Japanese news correspondent, Guadalcanal

Ryosuke Nomura—Air staff, Southeast Area Fleet, Rabaul

Robert T. Orman—U.S. Marines, Tulagi landings

E. Douglas Otton—AIF detachment, Coastwatcher, Bougainville

Gordon Pabulu—Coastwatcher network, Choiseul

Willie Paia—Coastwatcher network, New Georgia

Patricia Rattray Penrose—Allied Intelligence Bureau cipher clerk, Melbourne

Capt. Edwin L. Pierce, USN (Ret.)—PBY supply and rescue missions

Otis B. Point—*Helena*

Cdr. Floyd R. Porterfield, USN (Ret.)—*Nautilus*
Daniel Pule—Coastwatcher network, Guadalcanal

W. J. Read—Coastwatcher, Bougainville
Cdr. F. A. Rhoades, RAN (Ret.)—Coastwatcher, Guadalcanal
Norman Robertson—RAAF Catalina supply missions

B. Gen. L. G. Saunders, USAAF (Ret.)—rescued U.S. flyer, Vella Lavella
Joe Sciarra—Marine Raider patrols, New Georgia
Jesse Scott, Jr.—rescued U.S. flyer, Mono
Loren A. Sherman—*Helena*
Philip Shuh—*Helena*
D. Lyle Sly—AIF detachment, Bougainville
Capt. Archibald M. Smith, Jr., USMCR (Ret.)—rescued U.S. flyer, Santa Isabel
Robert E. Smith—*Helena*
John R. Scott—rescued U.S. flyer, Choiseul
Lt. J. F. Sutherland—*Enterprise* and Henderson Field
Toshio Suzuki—229th Infantry Regiment, Munda
James Raymond Swanbeck—*Gato*
B. H. Swanson—AIF detachment, Bougainville
Rear Adm. John D. Sweeney, USN (Ret.)—*Helena* rescue mission
Col. James E. Swett, USMC (Ret.)—rescued U.S. flyer, New Georgia

Job Tamana—Coastwatcher network, New Georgia
Capt. Henry Tamblyn—RAAF Catalina supply missions
Capt. LeRoy Taylor, USN (Ret.)—PT-boats, Rendova
Capt. Donald B. Thomson—Liaison Pilot 37th Infantry Division, Bougainville
Oremo J. Tonarelli—*Helena*

Rear Adm. George van Deurs, USN (Ret.)—Chief of Staff, COMAIRSOPAC

Sir Alexander Waddell—Coastwatcher, Choiseul
Rear Adm. Norvell G. Ward, USN (Ret.)—*Guardfish*
William H. Warden—rescued U.S. flyer, Guadalcanal
Arthur B. Wells—rescued U.S. flyer, Rendova
Capt. Irving E. Wetmore, USN (Ret.)—*Nautilus*
C. D. Williams—*Helena*
Hal M. Winner—*Nautilus*

Col. Michael R. Yunck, USMC (Ret.)—rescued U.S. flyer, Santa Isabel
Satoru Yunoki—Staff intelligence officer, 8th Combined Special Naval Landing Force, Munda

Index